I Wake Up Screening

What to Do Once You've Made That Movie

John Anderson and Laura Kim

WATSON-GUPTILL PUBLISHING • NEW YORK

Our Gratitude

To Bob Nirkind, for his support and patience

To Sylvia Warren, for her eagle eye and patience

To Eric Myers, for his faith and patience

To our subjects, for their time, their devotion to film, and for
all that they do to help films find their way

To Diane and Betty, for their love, time, and support

Executive Editor: Robert Nirkind

Editor: Sylvia Warren

Senior Production Manager: Hector Campbell

Designer: Leah Lococo

ISBN 13: 978-0-8230-8898-0

ISBN: 0-8230-8898-7

© 2006 by John Anderson and Laura Kim

First published in 2006 by Watson-Guptill Publications,

a Division of VNU Business Media, Inc.

770 Broadway, New York, N.Y.

www.wgpub.com

Library of Congress Control Number: 2005908033

Printed in the United States

First printing, 2006

1 2 3 4 5 6 7 8 9 / 10 09 08 07 06

Kramer, Jeffrey, producer, *The Big Empty, A Time for Dancing*

Laemmle, Greg, president, Laemmle Theatres; copresident, Laemmle/Zeller Films

Levy-Hinte, Jeff, independent producer, Antidote Films, *Thirteen, Mysterious Skin, The Hawk Is Dying*

Libby, Chris, publicist, B|W|R

Lin, Justin, filmmaker, *Better Luck Tomorrow, Annapolis, Fast & Furious 3*

Linklater, Richard, director, *Slacker, Dazed and Confused, School of Rock, Before Sunrise, Before Sunset, A Scanner Darkly, Fast Food Nation*

Luddy, Tom, director, Telluride Film Festival

Macaulay, Scott, independent producer, Forensic Films, *Raising Victor Vargas, Idlewild, Julien Donkey-Boy*

McCarthy, Todd, chief film critic, *Variety*

Millard, RJ, former head of marketing and publicity, IDP Films

Nadler, Maud, SVP Independent Productions, HBO Films

O'Haver, Tommy, director, *Billy's Hollywood Screen Kiss, Get Over It, Ella Enchanted*

Peña, Richard, director, New York Film Festival

Pogachefsky, Mark, copresident, mPRm Public Relations

Pogodin, Fredell, publicist, Fredell Pogodin & Associates

Pulcini, Robert, filmmaker, *Off the Menu: The Last Days of Chasen's, The Young and the Dead, American Splendor*

Raphael, Steven, producers rep, Required Viewing

Rappaport, Irwin, entertainment lawyer, Irwin M. Rappaport, P.C.

Rhee, Karen, entertainment producer, *Good Morning America*

Rosen, Rachel, director of programming, Los Angeles Film Festival

Scarlet, Peter, executive director, Tribeca Film Festival

Schamus, James, copresident, Focus Features

Schwarzbaum, Lisa, critic, *Entertainment Weekly*

Sloss, John, sales agent, attorney, Sloss Law, cofounder Cinetic Media

Spence, Carl, director of programming, Seattle Film Festival

Springer Berman, Shari, filmmaker, *Off the Menu: The Last Days of Chasen's, The Young and the Dead, American Splendor*

Taubin, Amy, critic, *Film Comment*

Turan, Kenneth, critic, *The Los Angeles Times*

Vachon, Christine, independent producer, Killer Films, *Boys Don't Cry, Far from Heaven, Mrs. Harris*

Walker, Jeremy, publicist, Jeremy Walker & Associates

Waxman, Sharon, Hollywood correspondent, *The New York Times*

Introduction

Location: **Los Angeles.**

Time: **A Saturday in June, 2002.**

Setting: **Interior of a car. The car is winding its way through the lower hills of Hollywood, the sun shining, the birds singing, the entire scene in contrast with the dour atmosphere inside said automobile.**

Dramatis Personae: **Laura Kim, a publicist and longtime member of mPRm, a prominent public relations house in LA specializing in independent film; and John Anderson, daily film critic for Newsday in New York, who has answered the summons to jury duty at the Los Angeles Independent Film Festival (now Los Angeles Film Festival).**

THE MOOD WAS BLEAK that sunny day in Los Angeles. Two longtime friends and professional associates were making their way home from another day in Festival . . . well, Hell is an overstatement. But there was a decided sense of fatigue informing the conversation, the two having dealt with yet another movie with less of a future than a full keg at a frat house.

One of us was representing it, one of us was judging it, as part of the festival's First Feature competition. ("Why don't they ever have a Last Feature competition?" we asked each other. "That would be something to see.")

We'd been in the business of indie cinema long enough not to kid each other; we had seen enough films together, worked together on enough interviews, and had done our share of festival duties, be they at Sundance, Cannes, or Toronto, to know that what we'd just seen was not great, and not terrible, but just somewhere sadly in between, like so many films we had seen. We both knew the film would never go anywhere, also like so many films we had seen, which was really depressing and aggravating at the same time.

What was getting us down wasn't just the movie in question, which was far from the worst thing we'd ever looked at, written about, or tried to sell. Of course, there are plenty of bad ones out there, including those made for much more money, with more resources available to the filmmakers. This lackluster attempt at comedy/profundity was more sad than bad, mainly because it had had so many advantages: The script had been workshopped; its director had been mentored; some members of its talented cast were famous; and the story, though a bit nonsensical, had elements of intelligence that merely needed . . . well, a real filmmaker. That no one had told this particular artist *somewhere* along the line that the film didn't work, or that it needed more work, was both another example of the yessing that goes on throughout the industry and a testament to the results of a blinkered ego.

But the other thing that got us down was that there were really worthy movies out there, little gems that needed—and, more importantly, deserved—real, practical, affordable advice. The movie in question—let's call it *Bewildered*—could afford a publicist and had one: Laura. In suggesting that the movie didn't need one, she was violating the First Commandment of public relations: "Thou shalt never advise anyone not to seek representation." Not only that, but after admitting that this film could have lived without a PR agency, she suggested that many other directors and producers (not a lot, perhaps, but some) could do for themselves everything a publicist could do—if they just took a hard look at the film they had on their hands, set reasonable expectations, and rolled up their sleeves and just did it.

John, in turn, realized that what got him interested in seeing a film—or at least willing to see it—wasn't the glossy press kit, tchotchkes, or screenings with free popcorn. It was—as in cuisine, landscape gardening, or overpriced real estate—all about presentation. How the film was brought to his attention. Ultimately, a film has to stand or fall on its own merits. But if a good filmmaker can at least get his or her work traveling through the right channels, with a strategy in mind, he or she has won their first battle.

We came to the conclusion that the only thing worse than seeing an undeserving film like *Bewildered* get attention is to see a really worthy film go without. And it happens. Festivals, those great showcases for unattached cinema, are only human (sort of): Just as squeaky wheels get the grease everywhere else, at festivals the persistent, dogged, crafty, and strategically savvy moviemaker gets the right kind of attention—from both the press and from buyers. If you have a movie, you want to be squeaking. And squeaking the right way. And for the right reasons. And sometimes not squeaking.

This book might have been called *How to Squeak.* Instead, it's called *I Wake Up Screening* because it's a lot funnier, and catchier, and may sell more copies. Presentation, remember, is everything.

What we hope to do within these covers is take a mental machete to the seemingly impenetrable thickets of fear, intimidation, and bad information that envelop the whole hype-driven marketplace of independent cinema. And, being small-d democrats bordering on Marxist radicals, we hope to do it for filmmakers at every stratum of economic privilege or need. You may be able to afford great PR representation; if so, go with God. But you may also have sold your mother's iron lung to finance your movie and need to take the self-help route to the Palme d'Or and your enshrinement as the next Tarantino/Linklater/Soderbergh/Anderson (P. T. or Wes, take your pick). The aim is attention, the right kind of attention from the right people, at the right time. And at some point, the playing field is level, and no amount of squeaking will make someone like it, buy it, or write about it. Your film will speak for itself, and there's no better time to be heard.

While the reality is that most American independents and art films will never break even theatrically, let alone be released, what we're looking at is a film world with new and expanding opportunities. "The marketplace now is better than it's ever been for independent films," said Bob Berney, one of independent cinema's more successful distributors. "There are more theaters, more distributors—maybe not big distributors, but micro-distributors. There are more opportunities for a film to get distributed, especially with the advent of digital. . . . Among mainstream exhibitors there's more risk-taking. There are bigger grossing independent films than there have ever been, so the market is pretty good. And DVD is stronger than ever, and that's a major boon to the theatrical business, just knowing that sort of safety net is there."

"What's happened since the '80s is the emergence of home video and now DVD as another way of making money," said Karen Cooper, who runs Manhattan's premiere art house cinema, Film Forum. "Which means that after you've produced a small film, you don't have to make your money on theatrical. You can really expect to make it post-theatrical. It used to be that post-theatrical was the educational market, schools, libraries, film societies. Now, it's really the home market. I think that huge, huge market, which was really only created in the last twenty years, has meant that many more movies are produced. Most of them, absolutely dreadful. Or at the very least banal."

Or—sometimes—inspiring, provocative, and important, either in their contribution to cinema or to how we, as responsible members of society, look at ourselves and our culture. Yes, technological advancements and the phenomenon of the homemade moviemaker have meant that the theaters have become cluttered with claptrap. On the other hand, without the cinema revolution of the last fifteen or so years, American movies wouldn't have Todd Haynes, Paul Thomas Anderson, Wes Anderson, Richard Linklater, Quentin Tarantino, Ang Lee, Miguel Arteta, Alexander Payne, Rebecca Miller, Kevin Smith, Todd Solondz, Nicole Holofcener, and many others.

Ultimately, we can do nothing about *Bewildered*, or films like it. In some ways, film has become *too* easy to make—there's a lot of loose money out there abetting bad ideas; digital has enabled almost anyone to point a camera at Grandma and make what they're sure will be a riveting expose on the dark side of the AARP. Struggle, which we believe is always an important ingredient in art, much of the time goes AWOL in the making (if not the selling) of motion pictures.

As long as Sony keeps making new cameras and the great two-headed deity, Kodak-Fuji, continues to supply hopeful auteurs with the fodder of cinema; as long as filmmakers, festival programmers, distributors, exhibitors, and audiences exist, all we can do is use our powers for good. And maybe even the good of cinema.

What we've learned in the making of this book is that once filmmakers have finished a film, the process of showing the film and finding a buyer is filled with countless landmines, and that the independent film community has little patience with, and sometimes contempt for, the hundreds of films that crowd the marketplace. But even among the beleaguered journalists and distributors, we found that many people are extraordinarily protective of good films, and passionate about making sure filmmakers with real talent have enough knowledge to navigate this journey, and that as tricky and crowded as the marketplace may be, there is always room for a film that deserves to be seen.

It's been revelatory. We hope you find it so as well.

1

Evaluating Your Film

Is It Too Late Now?

If God wanted us to sell ourselves, he wouldn't have given us agents, publicists, advertisers, or evangelicals. That's because no one is the best judge of their own work. That's why writers have editors, to tell us where we've gone wrong (and tell us, and tell us).

Filmmakers have editors, too, but their job isn't really to tell directors that their films aren't working. Their job is to fix the film, and—if you believe the memoir of someone like editor Ralph Rosenblum (*When the Shooting Stops*)—it can mean as much as turning a calamitous collection of contiguous film images into something coherent and watchable. As he did with *Annie Hall*. And the original *The Producers*.

While not everyone can afford a Ralph Rosenblum, sometimes one is fortunate enough to have the ultimate assessment of one's work come from on high. Very high.

BOB BERNEY, president of Picturehouse and former head of both Newmarket Films and IFC Films (the guy who distributed *Monster, My Big Fat Greek Wedding, The Passion of the Christ*, and *Whale Rider*), remembered one such case.

"This guy that directed *Chumscrubber*," said Berney, referring to Arie Posin and his independent feature, which played Sundance in 2005, "somehow he was mentored by Billy Wilder. And he showed Wilder his first short. And Billy goes, 'Wrap it in a box, carefully. Put it in a safe. Never show it to anybody again. And start over.' And he did."

Few, of course, would be so privileged as to have someone as lofty (or in this case, one suspects, as gentle) as Wilder to tell them what was wrong with their film. At the same time, not everyone would have followed the late writer-director's advice (although it's perhaps as hard to imagine why as it is easy to imagine happening).

No one, really, wants to know what's wrong with his or her film. But there *is* usually something wrong—at least, there almost always is a way to make it better. Love for an individual film is never universal—Hate? Yes. Love? No. And before investing thousands of dollars and man-hours and buckets of perspiration and tears wept in your pillow, it is essential that the filmmaker take stock of what he or she has done—honestly, patiently, candidly, frankly—and figure out what's in the can (or camera).

"Make sure the film is truly finished, that it's the best cut possible from the footage you shot," said producer Scott Macaulay, of Forensic Films. "It's sometimes hard for a first-time filmmaker to gauge when a film's picture is ready to be locked, or what the strongest film is within the footage. A lot of people making their first features are telling stories that have a personal significance for them. Maybe they've been dreaming of making this film for ten years. But in a well-edited film, a level of brutality with regard to the shooting script and even the footage always comes into play. You have to lose things in the edit that might have been great on the page, or even great when they were shot. Maybe you wrote the whole movie around this one scene, and maybe that one scene doesn't work. The editing process is about being really rigorous in terms of the footage you have, the story you want to tell, and the effect you want it to have on an audience. And that audience should be an audience bigger than just yourself."

One might say you have to finish your film so that your audience isn't finished with it five minutes after the opening credits. But it also has to be in its most viable state for the festival, market, or other acquisitions environment at which it's aimed—whether you want it to be picked up by the most mainstream of distributors, or screen only at festivals, or find some comfy niche in between, such as New York's Film Forum. Or perhaps exist in an ethereal experimental-film atmosphere, screening only at certain kinds of European cinema festivals. That's OK, too.

"There are different hurdles people have to clear, and getting into festivals is one of them," Macaulay said. "But then being successful at a festival and getting distribution are others. I think a lot of films go to film festivals before they're ready. The producers submit them before the cut is at its strongest. You have to make sure you've screened it for audiences, you've gauged the reactions, and that the film is as tight and as well made as can be."

Before taking a film to a festival, screen the film to get good, honest feedback by doing some screenings with smart, trustworthy colleagues—a private screening, full of friends without agendas, friends with discernment—who would give smart story advice and be able to articulate exactly what doesn't work, before a batch of film festival programmers see the film and its flaws, and tell you the same thing. Fix what doesn't work. Imagine the aggravation in having your film reviewed in *Variety* in January, repeating the same comments that half the people who were in your living room back in September said. Start even earlier with your script.

"So many people will test the hell out of their movie when they think they have a cut that they like, but they don't work on their script," said Irwin Rappaport, an entertainment lawyer based in Hollywood specializing in independent film. "What they end up with is a film that has problems and the problems stem from the script. They could've fixed it before they spent a million, two million dollars, by spending another three weeks doing rewrites. Actors don't necessarily know, and first-time filmmakers don't necessarily know, so do the table reads. Get a lot of people to read your script and give you input. You don't have to listen to all of it, you don't have to incorporate all of it, but it saves a lot of time and money, it avoids reshoots and bringing on all sorts of different editors to see what they can salvage, cutting around things."

Cutting back to 1981, Jeff Dowd said that the reason Sundance was started—"and I was around then, with a bunch of people sitting in a room like this—was because [Robert] Redford, and all of those involved, wanted to do something, because they were seeing indie films that had a lot of independent vision, which were really trying to say something, and had unique qualities to them, but didn't quite work. A movie would rocket along until the third act, and then miserably fall apart.

"And everybody would be like, 'Jesus, if only they'd done this,' 'If only they'd done that.'"

Dowd said Redford based a lot of what he wanted to do on the Eugene O'Neill Theater Center, which takes new plays, subjects them to a summer month of readings, dramaturgy, and start-up performances, and then presents the finished products.

"The idea was if we could bring some of these filmmakers to Sundance and be able to dramaturge these movies with some of the best and the brightest—writers, particularly, but also directors, go to Sony to get some equipment to put them on their feet—we'll shoot, we'll edit two or three scenes, and we could do some preventive medicine. Basically, tell people, 'Stop. Do not make your movie. You're not ready. Make it three months from now. Make it six months from now. Make it a year from now. But make it the right way. When you'll have a better chance of doing it right.'"

It's a philosophy that continues at Sundance, with, for instance, the screenwriters and directors labs for feature-makers, the editing and music labs for doc-makers, and the composers labs. Institute Fellows are invited, mentors are assigned to them, and embryonic movies are nurtured into being. This is not to suggest it's a fool-proof system, but it certainly helps, and there is plenty of testimonial endorsement of the labs, as there would be for any program that so tenderly massages projects into being self-sustaining works—and keeps the postproduction experience from turning into an absolute nightmare. If there was one thing that was repeated as advice to filmmakers, it was that even if your film is finished, it may not be done. That there are always things one can do to make it better.

Independent producer Ted Hope said, "You don't want to do any kind of screening that's going to affect the film in the marketplace—you want it to be done in a hush-hush way. The first step is actually screening your movie in front of an audience, which isn't always a luxury that people have, but luckily the technology exists where even on a good monitor you get a good response. And try to do as many of those screenings as you're finding a positive result from. I can't tell you how many times I've heard from people that Sundance is their first public screening of a movie."

And the effects of that on a movie can be disastrous. "It doesn't need to happen," Hope said. "You can have a real feeling of how your film plays with an audience by assembling a screening in a screening room in a natural environment and people frequently do that for their friends and family, but there's no way those people aren't affected by that relationship. Showing it to people who will actually speak up is a far more important thing. And once people have gone through that process—and I personally recommend going through it three or four times—they'll see it's not about test-marketing. It's about watching the audience, hearing how they talk about the movie, what moves them, what doesn't, what points are getting through. As filmmakers, we are trying to have some kind of dialogue with the audience, and we want to see whether that's happening or not."

Of the films that are going to come to market without distribution, "Seventy percent of them are a kind of specialized art film of some sort," Hope said, "and getting response from the cognoscenti is critical."

"We took ten minutes out of *First Love, Last Rites* after premiering at the Toronto Film Festival," said Scott Macaulay. "That may have been ten minutes we could have taken out before that screening. But when we saw the way it played, it was too slow. There was a distributor that liked the film, and his requirement before he would agree to acquire it was that we lose ten minutes. After seeing it with a large audience, though, we didn't disagree with him and went back and made the cuts."

"It's really important for the filmmaker to do the research and make an honest evaluation of their film—although I have to say that this is virtually impossible for them to do," said Marcus Hu, copresident of Strand Releasing in Los Angeles, distributors of edgy, gay, foreign, and generally esoteric cinema. "Every filmmaker seems to think that their impossible movie is going to be so commercial and they all think their stories are universal. You just sort of sit there and kind of glaze over when you're listening to their idea. You go, "Oh my God, they have no concept . . . ' "

But that, of course, comes with the territory.

"Yeah," Hu agreed, anticipating the point, "because they otherwise wouldn't have made the film in the first place. In order to get that film made, they have to have these blinders on. Otherwise, they'd get stopped at every impasse."

"One story I find myself telling filmmakers over and over again comes from an article Caryn James of *The New York Times* wrote in the wake of the Sundance Film Festival a number of years ago," said publicist Jeremy Walker. "The story ran on page one of the Sunday *Arts & Leisure* section, and it was the year I think Miguel Arteta's debut *Star Maps* had its world premiere and was picked up by Fox Searchlight—then headed by Lindsay Law.

"It had been a storybook acquisition," Walker said. "The film had had a technically very rough first screening, with projection problems in a motel ballroom that had not quite been transformed into a makeshift movie theater. Miguel and his producer, Matthew Greenfield, were very upset. But a junior Searchlight acquisitions exec was in the audience, loved the film, and this brought Lindsay Law and the rest of the Searchlight team to the film's second screening at the [Park City] Library, where it played like gangbusters. The deal was completed the same night and was announced the next morning.

"The thing is," he said, "when *The Times*'s James quoted Law in her story, he talked not about the film they acquired, but rather the films they did not. He alluded to the idea that he'd seen many films that year that were almost there, but not quite ready. He got the sense that more than a few filmmakers had rushed to finish their films so that they could physically have something to screen at the festival, to their great detriment. No executive, he explained, would spend hundreds of thousands, or millions, of dollars on what was an even riskier proposition than it needed to be. And his main point was, hey, guys, you only have one shot."

Films are like fruit, Walker said: "If it ain't ripe, no one's going to go near it." But if a filmmaker has done the research, made whatever kind of evaluation he or she can, and still wants to continue, the next step is figuring out who else might possibly want to see that movie. Or cruelly rip the blinders off.

Producers rep Jeff Dowd is a burly, shaggy, instantly recognizable figure at film festivals around the world. He's cut a wide swath; he was, famously, the model for the Jeff Bridges character, The Dude, in the Coen brothers' *The Big Lebowski*. In fact, he was on his way to the 2005 LebowskiFest when we sat him down at the fabled Chateau Marmont in Hollywood.

"A general estimation," he said, "is that there are about 5,000 films out there right now that are not going to get a release of any kind, whatsoever. They're not going to get theatrical. They're not going to get video. They're not even going to get on cable. They're not going to get a DVD release, they're not going to get on Netflix, and they're not going to get foreign."

Estimate each film as a $100,000 shot, Dowd suggested, and what you're looking at is a total of five billion dollars.

(As producer Jeffrey Kramer once said about the selections at an unnamed film festival, "If they'd burned the money, at least they'd have produced heat.")

"That's a lot of money," Dowd added. "That's a lot of money to have fall off the planet."

But it's a serious matter. "I think some of those people," he said of the unsuccessful filmmakers, "lost their wives, lost their husbands, their parents won't talk to them. Neither will the friends they got their money from. . . . A lot of people go in with the attitude, 'Hey let's make a movie,' but unless you're one guy—like the guy who made *Tarnation*," he said of Jonathan Caouette, whose film is a kind of home-movie memoir, "one guy who's on his computer and has a lot of stuff—mostly you're putting a lot of burden on other people's lives. And you're asking them to do things for free. So with that comes a certain awesome responsibility."

Dowd said it all starts with asking yourself a couple of questions: One is how good is your script? The second is whether there's any market for your movie. "What I find is, ninety-five percent of the independent filmmakers don't really do either of those things as much as they should."

The purpose of all this precareer preparation is to draw an accurate bead on your work—how is it going to play? Are there rough spots that can be smoothed out with a little explication? A dropped scene maneuvered back in? An included scene sent off to Siberia? The timing on a joke rejiggered, or some narration imposed? Festivals are a great way to figure all this out—if you've got the nerve to face what may just be a hostile audience.

"When I view a film for the first time," said veteran publicist Harry Clein, "there are essentially three films spooling in my head. I use the analogy that it is like the old three-strip Technicolor camera, which recorded a red, a blue, and a yellow image to make the full range of colors. In my head I see three films: one, for myself; two, for the audience; and three, for the media.

"The film for myself is my personal reaction. Just for my own enjoyment. My personal taste. What I like, love and don't like or love.

"The film for the audience is often different from the film I see for myself," Clein said. "There might be moments that I think it has gone too far, or not far enough, but often I feel these are the moments that will make the film work for an audience. The audience might need more information. They may need things repeated twice. I like a leaner film. But sometimes you just have to hit an audience over the head making sure it doesn't miss a big moment.

"The film for the media is usually closer to my own feelings about the film. It is about the artistic affect and effect. However, I must feel that it is something the media can get behind, can write about in such a way that entices audiences to leave their homes and buy tickets. Is the subject matter interesting? Are the performances and direction special? Is there anything that raises this film above other films? Is it coming at the right time to get space? Question after question arises, as I search for angles.

"Sometimes even if I don't like a film," he said, "I know audiences will and therefore I can hook the media. For instance, I sought out Hugh Wilson to work with him on the first *Police Academy*, because I thought it was the best of all the slob comedies. And I was able to get exactly the media I promised him.

"As I got involved with more films at Sundance before they had distributors, I began color correcting my three-strip mental process. I had to figure out if the film contained elements that would make it marketable, as well as playable. No matter how good I thought the film was, it had to possess elements distributors needed. For instance, was there an image that might make a great poster? Since I worked on so many films that made stars out of new faces, the one thing that never fazed me was when a distributor said they couldn't buy a film because it didn't have star names. I always felt if the performances were good enough in a strong enough film, I'd find a way to turn that negative into a positive. The media loves to discover new talent. Or at least they used to when I started working on films in Sundance.

"So another strong element of my mental 'color correction process' is whether or not I find a strong subtext. That is the way I am able to project whether a film can appeal beyond a niche audience and reach a larger audience. As I have worked on film after film, it is always the subtexts that keep me interested. Even now I am talking to producers about new films, and constantly I am detailing the many stories/themes I find in the central story of their scripts. Perhaps there is the film that will appeal to teenage girls, but also there is the film that will appeal to older women, and there is the angle that will appeal to older men. And, usually, I will find the story that will not be objectionable to teenage boys."

"You make discoveries with audience members about why they like movies," Dowd said of first-time screenings. "Filmmakers never really know what they have. The first thing I say to them is, 'Have you shown it to an audience yet?' 'No.' You don't know what you have until you show it to an audience. Let's make the assumption it's a very good movie. When you screen it you're going to make discoveries that are better than your expectations. You're going to find why a movie touches or moves people in ways you didn't know, and how they articulate it in ways you never would have imagined. That's what happens all the time with the success stories."

"Screenings can also confirm that your instincts are right," Hope said. "With *American Splendor*, our first screening was mostly for editors, producers, one or two directors may have been there. We were planning a lot of work on it, but when we saw the effect the film had on people, it was incredibly encouraging. We felt that we were doing the right thing, and it pushed us to continue with our plan with even more conviction.

"The first time I saw *Brothers McMullen*, Eddie [Burns] had it cut almost as a melodrama; it was almost an hour longer when I started working with him. There was a very short period of time, but they got what I was saying and took tremendous leaps with the footage."

The problem was, Burns and Co. had already accepted an invitation to screen at one of the IFP's (Independent Feature Project's) Independents Nights at the Walter Reade Theater at Lincoln Center, an event that would have constituted a premiere and made the film ineligible for competition at Sundance.

"We knew we couldn't screen it," Hope said, "but they had the screening booked, and information had gone out, and we didn't know what to do. We hadn't finished recutting the film but we knew we had the first twenty minutes and it just happened to end, if you remember the film, at the banana-cutting scene. So we kind of planned a 'technical difficulty' to correspond right where that cut ended.

"The first twenty minutes played like a comedy, and it went over like gangbusters, and the crowd was all excited, everybody was really upset about the technical difficulty, there were buyers in the audience, and all of us walked away really confirmed."

And the fact that they hadn't actually shown the whole film meant it was still eligible for Sundance, where it went on to win the Grand Jury Prize.

"It was one of those things," Hope said, "where we really didn't have the money to finish the film—at Sundance we only had a couple of music cues that played over and over but nobody seemed to notice because they were laughing so hard. The money had come from Eddie and his family and they had turned away finishing funds from other sources that wanted a big cut of the back end. And that screening gave us the confidence that it was worth the remortgaging of their house, or whatever they did to get the money."

In many cases, independent films just don't screen to test audiences the way they screen to audiences who love art films or independent films. "You have to have the courage of your convictions," Hope said. "When we were screening *Happiness* in the early days, we had some really negative responses, but you were able to discern why they were responding that way. And it wasn't about the film-making. You always have to remember when you're doing these audience screenings, that independent film—art film, specialized film, whatever you want to call it—the people who see these movies are an audience where 50 percent are arriving already knowing what they think because of the reviews they've read. Their minds are made up. But an audience that sees a movie in a raw state is never going to respond in that same sort of way."

The point is, in postproduction, it's not too late to hunker down and make a film better, just by listening to audiences a little. If the film is great the way it is, hallelujah. But there is nothing wrong with fine-tuning a film and really getting it ready before its long trek into the mouths of strangers. A classic Hollywood example movie was *An Officer and a Gentleman*.

"They went out and tested the movie," said Dowd, "and it did forty-two percent in what's called the top two boxes—'very good, excellent/recommend' and 'definitely recommend.' They went back, based on this information, and shot the back-story which shows Richard Gere's father is an abusive whoremongering alcoholic guy, his mother's a prostitute or something, he gets beat up by these kids in the Philippines. Not the most elegant of filmmaking. Everything else in the movie is the same except the first four minutes. And it goes up to ninety-three percent top two boxes.

"Why? Because it gave it an emotional context. We now understood where Richard Gere was coming from. 'Oh, I now understand why he wants to be an officer.'

"They didn't put it together till they started to test. But three or four minutes at the beginning of the movie. . . .

"Another one? *Blood Simple*—'It'll never play for women.' Women get it. Hoosiers—the assumption at Orion was, 'This movie will not work because women will never go see a movie about basketball and sports movies don't work.' Guess who likes the movie the most: Women, even more than men, because it's got vulnerable men who deal with their problems, and basketball is the sport women like the most 'cause there are good-looking guys running around in their shorts.

"So anyhow, we learned this through those screenings, so therefore that informed the entire strategy of how you approached that movie. The results informed everything we did. So the first thing you've got to do is when you're a filmmaker—*especially* before you go to a film festival—let's really back up. You want to make changes in your film before you show it to the programming committee of a film festival. Because as rushed as you are, back up your schedule so you're not showing your first cut to the Sundance committee on October 5. Back it up so on August 15, you're showing that first cut to someone—so you're tweaking it, and by October 5 it's a better cut."

"Make sure your film is as short as you can humanly stand it," said director Miguel Arteta (*Chuck and Buck, Star Maps, The Good Girl*). "Every minute beyond ninety is a fucking unmerciful splurge. Every millisecond that you're demanding attention better mean something really special to you, because the audience is smart and knows everything."

If there was one thing that was always true, Arteta said, it's that during your first screening "every second of celluloid will reveal all your intentions and planning a lot more transparently than you could have ever imagined, once it's up there in front of a big, discerning audience."

A really good lesson in prescreening tweaking can be learned from Heather Juergensen and Jennifer Westfelt, the writers and stars of *Kissing Jessica Stein*, who screened their film a few times in an edit bay to friends, and asked for really constructive advice from them. Dowd, after seeing the film in one of these screenings, urged them to go back and make some changes, involving some reshoots, before the film was to be unveiled in a few weeks time at the Los Angeles Film Festival. The filmmakers were wary of spending more.

"It was four weeks before that screening," Dowd said. "And they were saying, 'We don't have enough money, we don't have enough time . . .' and I said, 'Well if you want to end your career now, everybody else's career, lose all the money, etc. etc., don't listen to what those people are saying at the screening.'

"'Or you just might listen to them.'"

The two women eventually agreed that the film had flaws, and understood the importance of making the movie better before presenting it to buyers.

"At the end of the day, we're marketing emotions when we market films," Dowd said. "Very often, in a lot of indie movies, there's a lack of craft in storytelling. But there's also a lack of depth of emotion, and the place to make all these changes, the cheapest and easiest, is at the script stage. You could take a situation like *Kissing Jessica Stein* which, parenthetically, was dramaturged a lot. It started at a workshop in the Adirondacks as a one-act play, went to off-off-Broadway as a one-act play, was developed into a screenplay, developed into a . . . development deal within the system here a few years ago and then went back to an indie thing. But there were constant changes, because Jennifer and Heather were writers, but also actors. They kind of naturally would dramaturge the piece. Some of the better movies ever are by writer-actors—Woody Allen, Carl Reiner, whoever. Mel Brooks."

The situation with *Kissing Jessica Stein*—one of those break-out indie hits that prompt one to say "it came out of nowhere" (when in fact it was a intense, laborious process)—involved a movie that worked all the way to the very end, and then didn't. (See "Case Studies," pages 185–189.)

"So they went back and shot for a day," Dowd said, "and it made the difference between no sale, and what was the biggest sale of the year for any indie filmmaker. So you can dramaturge early, or fix it later, but so much depends on the script. But that's a success story because they had so much that was working they could fix it in one day."

Some filmmakers, in getting an assessment of their film, might forsake their friends and choose to work with a group like NRG (National Research Group) or OTX (Online Testing Exchange) to (1) get a sense of what they have and (2) if the results are good, get numbers in hand that would help convince distributors of a film's virtues.

As screenwriter William Goldman famously said, "Nobody knows anything." He was talking about Hollywood, but his axiom applies to film in general.

"What was Bingham Ray's quote on *Blair Witch*?" Dowd asked, referring to the cofounder of October Films. "'The only thing scary was what they paid for it'? Even the experts don't know."

Many people we spoke to echoed the same sentiment—that before you even start production, work on the script, and don't rush into production. To test a film when it's done can be too late; why not test the script before you shoot? Send your script to smart people and get lots of good advice, do readings and see what works and doesn't before you start production so that you can fix problems before spending more on rewrites, reshoots, salvaging and cutting around things. Have you done everything you can to make the film as good as it can be? Do your homework first. It could save you heartaches and headaches later.

Other questions to ask yourself: What kind of film is it? What kind of buyer would be interested? Who has distributed similar films in the past? Who is the audience, and who will really respond to it?

"If the goal is to have a filmmaking career," said Dowd, "the misconception is, 'Well, I'll make my first movie, and listen to people who say, "Whatever you do, don't listen to anybody tell you what you can't do. Just go ahead, listen to your inner voice and go for it."'" Well, what if you end up with is a movie that embarrasses you? (A) It doesn't get released and (B) it is counterproductive to your career because you wouldn't want to show it to anybody. You couldn't show it to an actor; they'd say, 'Hey this person doesn't know how to work with actors. I wouldn't trust my career to this person.' It's not even a good calling card, necessarily. Not only because it didn't get released, but because it doesn't work. So the quickest way to get to a career, if that's your goal—and I think it is the goal of most filmmakers—is to get to first base. And a foul ball, or a strikeout, is not the best way to get on."

Start before you shoot. Start with your script.

"Be willing to be really critical of your material—not unrealistically so, but to really look for ways to make it better," said Greenfield. "Never be satisfied that it's good enough, because movies are complicated, but they can almost always be better. And figuring that out, every little way you can make it better, makes it more likely that it will survive, and get out there to an audience, and that you'll have the opportunity to make another one.

"Really," he said, almost pleading, "make sure your movie is the best possible movie. That it's really finished and it's the best movie you can make. Don't make something kind of like the movie that sold last year, or like another movie you liked. Finish the movie first, and make it the best movie before you worry about all of the other stuff. Get really good advice from people who are in this business now, and really get their take on it, and how to do it. It changes every year. Every week."

Andrew Jarecki, who made *Capturing the Friedmans*, said, "Filmmakers often think that when they finish making their film, they've completed the artistic part of the process, and that some businessperson will be poised to swoop in and carry it off to the world of deals and getting it seen. But the process of finding the right distribution approach is far more art than science. If it is your first film, you will be new to the process and feeling of letting it out into the public. It's invigorating and wonderful and necessary, but also one of the most nerve-wracking experiences you'll ever have."

Jarecki described the first public showing as "not unlike sending your three-year-old child to his first day of school. He's been in your care for a few years already, and the only reactions he's really gotten have been from you, or friends who come over and meet him, under your watchful eye. Now, he's going off to a place where other kids will meet him for the first time: Most will not even notice him, some will love him like you do, and others will take him out to the playground and beat the shit out of him.

"It can be unsettling for our parent-filmmaker to watch him toddle off into the playground for the first time, not knowing what will happen and that as soon as he's out of your sight, you won't have much control over it. So all you can do is make sure he gets some sleep and brings a good lunch."

Scott Macaulay said, "Filmmakers need to be able to define success in a way that is empowering for them and that is meaningful for them. . . . The difference between success and failure can be very subtle. There are films that we may perceive as huge successes, but that have actually lost a lot of money. There are films that we may think underperformed, but that have been in profit before they opened on a single screen. Getting into the Sundance Film Festival, getting into competition, is not the only barometer of success. If you adjust your expectations and have a modesty about yourself and your film, and you can figure out how to place it in the market, you can make it seem successful, and that's important."

"At some point, you have to take a real hard look at what you've got and what its chances are," said longtime indie publicist Mark Pogachefsky. "I've seen really good movies, with no stars, and they're good, but they're not going anywhere. I think we've unfortunately gotten to the point where everyone can make a movie, but it doesn't mean they should."

"The reality about selling your film is that it's an incredibly tough market," said producer Matthew Greenfield. "It is now and always has been. The buyers are really careful, and there are not that many of them. Some buyers have very specific kinds of movies that they pick up."

Dowd continued, "You ultimately have to ask yourself, 'Why is this movie so special that somebody is going to come see it on the opening Friday night?' It can be, literally, four hundred people in the New York metropolitan area. Or metropolitan Los Angeles. Or Seattle. Four hundred people—that's good enough. Out of what—twenty million in metropolitan New York? But that'd be all right for the Sunshine, or something like that, the Angelika.

"But if you can't get, for some reason, four hundred people out of twenty million to show up for the first weekend, with the infrastructure of support that is there, even on a very challenging movie, one might ask, Who are you making this movie for?

"So you should try to ask yourself what's so special. Not that it's like 'interesting'—'interesting' is the code word for 'I didn't like it, but I better call it interesting in case John Anderson or Manohla Dargis tells me later it was the greatest movie of the year.

'Hey! I always said it was interesting!'"

2

The Delegation

Putting Together the Perfect Team

"**F**ind someone you trust to navigate you through this process," said producers rep Steven Raphael of Required Viewing. "You only have one opportunity to premiere a film."

Someone. But who? Nowhere in this book is there likely to be a greater diversity of opinion—which is putting it politely—than about who you need beside you when you set out to conquer the world.

Genghis Khan had horsemen, archers, swordsmen and an unconquerable hunger for domination. You will have—if you choose—a publicist, a sales rep, a producers rep, and a lawyer.

Which team is fiercer—yours or Khan's—may end up being a matter of perspective.

"PROBABLY THE MOST IMPORTANT PART of this side of the business, from where I sit," said James Schamus, copresident of Focus Features, "is for filmmakers, who don't have to be businesspeople, to be smart enough to surround themselves with the best advisers."

Schamus said filmmakers should have some knowledge of the business— both general and, if they're courting Focus, specific. Such as "knowing the kinds of films we distribute here, what kinds of films we distribute well, they know the ones we struggled to distribute well, they know our track record, they know the way we put movies out, they know the way we *don't* put movies out. So that when we're talking, either before or after we've seen the film, they have a sense of who we are and what we do. And there's a reason they're talking to us, because they probably think we can do well with their film—not because we're going to bid higher than the other guy.

"It's not as if I ask filmmakers to be experts in marketing and distribution, and publicity and ancillary exploitation. They don't have to be. What would be great sometimes is if they could be interlocutors, if they do have a team of sales agents and managers and publicists. And number two, they aren't rabid, dollar-chasing egomaniacs."

Independent producer Ted Hope of This Is That said, "The first question is always, what type of film? But to get access and doors to open you still generally need someone who's traveled down those waters before. Ten, fifteen years ago there weren't many people—now there's a plethora of them, and many different paths you can take and generally you want advice from the different segments."

A four-headed beast, he called it. "Someone on the business side," he said. "Someone on the creative side and someone on what I'd call the 'appreciation' side, whether it's someone who does exactly the same thing, or a critic or someone who loves the kind of movie that you believe that you've made—and then someone to help you position it."

Most films don't need a "delegation" or an "entourage" of well-paid accessories, and that's good because in most cases the people you want aren't going to want you either.

Which means—obviously—the competition for their attention, and the attention of top-shelf publicists, producers reps, et al., is brutal. It means that just getting them to look at your film will be a challenge. Never mind the idea of you picking them. Although, of course, a lot of what happens has to do with not just the quality, but the salability, of your movie.

"Twenty years ago," said Michael Barker, copresident of Sony Pictures Classics, "you'd have a producers rep, and Producers Rep was the producers rep title. In the last few years I have noticed that experts in many different professions have helped filmmakers realize what they desire in distribution. It could be a lawyer, it could be a publicist, it could be a manager, it could be an agent. This is happening much more as we go forward. But what I think is so important is that a filmmaker has—whether it's an intermediary or an adviser—someone who has expertise that the filmmaker respects and who also has a feel for the filmmaker and the filmmaker's film. I don't think it matters what that person does, just so long as that person has the business expertise to be helpful.

"By the way," Barker added. "Mr. Sloss [John Sloss of Sloss Law and Cinetic Media] took great exception to that on a panel at Cannes."

On hiring help, director Gregg Araki said, "I would find out what films and what filmmakers they've worked with before and check out their references. Talk with the directors or producers they've repped in the past to get the

411. That's the great thing about the socializing/bonding experience of festivals: You develop these relationships with your fellow filmmakers and can call or e-mail for references on these people—not to mention actors, potential crew, etc. It's important to get an opinion, preferably a few opinions, to find out what you're getting yourself into."

Producer Jeff Levy-Hinte added, "Once you're in competition you have tremendous leverage. Until you've spoken to everybody, you shouldn't make a deal and negotiate the rates. It will never make the difference between whether the film will sell or not, unless someone is completely incompetent and they prevent it from being sold; it can make the difference, if there is interest, in how strong a deal you can craft by working with a specific person, and how dedicated they are, if it doesn't go in the first round. I think you just need to be realistic as to what kind of film you have, and similarly allow the market to speak for the film. Not to assume that you're being dealt with incompetently because you don't have million dollar offers before the first screening is over. Frankly, a lot of films don't sell at all. A lot of fantastic films don't because distributors don't see them as viable."

Before going much further, let's explain who is who and who does what:

Publicists

Publicists get word out to the press about your film. They are servicers of information. Which doesn't necessarily mean that the press will write about it. When selecting a publicist, check their reputations and meet them. Do you get a good vibe from them? Do they get your movie? Are they able to think strategically? What kinds of films do they do best with? The truth is, there are no guarantees in publicity—if anyone's making promises, think twice. In the world of independent film, publicists, in most cases, have made a decision to work in this arena for their love of these kinds of films and in order to be fairly successful, they have to be at least pretty good. It is a lifestyle choice of the unglamorous kind—and definitely a different breed than the Hamptons-bred, *Sex-in-the-City* Samantha types.

The old-style image of the cigar-smoking, baggy-pants-wearing press agent is, film critic Roger Ebert said, "far from the truth. In my early days I did meet some of the old-style press agents, and they were colorful and sometimes outrageous, but the new-style PR people are professionals, and very useful. I am talking mostly about the publicists I meet at film festivals or in the course of covering independent, foreign, documentary, and alternative films. The studio and agency publicists are excellent people, too, but they are handling whatever their client has to open. What I like to call 'indie publicists' often choose a film because they believe in it. They have taste. For them, a good film is a cause."

Jeremy Walker cleared up some of the mystique, and explained what constitutes a good publicist. We "tend to be viewed as everything from charlatans and snake-oil salesmen to gurus with magical powers who can save a film. Like anything in life, the truth is somewhere in between. In the most clinical terms, we are paid sources for the press, but just because we are paid does not make us any less valid as sources. Indeed, my feeling has always been that the best PR people are the most reliable sources: honest and straightforward people who provide accurate information and who have a healthy respect and empathetic understanding for at least some of what journalists need to do their jobs. The best PR people keep their clients honest and, in our cases, champion the work of filmmakers about whom we are truly passionate.

There are a lot of fallacies that come with the territory. Among them: "Greasing palms, wining and dining, calling in favors," said B|W|R's Chris Libby. In fact, he said, "Successful film publicists respect the role of the media and interface with press contacts thoughtfully. Journalists hate cheerleaders. Smart journalists demand honesty and smart publicists handle the media with integrity, selling journalists on a film's highlights—what makes a movie newsworthy—without overselling the film itself.

"A good publicist," Libby said, "will collaborate with the other assorted reps; they can help set the tone for a film and create 'the message' or, more simply, decide how the film should be talked about among the group, and then to outsiders. Publicists can define the media strategy that would best serve a film's needs, and in most cases, during this time, getting all the press you can may not be time and ink best spent."

All of these things are done in an effort to get films seen and seen in the right way, to better any chance they might have. Micah Green, formerly of Cinetic Media, the most prominent consulting firm involved with the sale of independent films, and now at CAA (Creative Artists Agency), said sometimes a publicist can make the difference. "To be honest, even on a film that we are handling, more often than not the publicist will play the most important role in setting the stage for a great sale by positioning the film with key critics and keeping the filmmaker up to date on press response and reviews."

On how important PR weighs in on a sales strategy at a festival, William Morris agent Cassian Elwes admits, "That's a loaded question. I think it's enormously important. For me, PR is critical, because you need to know what the critical response is going to be to your film when you're in the environment of trying to sell the film. If the film is going to be poorly reviewed, then you know you need to hurry up and get it done. If it's going to get great reviews, then you can maybe play the field a bit more."

Bill Condon, director of *Gods and Monsters,* will tell filmmakers before going to a festival like Sundance, "One of the crucial things going in, and I'm sure every filmmaker knows, you've got to hire, especially if you don't have a distributor, to get the most out of this, you hire a publicist, and we had Jeff Hill and his company, and they were great. They worked as hard as the people who financed the movie, in terms of trying to bring the deal together, and they know more about what's going on than anyone. And they took the movie on because they believed in the movie. They were the best allies we had during that whole experience."

Hill modestly described his role," I am the middle man between the press and the art. Leading them to it is easy if the director has made a good film. You can lead a horse to water but. . . ."

A dedicated publicist may be a necessity at many festivals; for others, like Seattle and SXSW [South by Southwest Film Conference and Festival], you may want either to work with the festival's press office or with someone locally. Carl Spence, Seattle Film Festival's director of programming, said, "It does help to have a publicist or additional help, but they do need to know the local press or the way the festival works. The protocol here and at a lot of festivals is just different and if you don't take that into account you risk alienating the local press."

Each agency has its strong suits, but here's a short list of PR agencies known for their work in film, particularly independent films at festivals without distribution:

B|W|R	**mPRm**
Falco Ink	**MRC**
Fredell Pogodin & Associates	**Murphy PR**
IHOP	**Sophie Gluck & Associates**
Jeremy Walker & Associates	**TCDM**
Mickey Cottrell	

There are many others who primarily work with films that have distribution, and each has their specialty.

"Not all films may need a publicist," said RJ Millard, former press office manager at Sundance and former publicity and marketing VP at IDP Films.

"But they need someone to guide them—Bob Hawk or Peter Broderick maybe"—he said of two veteran consultants, "but they need somebody. Otherwise, you walk into a festival environment not really knowing what you should accomplish. If you want to have that experience, fine. But you may not get much out of it. You might just go and have a great time. But aside from that, you have to be focused on 'What is my objective?' Do you want to sell your film? Do you want good publicity so you can make your next film? Will you use your film as a calling card? Take an objective look at your film, and figure out what you can do with it, and what you want to do with it. Where do you want your career to go? And you should know that going into a festival. It can't be an afterthought."

"When the publicist is good, it's strategic," said John Sloss. "A bad publicist will just try to get as much publicity as possible. A good publicist will understand that they have to work in league with the producers rep or the agent for the film. At any given festival, there are thirty people you're marketing to, and those are the buyers, not the public at large."

Sloss said that the press or publicity has to be positioned, and used as an instrument in service of strategy, not just in service of the broadest possible awareness of a movie. "That means getting the right press there, keeping the wrong press out, getting the right press into the proximity of the buyers and getting them in the mood to talk about their good feelings, prescreening before the festival.

"We are extremely bullish on the idea of involving a smart publicist in the sell," Sloss added. "We think they're essential."

Jeff Levy-Hinte said that working with a publicist is essential, simply because "those first reviews and stories and the way people talk about it are going to set it up for its entire life. It's like prenatal care. If you screw it up, your child will be autistic or retarded," he joked. "I certainly have people I work with. Show them the film, meet with them. See who understands the film and will work really hard and there's always the monetary side, so that's going to limit who you can work with."

New York Times entertainment reporter Sharon Waxman recommends a little investigative journalism: "Do your homework. Do your research. Find out who their clients have been, find out who they represented, call them, find out if they were happy."

The right publicist or rep really matters, Waxman said. "If it's someone I know, whose opinion I respect, then I will listen to them more. If it's someone who talks about every single movie they're working on, then I can't give them much credence because they're pitching every project they have to me, just because it's their job. Certain journalists and certain distributors will respond to different things. Having a publicist or a representative who's savvy enough to know the landscape you're dealing with is really important."

It's the boy-who-cried-wolf phenomenon. "There are publicists whose advice I trust," *Los Angeles Times* critic Kenneth Turan explained, "and when they call, they are really going to have an impact on you. When they say, 'You should really see this,' it means something. I have learned over the years who I can trust and who I can't—trust in the sense of having an idea of what kinds of things I might like to see, and not trying to spin me. If someone is inaccurate in their representation of a film, and hyping it, it's not like we're not going to know. We're going to see the film; it's not a big con that you can get away with. Publicists and critics are going to have to deal with each other for years, so honesty is really very important."

"It makes all the difference," said Karen Rhee, entertainment producer, *Good Morning America*. "Especially if it's a smaller movie, it really matters who's calling me. Am I going to take the pitch seriously? It depends on who's doing the pitching.

"I get so many pitches a day, press kits, e-mail pictures, phone messages," Rhee said. "But out of six hundred pitches a day, what am I actually going to consider? I'm going to consider the ones that are coming from people I know—because if I don't know the name, I probably won't even read the e-mail pitch. That is the bottom line. People say that this is a relationship business, and it is. If I trust the person, then I know they're not going to waste my time with something that doesn't make sense for my audience. So it's all in who you hire to work on your movie."

"This is a sore point," said critic Amy Taubin, a longtime supporter of indie film. "I don't like that everyone thinks they have to spend all this money. But on the practical level, if a publicist I know calls me up and says, 'I took this movie on because I really love it,' I'm more likely to go see it than if it's a movie no one's telling me about. What do I know? It moves up on my list of priorities. So if Jeff Hill calls me up and says, 'This is a movie for you,' I'll go to see it."

She said it doesn't have to be a publicist. "It could be the producers rep, or the sales agent. Just someone you know, who knows what you like."

Not that anyone can necessarily control the media, but "You have to strategize," said Strand Releasing's Marcus Hu. "You don't want a *New York Times* feature eight months early. The public has such a short-term memory, they won't even remember. What you'll have is a nice clipping. And you probably won't get that again, when the film opens.

"But that's the value of having a great publicist, to walk you through these things and stop you from doing something stupid."

Depending on what festival you're going to, you might not get a publicist to work your film, and in that case you'll be working with the festival's press office. Which is fine, in many cases. Do you need a publicist at SXSW? No, in most cases. People are either going to see your movie, or they're not. The filmmaker will send tapes to whoever is interested, and the festival press office will let you know if there are any inquiries.

Some festival press offices are staffed by individual publicists who are pitching stories to major dailies, regional papers, and the wires, such as Associated Press. When Laura worked with them, they would formulate story ideas—let's say a festival had a lot of minority filmmakers one year, or a lot of movies about alienation, or a lot of really introspective films, or maybe 9/11 films. You look for hooks. Publicists can help get films noticed and highlighted by thinking of story ideas that help journalists cover a lot of films in a way that makes sense for them.

As a filmmaker, the press office should have a cell phone number where you're available, and an e-mail address where you're available, as well as information about general availability and cast availability. A few weeks before the festival you should have a conversation with the press office, introduce yourself and describe your film, and let them know you are available should anything come up.

Producers Representatives

A producers rep will guide you toward the acquisitions strategy that best suits your film. He or she may call and put in a word at a festival, and will push buyers—and press—to come and see your film.

"Producers reps can help filmmakers get into a festival, and create buyer awareness," said Paul Federbush, SVP of Production and Acquisitions, Warner Independent Pictures. He explained that while producers reps are paid a combination of retainer and a percentage if a film sells, "You're basically paying for their relationships."

"A couple years ago, in a matter of three days, we had *Garden State, Open Water, Riding Giants*, and this doc, *Deadline*, all of which were selling out of our house," said Sue Bodine of Epstein, Levinsohn, Bodine, Hurwitz and Weinstein, LLP. Bodine is a lawyer, but admitted, "We do sometimes act as producers reps or sales agents.

"It was insanity," she said. "You have to be ready for that and you certainly want to be able to take advantage of any opportunity to have that kind of situation happen, where there's that kind of competition, and where you can really maximize the deal you're going to make.

"But I've found—and I have no idea what Sloss would say—that a sales agent or producers rep doesn't really create that. You can help create the atmosphere of desire, and that's really important, but these guys who buy these movies, they're smart guys who've been doing it a long time, and they want the movie or they don't. And that's why you find that there are certain films that catch on, and it's basically because of the movie.

"Again, you have to manage the filmmakers' ideas about expectations," she said. "You want them to be ready and know that you're ready to really jump on any opportunity that might present itself, but also understand, and be prepared, for a more likely reality."

"Producers reps can maximize your success," said producer Scott Macaulay, "especially if you have to answer to investors: If you have a professional in that position who knows the marketplace, and knows the buyers, you can at least have the peace of mind that your film is being professionally handled, that every rock has been uncovered in the search for a distributor.

"Going to a festival," he said, "I think having a producers rep is very important. There's a value to each member of the team—the director's agent, the lawyer, the publicist. Funnily, though, depending on the film, the job of the producers rep can be both the easiest and most lucrative. They show up at a festival with a print fresh from the lab, it screens at the [Sundance] Eccles Theater, it's a huge hit, the offers start flying, they have an all-night session, and they make the sale in the morning. In twenty-four hours, they've made a lot of money. Of course, they're able to cut a smart deal based on their years of experience, so even though they might wind up making more than the director, it's ultimately worth it. But a film that is more difficult, more challenging, and less audience-friendly can take months and months to sell, and some reps will lose interest. In those situations, filmmakers need to know that they have to do as much work as the rep in terms of hustling to get the film out there."

Justin Lin, director of *Better Luck Tomorrow*, added, "I had no idea who was who, but John Sloss was the first person I called. All I knew about him was that you read about him and he was everywhere in the books about independent film books and magazines but I didn't know him."

Producers reps are only really going to want to rep movies that they believe they can sell, or that they really believe in, which makes sense. You can't persuade or force someone to come and work on your film when you don't have anything to offer.

"I had a small, dark Asian-American film and passion was really the only currency I had," said Lin. "The actors, the crew, everybody came on because they believed in the project, and they believed in me. I felt so lucky because I really had nothing to offer except the film. That's something I cherish. It's very unique, and now making these studio movies, I'll never have that again. I will always treasure that—to feel like everyone is just there to help."

Of why he chose to represent the film John Sloss said, "First it was a film which we all loved. Then I met Justin and that sealed the deal."

Ask around. See if you can get a consensus on who's out there, and who's right for the type of film you have. Call them, show the movie to them, and follow up. If you think you need a producers rep, you will want the rep in place before you publicly screen. They will most likely not watch your film until you are accepted into a film festival. Please note: Any producers reps, publicists, sales agents who are good practically audition you. There are so many films out there, and so few places that will buy them, that it's not worth it to them to rep your film unless they think they can do something with it—that is, sell it. Getting someone they know and trust to refer you would be a good idea.

"When all is said and done," Lin said, "having someone to represent your film doesn't hurt, but it has to be the right relationship. There's no template— it always comes down to the people and how much they believe in you and your film. Their names can only go so far—they can get people into the room. But the buyers—they have to really love the movie."

Levy-Hinte added, "Every film is different. In the Sundance environment, I think a producers rep is essential for a few reasons: They have intelligence of the marketplace, particularly if they're supporting a few films. There are only a few good reps that are worth dealing with—Sloss is the gold standard. I've enjoyed working with him in the past. The disadvantage is that he has a lot of films and the advantage is that he has a lot of films. He has good taste. The fact that he controls up to half the films which are being sold seriously really means that he can shape the marketplace unilaterally and prevent one film from being played against the other. The disadvantage is that he probably is not able to give every film all the attention all the time. I also like Cassian Elwes, Andrew Herwitz, and Bart Walker, who is amazing, but doesn't really play the same roles as a Sloss or Ken Kamins."

While they are referred to as sales reps, producers reps, lawyers, etc., Cinetic Media consider themselves a consulting firm. They have a theatrical sales department and an ancillary sales department that explores television and video values on their projects and can assess split-rights opportunities—which separate TV, video, and theatrical rights—as they sell the film. They also consult on film financing. "We watch every movie that's submitted to us," said Sloss. "We watch about a thousand films a year, in one form or another. It's true that I don't watch all of those films, and there is a process, but we have reliable, well-trained staff who watch them."

The reps with the best reps say persistence is really important, because most films don't sell right away. "We stick with films," Sloss said, "because we're committed to movies and we feel responsibility, and have a lot of personnel and if it doesn't sell immediately, we'll redouble our efforts and we don't give up."

Cassian Elwes added, "The difference for me is just experience. I feel like I've been in the trenches longer and been involved in bigger deals than a lot of competitors in my field. And I'm very picky about which films I work on, but once I actually get onto a film, I stay with it until the deal gets done. There are no films I've worked on that haven't gotten deals eventually in some form."

Even if you don't get one of these reps on board, remember the advice of Eamonn Bowles, president of Magnolia Pictures. "Don't sign anything," Bowles said. "As soon as you have any interest on any level, get someone who knows the process. If not, you will most surely be taken to the cleaners. Conversely, you may have some notion that something's unfair that is pretty basic in most contracts. You need someone who knows the lay of this very complex land."

Producers reps/sales reps/consultants include:

John Sloss and Erin Heidenreich at Cinetic Media
Rona Wallace
Steven Raphael at Required Viewing
Josh Braun and Rosanne Korenberg at Traction Media
Andrew Herwitz at The Film Sales Company
Jeff Dowd
Jonathan Dana

Agents that sell films include:

Cassian Elwes and Rena Ronson at William Morris
Micah Green and Kevin Iwashina at CAA

Rich Klubeck at UTA (United Talent Agency)
Sean Redick at ICM (International Creative Management)

Entertainment Lawyers

An entertainment lawyer represents parties involved with the film, provides production counsel, financing deals, above- and below-the-line deals, clearances, distribution legal, contracts, guild dealings, distribution licensing. (See Chapter 3, "Legal Matters.") In many cases, a good attorney can also help with foreign sales.

While attorneys will help you close your deal, they do not necessarily have the time to help position the film with buyers, etc. Some attorneys who work in independent film are:

Sue Bodine	**Linda Lichter**
Tom Garvin	**Irwin Rappaport**
Jonathan Gray	**Shelley Surpin**
Andrew Herwitz	

Foreign Sales Agents

A foreign sales agent will sell your film to other territories and for rights around the world. While you will want to have one in place before you screen at any festival at which there are a significant number of potential buyers from around the world, if you have a film with very little international awareness, you may not get anyone on board until you've had a successful first-festival experience. Once they've heard about the film, they may be more approachable to selling that film to the rest of the world. If you are going to sell your film in a market, you are better off working with a sales agent. Few American independent films will generate enough money to make it worthwhile for a sales agent to take them on, so finding one who will act on your behalf may be difficult. Among the top-shelf foreign sales agents are:

Celluloid Dreams	**2929**
Fortissimo Films	**Jan Rofekamp**
Kathy Morgan International	**Summit**
Arclight	

"Usually you bring in a foreign sales representative after it's world-premiered," said Jeff Levy-Hinte, "at least in the indie mode. You bring it to a festival to sell it. It's a hard balance between being humble enough to be realistic about what the possibilities are but then to also be steadfast, and not be conned by people who are trying to make a quick buck by getting involved with your film and taking advantage of you.

"The best are Celluloid Dreams and Fortissimo Films," he added. "Those really are the premiere foreign sales agents for small films. Depending on the genre elements, Lions Gate. There are hundreds of foreign sales agents all vying for your attention. If someone is overly interested, it can be as bad a sign as if they're underinterested. There are so many people who will just lie about what they're able to do and what they're able to offer."

"I would say that in this business there are so few good sales agents out there," said Strand's Marcus Hu. "Maybe ten. Ten in this world."

"It depends on how marketable your film comes off to these prospective sales agents," said Hu. "If they all look at this one movie and see the hook, they'll jump on it. Or they see the cast. Or they see the creativity the movie has—something like *Mean Creek*, where someone says, 'There's a way to sell this movie.' Or something really difficult like *I Stand Alone* [Gaspar (*Irreversible*) Noe's first feature]—'How am I going to *sell* this movie?'

"And then, if you have a movie like *I Stand Alone*, maybe you'll get John Sloss. But maybe the best person to sell that movie is a company like Celluloid Dreams, where Hengameh Panahi is just so ferocious about supporting these impossible movies because she so believes in their artistic merit. She's certainly not out just to make money, and she has a museum curator's taste."

Again, it's complicated because, by and large, many of the smaller films aren't going to attract the interest of these heavy hitters—and if you haven't gotten into Sundance or a comparable festival, it's going to be very hard to get one of these guys to even watch the movie.

On the acquisitions side, they'll all get watched—but it might be by an intern or assistant, unless the film is of a high pedigree or has a high-profile producer. But in that case, the filmmakers wouldn't be sending out tapes. They'd have an acquisitions screening.

Micah Green encourages filmmakers to work with their reps, saying, "It behooves filmmakers to accept that they will need to take a much more proactive role in studying the industry and festival circuit, coordinating the press and marketing of their film at its festival premiere, and monitoring every element of the sale. Too many filmmakers turn a blind eye to their agents or reps and assume that they are working in their best interests."

As far as putting together a team, you have to consider whether you really want or need one, because they will somehow have to be paid. Sales reps and producers reps usually get paid in points. Entertainment lawyers are usually paid by the hour, but you can set a cap if necessary, or a fee per job. Publicists are paid a fee or retainer, and, depending on the festival, the costs will vary.

"Certainly, there are lots of examples of filmmakers who have gone to these festivals without anybody or anything and have worked tirelessly to promote their films," said Sue Bodine. "And I think ultimately, if you have a really great movie, it will show."

On the other hand, "I can't imagine a more hellish way to spend a Sundance than chasing distributors or key press people on your own," said director Gregg Araki. "That's what the reps and publicists are paid for. But you do have to keep track—make sure that your representatives are doing their jobs and getting your film seen by the necessary people."

There have been cases, Bodine said, when unrepresented filmmakers have gotten offers and then called in an SOS. "We've had that happen, where we've gotten calls at Sundance from filmmakers we haven't even met, right there on the scene, having to deal with decision-making with regard to deals, and they need someone immediately," she said. "It's always nerve-wracking for them to be in that position."

Sometimes, Bodine said, her firm has made arrangements beforehand with films "that we don't for whatever reason feel that we have the time, or energy for, or the filmmaker doesn't necessarily know what they want. But we can be backstage in the wings.

"If I make that commitment to someone ahead of time, of course, we're going to be there," she said. "But depending on what's going on, it can be a little bit chaotic—obviously, it's not the preferred way."

The fact is that for a lot of the smaller films, and new filmmakers, there is very little likelihood that they are going to get into some kind of major deal-making—so it might make sense to have this type of looser arrangement.

"Filmmakers, of course, feel like if something happens right then and there, it needs to be dealt with immediately," she said. "Sometimes that's the case. But a lot of times, it's really not the case. We've had this plenty of times— you have a film, and there's one distributor that's interested in it, and it's not going to be a big-money deal—which is not to say you want to let it lapse, by any means, but it's not urgent. You don't have to lock yourself up in a room with the distributor, and stay up all night and make the deal."

Those are the legends filmmakers have heard, she said—of the all-night deal-cutting in the sweat-lodge atmosphere. "And they want that," she said, "even when it's not necessary, or appropriate. Personally, in terms of style, I really don't like to be in a situation where filmmaker expectations, and reality, and how we are going to be involved, are out of synch."

Regardless of your situation—and the budget of your film, and who's in the credits, and how compelling your story is—you do need help, or at least the advice of some professionals. If you're a filmmaker, and you're just finishing your film, and you're planning to submit it to a festival—or you have just submitted it and gotten a pretty good indication that you might be accepted—*that's* the time to start making calls. You should have it clear in your mind who it is you would really like to work with, as well as who you want as your second and third choice. Needless to say, don't screen your film for all of them at the same time.

Go to your dream publicist, sales, or producers rep, and see if they say yes or no. If they say no, go to your second choice. But you don't want to just throw it in a blender and expect to get lobster thermidor. You want to go to the people, strategically, who make the most sense for your film. They all have Web sites that indicate what they've worked on. Does your film fit their taste? (And it's largely about taste, unless you have a *lot* of money.) At the same time, when they've seen your film and you meet with them, see if you get a good vibe. See if you think they "get" the film. There has to be a personal connection.

And remember: Your team is only as good as your movie. They won't make it any better.

You also have to remember that the competition among filmmakers and distributors—the whole scene—has become intensely competitive. And the competition begins long before festivals, sometimes before films are finished. Those who have an interest in new films and filmmakers are tracking things like a pack of Republican bloodhounds.

"Absolutely," said James Schamus, at the Greenwich Village offices of Focus Features. "It's very, very competitive out there. [He shuffles some papers looking for a certain bundle. He finds it.] This is just literally stuff that's coming out, not even at Sundance; this is a hot list and you'll see on each page there are four films, and each page [he flips through] gives you the information, including the various notes of all of our various contacts with the filmmakers. And that's just this month's. That just comes regularly and we sit and go through them and say, 'Here's an interesting group of people.'"

Is it people they're already aware of?

"No, no, no, no," he said. "It could be people you've just heard about or the log-line seems interesting or the sales agent is a respectable person. You try to stay in that loop."

Schamus said it isn't necessarily bad that all this is happening. "But we need to acknowledge that it's happening," he said. "That's why you have this new class of entrepreneur who has really always been part of the system—it was me for a while, and Ted [Hope] and David [Linde]; it was John Pierson; it was John Sloss and still is John Sloss, the so-called sales agents. And here again you have a really interesting situation. Along with the rest of the hyperinflation of the environment, you have a lot of these guys showing up in Sundance with ten or fifteen movies they're supposedly representing, but what we're really talking about is a lot of spaghetti being thrown against a very large wall. Some things stick. With some, it's 'Oops, I lost your cell number.'"

The scary, or at least ironic, thing about all this "development" is that the very films that should be benefiting from the so-called blossoming independent movement are oftentimes being lost in the shuffle. Due to the rise of the middleman—the producers rep, the sales agent—what's become of paramount importance is the film that will sell the most tickets. Business is business, of course, and people have to eat, but this was never the point of indie cinema— precisely the opposite. "Fringe" doesn't mean the last parking space at the mall; "edgy" doesn't mean you've had too much at Starbucks. When you have business people dictating what films will be given the greatest attention, and festival programmers and even journalists going along with their agendas, what you have isn't all that different from the kind of cinema you find on your better airlines. In other words, Hollywood.

It's an ethos that infects everything. "Here's what happens," said Schamus. "As with a lot of other things in our culture, you have the winners and losers and the middle ground is what gets completely neglected. I can walk into a screening, as I have many times, to a film represented by a very powerful, extremely capable super-smart sales agent who sits at a screening of a film where I just want to slit my wrists, just walk out, never look back. And then I walk into a film represented by that same person, fall in love, and believe me, I'm out the door on my cell, kissing that person's rear end and doing my best to buy that film.

"Meanwhile, somebody else might have liked that other movie, but there's no real heat on it. So I can guarantee you, those calls aren't getting through. They're not happening. So there's only so many auctions you can hold. It's not like e-Bay. So what happens is, as a buyer, your real frustration is with that film that "could." You say, 'You know what? This is a film I could really take a little bit of a gamble with' and then there's nobody around to answer the phone. Everybody's too busy with the auctions."

And the solution?

"I don't know if there is one right now," Schamus said. "Because I do think filmmakers need savvy and experienced people. The business is very complicated, and the deal-making can be brutal, and filmmakers have every right to have representation that's there to extract the best possible situation, including the biggest numbers, since that's part of the story. That's fair. And they should be professional people, who'll be there the next time. Some of them, as you know—you read the [Peter] Biskind book [*Down and Dirty Movies: Miramax, Sundance and the Rise of Independent Film*], and someone's saying, 'Then I lied to so-and-so about the bid I got from somebody else and they gave me *more* money!' Well . . . I'm not sure we all do business that way. But generally speaking, people in business for the long term, they're professional people."

"I have to say there are very few sales agents or producers reps I can't stand," said Marcus Hu, "and those I can't stand I won't talk about. I like dealing with UTA [United Talent Agency] and William Morris—they all basically have the same ideals and understand how it works. Any of the real seasoned pros know how this stuff works. If they're selling to Sony Classics, they know what they can ask; if they're dealing with Strand, they know who they're working with. With most of us, we've been around so long, Sony Classics, Lions Gate. . . . It's practically a template. 'OK, we're going to follow the model we used on. . . . ' Any of the ones who are out there and established they're all fine to deal with."

"I've sat at both ends of the table," said Schamus. "Usually it's with people, honestly, the people with the longer histories who aren't just there to drive up the price, who have an ongoing business of making movies and getting them out in the right way. There's a comfort level. 'Cause they've been around—even if the filmmaker's a first- or second-time filmmaker, the producers have that history of kind of sensing that, 'Look, this is a movie that's going to be in theaters, it's going to get good reviews. It deserves the best distribution, and probably these are the best guys over here.'"

The moral is to go with the people with the most experience and as a consequence may cost the most. So what do you do? If you can only hire one person, who will it be?

"I think you do have to have representation, either with publicity or a lawyer," said Bob Berney, president of the distribution company Picturehouse. "It's very tough to send things out on your own, and try to think you can do it yourself, unless you really have the experience. I suppose before you get into a festival is a good time. I think probably a producers rep, but if you were already accepted somehow then a publicist to manage that. . . . It's all pretty equal."

If you had to choose between having a lawyer, producers rep, or publicist when you go to a film festival, what should your priority be?

"Well, you can easily get rid of all that by just hiring John Sloss," said Marcus Hu. [How do we spell "evil maniacal laugh"?]

"John is great," Hu said. "When he's really behind a film there's no one more powerful than John for getting a filmmaker the best deal."

And for your side?

"I actually like working with John," he said. "I like working with Celluloid Dreams." Hu said that when a filmmaker gets to a festival he or she really needs to have a sales agent in place—"Unless they are really seasoned in being able to approach all the prospective buyers. In that case, they should do their research, find out who would be the best buyer for the film. It's all about doing research ahead of time. I think that's a real important thing, so they can target those people, figure out who the players are. Just get informed."

But again: If you had to make a recommendation to a filmmaker who did feel like he or she had to be surrounded by this machinery, is there a priority list of people like producers rep, lawyer, publicist, whatever?

"Hire a good publicist," said Steven Raphael. "Get as much press on the film as possible. Also send cards with screening dates to all distributors reminding them of when the film is screening."

"Honestly, I don't even know," said Christine Vachon, New York institution and producer of such films as *Far from Heaven* and *Boys Don't Cry*. "In fairness to a filmmaker who does think he needs those things, when I first started you didn't need them, and I moved past that point before you really did, so you could very easily say to me, 'Well, you don't know.'

"But I guess at the end of the day, I'm not sure those people really make any difference," she said. "I mean, with a publicist, the only difference I've ever seen is a publicist can tell a distributor who's on the fence that they know that so-and-so at *The Los Angeles Times* actually loves the movie, but I've found a lot of that information to not even be valid lately. I've certainly had my hopes dashed more than once about what A. O. Scott or Manohla Dargis [film critics for *The New York Times*] thought of the film, and it turned out not to be true. I guess what it comes down to is, if there's heat on your movie, those people are going to come after you. Those people cannot create heat. They might tell you they can, but they really can't."

In Vachon's opinion, there are only two things that create heat. One is anticipation (especially "if a movie has an element in it that is considered interesting"). The other thing, she said, is the old Cinderella story, "just coming out of nowhere and being great."

"People just really scratching their heads saying, 'Oh, my God, who knew?'" Vachon said. "Neither of those things is bolstered, in my opinion, by an agent, a manager, a sales rep, a lawyer, or whatever. I don't know a buyer in the world who, just because they hear John Sloss talking about what a great movie *Brick* is, is going to automatically think it must be a great movie. I really loved that movie. And I thought that there were people who went in with certain expectations about it, and in my opinion *Brick* was a movie that in some ways would've been better served by being discovered."

Berney has been to a lot of festivals. He's seen the thrill of victory. And the agony of defeat.

"You can't just accept any festival," he said. "Rob Devor, his first film was *The Woman Chaser*, it got into the New York Film Festival. And he called me and said, 'It's great, we just got in'—but without distribution, if you get bad reviews, a festival is not necessarily good news. All of a sudden you're in the limelight. That film, in a smaller way, might've built based on the pulp-novel stuff, but to suddenly throw it out there. . . ."

The Woman Chaser, which starred Patrick Warburton, was a very dry, noirish, black-and-white comedy.

"Then," said Berney, "Steven [Holden of *The New York Times*] called and said, 'I've seen five or six black-and-white films this week in the festival. I hate it!' and we were thinking 'Uh oh.' And then he said, 'You know what else I hate? Film noir movies!' It was a really bad week for Steven."

The filmmakers, he said, all went to Sardi's, and they all went down to get *The New York Times*. And they all shared cocktails and groans.

"That's why, if you just do it yourself and get into a festival, you can set yourself up for disaster," said Bob Berney. "So you need a producers rep or someone to navigate the festival world for you."

Has the rise of the sales/producers rep damaged the process or manipulated it in any way?

"No, I really don't think so," he said. "It may be that some of them can get a film [into a festival] that shouldn't get in, but I think for the most part, it hasn't damaged it. And you need some guidance. I'm a distributor; you're going to take advantage of anything you can. 'You don't have representation? Oh, you don't need it. Come on over.' Not that I would do that. But some people might."

"We stick to our business plan and we've always stuck to our business plan," said Sony Classics' Michael Barker. "And there are impediments that go away and are replaced by other impediments. So I don't think it's any different now than it was before; people's names change or they go to different places but the thing that I find difficult about certain sellers of films is that maybe they're handling too many films so they can't serve all of them. Maybe they have more agendas than the single film, because to a lot of these sellers it's a business for themselves as much as it is anything else. It's the same with publicists—in order to survive they have to handle a lot of films. So you have to make sure you're one of the films they're taking care of well, or you're going to feel resentful. I just don't feel it's any different."

"Nowadays," said Schamus, "even if your film has no distributor, even if it's seen by no one else in the world, there's enormous pressure to position your film in such a way that the media discourse is molded around the experience of your picture immediately. And you use that as some kind of leverage in your selling and buying. Now, there's much more pressure to pretend that you're some kind of a retail-marketing kind of person, in materials, presentation, the way your publicist talks about the movie, with the press notes. All those things."

Short Films

Let's get one brief detail out of the way: short films. There is no real market for short films in the United States. Someone asked us, hypothetically, "OK, so I've made my twenty-minute film. What do I do?" We said, "Go back and make a ninety-minute film." It is very hard to get people to pay attention to shorts unless your subject matter is so salacious, or has such an interesting hook that people can't help but fall all over it (or has a title like—we're not kidding—*Billy's Dad Is a Fudgepacker*, which played several festivals in 2005). A short film is something you would show to production people in order to line up your next job. Or that you would package with your next script, just to show you can direct.

Shorts can also lead to unrealistic expectations. "We have had quite a few student shorts in the New York Film Festival and other programs we've done," said Richard Peña, of the Film Society of Lincoln Center and Columbia University, "but one of the things that's often very difficult is that people make a very good short, and the immediate assumption is 'Now it's time to make a feature.' And it's a very different animal. It would be great if filmmakers could make two or three shorts, really hone their art, get a feel for their craft and get more comfortable, but the leap from a very good talented short to a similar feature is a very difficult leap, and not very many people have been able to bridge it right away. But that's just the way the system is set up. There's no life to shorts. Shorts are a calling card. You might get some festival play, you might get a couple of TV sales. But it's no way to make a livin'."

If you have a short in a festival, the advice here would be not to waste time or money on a publicist, but to concentrate on getting the people in the business—production execs, agents, people who could help you in terms of your next movie—get in to see it.

Having worked with many makers of short films in his years as the press office manager at Sundance, RJ Millard would not recommend that a short film have a publicist. "A publicist will most likely not get that filmmaker anything," he said. "At best, a few mentions—but most likely only if they win, and they'll get mentioned anyway. Sensational or celebrity driven—those are the shorts that might get written about. But that's not about the filmmaking."

The gravy would be distribution on Sundance Channel, HBO, IFC, IFILM, Amazon, Showtime, or one of the other few domestic or international outlets for short movies, or the Internet. But in those cases (see Chaper 1, "Evaluating Your Film"), you have to know what you've got, and where it might play best.

The questions about short films are posed all the time. One advantage can be getting yourself slotted before a feature, so people will be *forced* to watch it. But it's not always the good move: Keith Bearden's *The Raftman's Razor*, which went on to win the shorts competition at SXSW and play at New Directors/New Films at the Museum of Modern Art in New York, played in front of a feature at Sundance called *Steal Me*. There was no heat on the feature, so by the end of the festival no one was coming to see it. Or *The Raftman's Razor* either.

If you're in a shorts program you'll get a lot of production people looking for up-and-comers. If you're in front of a feature you have to remember that no one's buying their ticket for the short.

If you're in a festival, bring postcards with contact names and information and perhaps a note: "If you can't make these screenings, and would like a tape, please call." While the politics of handing out tapes is not the same for shorts as it is for features, one thing is constant: Most people don't want to carry tapes around a festival. They'd rather have you send it to their home or office. And they're probably not going to drive half an hour to see a twenty-minute film. Personalize your efforts. When you're out and about, when you have a conversation with someone you'd like to see your short, jot down the person's name. When you get back home, write a letter, include info that would help that person to remember who you are, and enclose the tape. Make sure to include your contact info, info about the project, and—with any luck—info about your next project.

Legal Matters

Please Release Me

Question: **What's the most valuable single piece of information a young filmmaker can have?**
Answer: **Knowing what he or she doesn't know.**

This is particularly true when it comes to the legalistics of making a movie, or—more importantly—releasing a movie.

SHOOTING A THING—a face, a product, an architectural landmark—usually doesn't present legal problems. Showing it to the public, however, might. And the myriad ways a filmmaker can violate copyrights, privacy, and the boundaries of intellectual property are so vast that unless you've gone to law school in lieu of film school (which isn't all that bad an idea), you're liable to commit such enormous, stinking, heaving, resounding offenses against both man and his inanimate objects that it will keep your film tied up for eternity and your future projects in perpetual turnaround.

Have you shot on the street at any time during the making of your romantic comedy/horror fantasy/coming-of-age drama? Were the starring couple in a car? Were they in front of a billboard advertising antiperspirant? Did innocent passers-by get caught in your frame? Please turn around. We'd like to handcuff you.

The point is, there are so many ways to get in trouble you may as well hire a lawyer now, 'cause you're certainly going to need one later.

There are lawyers out there, entertainment-savvy attorneys who specialize in cinema, even the independent type. Take Irwin Rappaport, for instance. He's an entertainment attorney whose clients include writers, directors, and producers. He's probably the best person to explain what it is he does.

"I do mostly movies, some TV," Rappaport said (in what we have to say was a pretty cool house in Hollywood; being the Virgil on the tour around legal filmmaking Hell has its benefits).

"I represent primarily what I would call independent filmmakers, although I do have some studio-type clients or clients that have feet in both worlds," he said. "I primarily represent writers, directors, and producers, not actors. In the independent world, I am frequently the production counsel, which means if you want to make a movie outside of the studio system with private financing, whether it comes from individuals or small companies or foreign presales—which doesn't really happen very much anymore—then you would come to me."

Were you making a movie, Irwin would have done your financing deals. All your above-the-line, below-the-line deals; all the strictly production-related deals, like locations, and clearances, etc.

"Then when the movie's finished," he said, "I do the distribution legal, which means that I do all the negotiation and contracts related to the distribution licensing of the movie, so I would often work with the sales agent, and I prefer to work with the sales agent or sales rep—you know, like [John] Sloss, or UTA [United Talent Agency], ICM [International Creative Management], CAA [Creative Artists Agency], William Morris—to sell the movie, so we're both in the room negotiating with the distributor at Sundance or Toronto or after a distributors' screening here in L.A."

Uh huh. And when exactly do you start all this?

"Well, if you're a filmmaker, and you don't have somebody as your lawyer," Rappaport said, "then I would get involved from the very beginning, before you hire anybody, when you're raising your money, when you're ready to get your mother, and your father, and your aunt and uncle and friends, and your associates to put money in a movie, then you come to me, and I create the entity, draft up the contracts. So I'm meeting filmmakers at a script stage, when they're packaging their movies."

By "entity," Rappaport means a limited liability company (LLC). Each film has a separate production company to own it and produce it because such a structure protects the individuals against liability. It also protects any other film assets that they have from being tied to this film—in case there's a claim against one, you don't want it to "attach" to the other.

"So I meet the filmmakers when they have maybe some money attached, maybe they have a script, maybe there's a director, or maybe not, maybe there's just a script, and a producer or a script, and a director looking to go from there," he said. "Sometimes I'll help them package elements, but usually not. I like to be the guy they come to when they're ready to go, because I don't pretend to be a person who raises money for people. If I did that, that's all I would do. Like Sloss doesn't really practice law anymore. He raises money, and sells movies, and he has lawyers who do the contracts."

Some readers will be asking, as they look wistfully at their already finished product, can my movie and I jump on the bandwagon of legal filmmaking? Or are my picture and I *both* finished?

"No," said Rappaport reassuringly. "In fact, I will often get involved at that point. Filmmakers will get a recommendation to come to me by an agent or manager, another lawyer, a friend of a filmmaker. Oftentimes that happens with really low-budget films and documentaries, where they really haven't had anybody except some lawyer, who's really not an entertainment lawyer, helping them here and there. I've had a number of those situations come about, but the majority of the films I get involved with I get involved with at the production stage, and I continue to work with them for distribution."

Generally (unless they've read this book, of course), first-time filmmakers aren't savvy enough to know they need legal representation, or at least some kind of lawyerly help. Or are they? Certainly since the early '90s, and the explosion of indies in America, would-be helmers (*Variety* "slanguage" for directors) have gotten wiser and wiser about the intricacies of various moviemaking machinery.

So awareness has changed since then?

"It depends," Rappaport said. "If filmmakers have connections with Hollywood, they're more aware of the legal pitfalls. . . . There are a lot of lawyers who will represent the director or the writer, which I also do, but there are not that many lawyers that get involved in representing low-budget independent films. Mine range from five hundred thousand dollars to—I guess I've had some that have been independent—to ten million. They usually hear about me because I'm just one of the few guys who will do this."

That Rappaport works in Los Angeles might make him seem like a foreign agent-saboteur to the legion of filmmakers based in New York City, which is, and has been, a much more fertile ground for indie filmmaking (despite the presence in L.A. of Gregg Araki and others). But Rappaport certainly has clients in New York. He represents, for instance, Antidote Films, which made *High Art, Laurel Canyon, Thirteen, The Station Agent*, and *Mysterious Skin*—all films that had major successes at Sundance (both critical and financial). He was working with director/writer/actor Larry Fessenden (*Habit, Wendigo*) on his project in

Iceland, and he represents Larry Clark, photographer-cum-cinema provocateur and the director of *Kids* and *Ken Park*.

Why all of this should be particularly interesting, if not frightening, to filmmakers in general is what happened—or almost happened—to one of Rappaport's New York clients.

"Tony Barbieri was a first-time filmmaker who came to me through [publicist] Mickey Cottrell," Rappaport said. "He had made a film with his then wife. They raised the money from friends and family, no lawyer involved, just running and gunning, no permits, you know, really low-budget. It was a brilliant film, got into Sundance, sold to Shooting Gallery, and made top 10 lists all over the country." It was called *One*.

Barbieri made another film called *The Magic of Marciano*, which was released internationally and got a video release in the United States. It did not get picked up theatrically, although it got some very nice reviews in the trades, which went out of their way to mention the fine performance that Barbieri got out of actress Natassja Kinski, not the most malleable actress in the world. He now has another project that's being developed. At the time we talked to Rappaport, Barbieri had found a financier, was at the casting point, and was trying to package his film.

Flashback (and cue the organist) to the situation with the now-defunct Shooting Gallery. "Tony Barbieri had his film distributed by Shooting Gallery," Rappaport said, "and then they almost optioned another project of his—and fortunately they didn't close the deal. And then they went out of business.

"I think it's important for filmmakers to be careful about who they go into business with, to ask around not only to find reputations for honesty—do they actually report to you, and pay money when they're supposed to?—but also, to the extent that you can find out, you know, how are they doing? Are they a small company that just released a big flop and went really wide? A lot of these new distribution companies go out of business very quickly. I often will tell clients not to—if they can avoid it—make a deal with a new distributor. 'Cause they may not be around. They may release another film, spend all their money, and not be able to release yours, or they won't have enough money to release yours in the right way."

Though Barbieri's first film was released by Shooting Gallery, if he had made a deal with them on his second film, the project might have been tied up, not forever perhaps, but long enough to be fatal.

"It would've gone through bankruptcy," Rappaport said, "and the project might've been sitting with some creditor of Shooting Gallery that didn't have any interest in making the film, and that option would potentially have . . .

you'd have to let the clock run out." Barbieri would have been prevented from making the film at all "until the option expired, theoretically. Because until you know what's happened with it—definitively, through the courts—you can't just go off, and try to make it somewhere else 'cause some creditor might say, 'Wait a minute, I own that option. I just got it from the bankruptcy court.'"

It's the script they have control of. "Yeah, that would be the thing they would control the option for, at least for a certain period of time."

"You've got to be careful about the money people you get involved with because they can oftentimes be crazy," said director Tommy O'Haver of *Billy's Hollywood Screen Kiss, Get Over It*, and *Ella Enchanted*. "Make sure you have a good contract with the producers before you make the movie because, in the long run, I've found I don't make any money off that movie [*Billy's*], because they basically owned it outright. I got paid a little bit once it got sold, but they're collecting all the residuals, and various other things. I don't know if they got anything out of Trimark, now Lions Gate. Have a lawyer involved from the outset, just to make sure you're treated fairly—not to screw anybody out of anything, but just to make sure you're treated right."

In addition to avoiding a distributor or producer who is going to go out of business (that should be simple), or anyone with felonious intent, the filmmaker has to be cognizant of any number of pitfalls.

"You definitely need someone to sort through all the legalese, deal terms, etc.," said Gregg Araki, director of *Mysterious Skin*, as well as *The Living End, Nowhere*, and others. "I have never heard of anyone who wrangled a distribution deal all on their own. That's basically insane. Pick someone reputable, with a track record. If they've never done a distribution deal before, for any movie you've ever heard of, keep looking."

Anyone who is aware of the concept of music rights knows that you can't just use a recorded piece of music (or a written piece of music, for that matter) without getting permission, or paying for it, or both. It can actually be distracting when a film has a huge soundtrack of hit songs—if the movie's not so good, you can spend more time tabulating the cost of the music than you do following the plotline. Even good movies can have you wondering—what do you imagine they spent for the songs in *American Graffiti*? Why do you think that Wes Anderson's original version of *The Royal Tennenbaums*, which had an alternate take of the Beatles' "I'm Looking Through You" over its closing credits, lost that track for the released version of the film?

At Sundance 2005, we watched *Rize*, a film with which Rappaport was associated, and wondered, although we didn't know all the artists, whether all of their music had to be cleared.

"A lot of it was original," he said. "Some of it's being licensed. The difficult thing is that on some of these music-based films—I did one named *Scratch* which sold years ago, it was picked up by Palm domestically, it had ninety cues in that movie. A nightmare. Sometimes filmmakers will put music in a film without having rights to it. That's one real pitfall—you've got to find music you can afford. I always think you find music that you can afford, and you put it in, and if the distributor wants to improve the music, they can do that. If you put music that you haven't cleared, or that you only have festival rights for, but you can't pay for it yourself, then you're in a situation where the distributor might or might not pay for it—and if they do pay for it, they're paying less money to you for your film. They're clearing your music, and less money goes back in your pocket. Because it's all part of a financial calculation on their part."

"Music licensing is probably one of the bigger post-sale issues for lower-budget films," said Magnolia Pictures president Eamonn Bowles. "When you are negotiating for your festival license, also negotiate for an all-rights license as well. This doesn't mean it needs to be paid up front, but the chances of you getting a favorable deal may well be better than with an established company attached later on. At least have something negotiated for the acquiring company to decide whether or not it's worth it."

It's one of the big mistakes filmmakers make, he said. "Mainly, get all your clearances and music licenses set up. Sometimes a film can't get released or becomes prohibitively expensive because certain rights haven't been secured."

"There are some famous examples of films that were really difficult to release because of clearance problems that weren't taken care of," said the well-respected entertainment lawyer Sue Bodine. "*Paris Is Burning*, among others."

"Jennie made a movie," critic Amy Taubin said of *Paris Is Burning*'s director Jennie Livingston, "and I've always told my students to use the music they want. Chances are your film is not going to get into a theater. You want to make the movie you want to make, and music is really important, so just use it. Don't be stupid and use Elvis Presley or Frank Sinatra. And try—call the rights owners up, and say you're a struggling student, it's only going to be shown in festivals, and you'd like to be honest about it. Or don't try. Jennie didn't, and she could have cleared all of those songs, because the film could have been considered academic, educational, an anthropological documentary that no one thought would make any money.

"When Miramax bought it," Taubin added, "the music companies wanted real money, so Miramax took her advance and used it to clear the rights. She didn't make any money."

"Avoid anything you have to clear," said Robert Pulcini, codirector, with Shari Springer Berman, of *American Splendor*, as well as two earlier docs, *The Young and the Dead* and *Off the Menu: The Last Days of Chasen's*. "If you can get away with it."

On the other hand, "You're talking to people who used Frank Sinatra and Dean Martin in our first movie.

"We used nothing but standards and jazz recordings," he said. "It's funny: We ended up getting amazing deals because the Sinatra family loved Chasen's so much, and they gave us a great deal for a song or two, and then everyone else had to match it, since the Sinatras did it. But for the most part, that is such a fairy tale. If you can make your film without having to deal with those issues, it just makes the sale of it so much easier. If you can use [an original] score, if you can *not* use prerecorded music, and if you can avoid shooting things that have to be cleared, it just makes your life so much easier. And it could make the difference between whether or not you get the distribution."

"That's the thing," said Springer Berman. "It's very easy then to get festival clearances, because there's no money usually exchanged. But then, when someone wants to buy your movie in order to get worldwide rights in perpetuity, suddenly the cost of the film is dramatically increased. And it might be the difference between the distributor wanting to take a risk on your film versus 'No, it's too expensive.'"

That being said, if the music is absolutely essential to your movie . . . just make sure to talk to a lawyer.

"It's important to know what you're getting into. People always think, 'well, I'll get it,'" said Pulcini, meaning clearances. "If taking something out is going to ruin your movie, you'd better be really careful, because you may be asked to take it out. You better have an alternate plan."

Deals can be made wherein the distributor agrees to pay for the music rights, "but the more they pay for that, the less they're going to pay as an advance," Rappaport said. "The more money they pay out to you, chances are, the higher their fees will be."

"Nothing will ever make it easy," said Greenfield, "and 'delivery' [all the elements required in a distribution deal] is always a nightmare, even when you're well prepared. One place people get tripped up on is in music rights. And really making sure what rights you have, and what rights you don't, and what you need. Ideally you should have everything you need before going out to buyers, and before going to festivals, because it's a very complicated part of the process, and something the buyers are particularly careful about, and there's just a very sticky legal issue that you have to make sure you're one hundred percent clear on. I think having really good help on the legal side of music clearances, and making sure you have all of those rights before you go out, is one big thing."

There is no "fair use" in a film—you have to pay for every piece of music you use, no matter how short it is. Someone sings "Happy Birthday," you have to pay. Someone sings a Beatles song, you have to pay Michael Jackson (or whomever he might have sold the rights to). But it's not just a music issue. Virtually anything filmmakers don't create themselves must be cleared.

"If you're filming in my house," Rappaport said, "you'd have to get permission from the artist who painted that painting [he points at a work], because I own the physical painting, but I don't own the copyright. You'd have to get permission for any music that's playing in the background."

And books or magazines?

"If it's featured in a way where the camera focuses on it, and it's an important part of the scene. . . . It's more important if that image is going to be used in any way in the marketing or advertising of the movie than if it's just in the movie itself. It's not a hard-and-fast rule, but I always err on the conservative side, and say, 'Clear it.' If you have this book, and it shows up in the movie, and the author of the book doesn't like the film, and thinks that it casts his book in a negative light, then he has a claim."

How about something advertised on a T-shirt? If you shoot the street, and you shoot a billboard, and the billboard is advertising another movie, how are you supposed to make a movie?

"You have to dress the sets," he said. "A lot of times, people will forget. . . . They will be shooting on the street, and there will be a mural in the background. You have to clear that."

Who is responsible? The filmmaker, ultimately. He or she has to do what's called a script clearance report. Or hire someone to do it: a company that will break down your script based on everything that's in it. They'll say, this character's name hasn't been cleared. If you plan on showing a Twinkie or there's a reference to Twinkies, they give you the contact at Hostess whom you contact to get permission to feature their product.

"I produced a film," said producer Scott Macaulay, "where at the first day's location there was a wall covered with dozens of different posters. I asked the production designer if we had cleared any of them, and the answer was no.

The production designer said it didn't matter because there were so many of them that none were specifically featured. Then I said, but we don't know what the shots are yet, and until you see a shot list and the actor's blocking, you never know what background element might be featured. And sure enough, the staging put an actor's close-up right next to the face of a famous sports star who we had to get a clearance from."

The laws within this area are really quite complicated, said Sue Bodine, because there are both federal copyright and fair-use laws, several different kinds of laws you have to think about, and several different jurisdictions.

"There are a lot of old wives' tales about what's OK, and what's not OK," Bodine said. "'You can use eleven seconds of this.' That's nonsense. Usually there are guidelines that you can go by once you have an understanding of what those laws are, and one of the major ways is getting E&O [errors and omissions] insurance, which is something that is usually required for distribution, and that basically covers claims based on those kinds of things. And the insurance company will determine which things they will cover and which things they won't based on their understanding of what they think the law is.

"You, as a filmmaker, either have to argue with them or you listen to them, and say, 'Fine, I'll go get the clearance for this, that, or the other thing.' But it's mostly a documentary problem, because that's usually where things tend to end up in the film that weren't necessarily intended. Or people aren't sure whether they need releases, or that kind of thing.

"In fiction filmmaking, for the most part, you have somebody whose job it is on the production to do clearances. It's a very general matter of really incidental usage of background stuff that is not in any way featured, or there's nothing derogatory in the way it's used or the scene that it's in. But it's certainly an issue, and certainly one that we have had any number of situations where people don't realize what they need ahead of time, and as you become a more experienced filmmaker you do realize that you're not going to finish a movie with all this stuff in it unless you're purposely doing that. . . . Morgan Spurlock on *Super Size Me* obviously knew he was taking on McDonald's."

There was a similar situation, she said, with *Bowling for Columbine*, and the clearances necessary from K-Mart (which Michael Moore convinced to stop selling ammunition).

"Most of these things get resolved, of course, when you have something that's that high profile," she said. "It's a different dynamic because you have a distributor involved, and you have someone who's basically standing behind the filmmaker, and it's not impacting negatively—it becomes everybody's problem. With a smaller film that doesn't have that kind of distributor support, the distributor's likely to turn around, and say, 'We're not going to distribute it, end of story.'"

For the filmmaker, the script clearance report is the first step. A lawyer then reviews the script clearance report with you, and identifies what, in fact, needs to be dealt with and what needs to be changed. Then, usually, someone on the production staff, either a production office person or a person in the art department, will call and get those permissions.

A good production designer and a good director will know that they have to get permission to use things. And that includes anything with a distinctive design element to it. You can't just cover up the name "Volkswagen" on a VW Bug and expect that no one will know what it is. Volkswagen will certainly know.

There is, of course, the option, at least in some instances, of flipping it: Making a rights issue into product placement.

"It's good for both sides then," said Rappaport. "You won't get money like you would on a big studio movie; you'll just get free product. You'll get Twinkies, you'll get beer, you'll get soda. You just have to avoid using a competing brand in the movie, or in the scene."

It's always preferable to deal with such clearances before you've shot your film. *Most* problems (having enough money, for instance) are better dealt with before shooting. Some things *have* to be considered before production starts, and even if the readers of this book presumably want to know what to do after that point, it seems silly not to take advantage of Rappaport's wisdom while we've got him.

Some things, on the other hand, have to be considered afterward, and while they aren't exactly legal matters, they do involve rules and regulations.

"Sometimes there is a lack of foresight or planning," said Andrew Herwitz, a lawyer who works as a sales rep at the Film Sales Company. "If there is a chance in the world that you think you might have a documentary with awards potential, be careful. I've had cases where people come to me after they've made a deal with a foreign sales agent, and the foreign sales agent—this is more true about documentaries—has already started to sell the foreign rights to the film, and the film then will be broadcast on foreign television even before it's theatrically released here. And then they are already ineligible for the Academy Awards."

Bill Condon's problem was not with clearances, but with rights issues in his contracts.

"We had in our contract with Regent that *Gods and Monsters* wouldn't be made as a cable movie, and somehow the Showtime [deal] got past them," said the director. "I'm grateful that they helped us with it, but in the long run, it turned out to be something that hurt us tremendously, because in making the deals, pay TV was already taken. So that made people less interested, because there was a whole revenue stream that was not available to them.

"And beyond that," he said, "when you have a small company like Lions Gate, when they've got two movies that they are releasing at basically the same time, *Affliction* and *Gods*, and they're both after the same audience, they're both in the awards game. . . . Lions Gate had more of an investment in *Affliction*, and more of an upside with *Affliction*, because they didn't have that Showtime thing. So they spent a lot more money on *Affliction*. It was always a struggle, and it all came out of that one thing."

One area of major concern for filmmakers—and of more than passing interest to the authors of this book—is how to control the copyright on one's ideas. If, as Rappaport and others have said, a filmmaker should get as many people as possible to read his or her script before the shooting stage, how does that filmmaker avoid having the work stolen? Sure, it's your friends who are seeing the script, but even if all the readers are family members, ideas have a way of escaping from the bottle unless the bottle has a big lawyer sitting on it.

Rappaport said you can, indeed, copyright a script before you have a final shooting script—but you usually want to copyright the script when it's pretty close to what's going to be made. "Filmmakers should show their script to people that they know and trust," he said, "but they should also—if they're not dealing with close friends they know won't come after them later—get them to sign a certificate of authorship that says that anything that you contribute to this script is owned by me.

"The reverse of that is a confidentiality agreement that says you're not going to take what I show you and use it in something else. There are two sides to that. What you don't want to do is have significant work done on your script by someone, and not have anything in writing with them because then they can later claim that they have some ownership."

And "chain of title"?

"Chain of title is ownership of the screenplay, and all underlying works," he said. "If it's an original screenplay that's not based on a book or a magazine article or a short story or something like that, or someone's life rights, then your chain of title is simply the link between the author of the script and the company making the movie—a contract whereby that company options or outright purchases the screenplay.

"If you are making a movie based on, or the screenplay is based on, something else, then you also need a contract with the owner of that underlying work, whether it's a magazine article or a book or a short story, there has to be a contract between that person, and the screenwriter or the production company that is hiring the screenwriter. There have to be these contractual links—that's the chain—between the underlying work, the screenplay, and the film company that is ultimately going to make the film."

What happens if all this isn't taken care of? Well, among the possible scenarios is the Screen Actors Guild preventing you from starting your movie until it *is* taken care of.

"That's one reason to get a lawyer involved," Rappaport said, "because the Guild won't let your movie start shooting until you have all your chain of title properly documented and registered with the copyright office, so you need some help doing that because if you do it wrong—you might do it in a way that satisfies the guilds, but it isn't really what you want for yourself. You as the filmmaker might want to retain certain rights, and not grant everything to the production company—even a production company that you have formed with your producing partner.

"You may want to retain sequel rights," he said, "but if you sign the form that the Guild gives you just to satisfy their requirements, you end up signing away everything to the production company. If you and the producer own that entity together, then you as the filmmaker have given the producer ownership of some rights that you don't necessarily want him to have.

"But on a more simple level, I deal with the guilds—especially SAG [Screen Actors Guild], but sometimes WGA [Writers Guild of America] and DGA [Directors Guild of America]—because you have to have their clearance before you can work with an actor. I've seen situations—and this is for first-time filmmakers—I've seen them make movies, and not become SAG signatories. Then the actors who are SAG members have violated their SAG agreement. If the Guild finds out about them, they can get fined, they can get tossed out of the Guild. Ironically, if the film turns out well, and gets attention, and someone at SAG finds out that it's not a SAG film, and yet SAG actors were in it, it can hurt the actors, which means that all of a sudden, your actor doesn't want to publicize your work, and has a terrible nightmare to deal with, because you the producer or filmmaker didn't do what you were supposed to do to get it approved by SAG."

At the time we talked, Rappaport said he had a client in a situation like that, and that the Guild does not want people to become signatories after the fact. "You do have to become a SAG signatory, and if your director is DGA or your writer WGA, you have to know that, and become signatories with those guilds. The other thing to watch out for is that the guilds are more and more often requiring residuals or reserves for higher-budget movies, but you're not talking about movies of five to six million dollars."

And the advantages to *not* becoming a signatory?

"Well, you can avoid the minimum payment obligations, and the working conditions that are required by the guilds. You would avoid residuals," Rappaport said. "There are certain benefits, but it's not worth it. Actors who've done yeoman's work for you for very little money are in a dangerous situation."

Another way a film can get stopped in its tracks is if, for whatever reason, someone was unaware of an underlying work, a previously written basis for their script, whether it's a short story, a television show, a novel, etc.—then, when he or she is selling the movie, or when the movie is in release, someone can come out of the woodwork and file suit. The film's release can grind to a dead halt.

And this is because "you're infringing on their copyright or whatever other rights—privacy rights, rights of publicity," said Rappaport. "Errors and omissions insurance protects you against claims of infringing of copyright and libel, and other sorts of intellectual property-type claims. If you have that policy in place during production, you're protected in case someone sues, or threatens to sue, you while you're in production.

"Low-budget filmmakers tend to get that insurance after the movie is made because it's a required delivery element for most distributors. You have to have it in order to deliver your movie. But it's frequently the case that the claims are made during production, so it's always better, if you can afford it, to get that insurance before the cameras start rolling. Ideally, you get it in prep.

"The situation has occurred that a producer has optioned a script from a writer, not knowing that the writer had worked with someone in developing the script but never thought that they needed a contract with that person. Or there had been another producer involved, and that producer claims to have helped develop the project, and is therefore making a claim of ownership of intellectual property. Things will happen that have a reasonable basis, or an irrational basis. It doesn't matter. They can still make a claim, and the filmmaker is still vulnerable to a lawsuit. People can sue for stupid reasons without a basis; this is America. If you don't have E&O [errors and omissions] insurance, then you're completely naked.

"A client had to sue a prominent writer-director who had made a claim that my client's script infringed on his script," said Rappaport. "The claim turned out to be baseless. My client had to sue him to erase the claim, because [the writer-director] had made a claim—never followed up on it, never sued—but the claim was still hovering out there."

Such a claim is excluded from an insurance policy because it pre-existed the coverage. "So my client had to sue that filmmaker at great expense—$15,000 just to file a lawsuit—in order to make this person go away, and sign a settlement agreement."

It is, in a word, crazy.

"People ask me, 'You know how to make movies. Don't you want to produce?'" Rappaport said with a smile. "I've done sixty-five movies or something. . . . *No!* Exactly because I know what it's like. You have to have a great burning desire, and think that you have something important to say. Even when I find great projects, I realize how difficult it is to make these movies, and how little money you make. You do it for the love of the project, and you do it to advance your career, but the job of an independent producer. . . . No one pays you any significant money when you set up a project at a studio, and if you're getting it independently financed, you're working on it for a year. . . . It's tough going."

Springer Berman mentioned Volunteer Lawyers for the Arts. "I think they have chapters in L.A., and New York—for film students, for people who are indie, for people who can't afford to pay a lawyer, and they will help you. I don't know if it still exists but I know it did when we were students."

It does, and can be reached at (212) 319-2787; or visit their Web site: www.vlany.org.

4

The Grand Unveiling
Using the Right Launching Pad

You're only a virgin once. And that's just a fact of life in the film festival meat market—where your newness, your freshness, your unblemished pinkness is a large part of your allure. It's like a new car: Once your film has been driven out of the showroom—or, in this case, shown in a public space—your Blue Book value drops precipitously. Not to mix metaphors.

The Festival Circuit

There are many, many film festivals in the world—new ones seem to pop up every month. There are also many kinds of film festivals. There are festivals aimed at specific audiences (the public in Telluride, the industry in Sundance), or which boast certain types of films: horror (the International Festival of Horror or Scotland's Dead by Dawn); comedy (the U.S. Comedy Arts Festival in Aspen), silents (Italy's Pordenone festival), shorts (Palm Springs), gay and lesbian (OutFest in L.A.); children's film festivals; films from various nations and ethnicities (Asian, Jewish, etc.); etc., etc. There are festivals that are specifically geared toward the entertainment industry—festivals that program a healthy mix of world premieres, which help attract press and film buyers who have to see these films. And there are festivals that are purely for audiences, or are meant to extend the tourist season at a given beach, spa, or game farm.

Peter Scarlet, who is Tribeca Film Festival's executive director, said, "Film festivals are becoming on the one hand, more important, as they're becoming for many filmmakers the only avenue to find a public, but on the other hand it's becoming trickier for both filmmakers and the public because the damn things are springing up like mushrooms in the forest after the rain." He added, "And I remain unconvinced that the great majority of festivals are really serving much need beyond the ego of the local mayor or the general silly excitement about movies that doesn't really help filmmakers."

Carl Spence, Seattle Film Festival's director of programming, added, "Filmmakers should be careful about where they choose to present their film, and they should know that there are only a few festivals that add credibility both from the industry and critically. There are some festivals that are really looking for quantity over quality and they need to be careful to not waste an opportunity. There are some places where presenting their film can actually devalue the worth or the perception of the quality of the film. They shouldn't just rush and accept the first festival that they've been accepted to."

Name a genre, a tactic—or a day of the year, for that matter—and there's a festival to fit it. It will be hard to resist the urge to send your film to any and all festivals. Many of them will call and invite you.

Filmmaker Richard Linklater said, "As a filmmaker, a big part of you simply wants to get your film seen, period, so there's a natural impulse to show it everywhere that will play it. If you think that is the most realistic audience you'll have, then do it, but be aware you'll be seen as more played out and have less a chance at a 'big discovery moment' by a distributor.

"Almost any festival could be really good for a film, or you as a filmmaker. Just getting out there and mixing it up with people and sharing your movie can have its own rewards. I'd avoid anything where you have to pay money for a screening, like a market screening."

But he warned, "If you think you have a good shot at a national distribution deal, you should be very strategic in planning what festivals can help you and in what way. For instance, premiering your film at your local festival in some ways gets you nothing in the industry. If it does well there it won't impress anyone because they will think it's just your hometown crowd. Better to get a good review or word of mouth from far away to seem more legitimate."

However, warned filmmaker Chris Eyre (whose debut feature, the Native American drama *Smoke Signals*, played Sundance in 1998), "Don't rush the film to make a festival, or show it to an interested distributor before it is done. Take the time to make the film the best it can be. If possible, taking the time to reflect a little bit in post [production] can truly enhance critical parts of the film, and help the story and plot. When your film is seen by programmers at a festival, or a distributor, the gig is up and, great script aside—because they are all *great*—your intelligence and efforts and luck will be the film's only merits. Take the time."

Scarlet agreed and said, "I tell filmmakers 'Look, if I like your film, don't kill yourself to get it ready for us. The most important thing for you is to have your film in the best shape you can have it in; to knock yourself out to make a deadline, whether it's for Tribeca or Cannes or Toronto or Sundance, is silly.'"

And remember: Your film's "world premiere" is something many festivals most desire. The most selective festivals have rules—some unwritten, some not—about when, where, and if your film can screen beforehand. And they may not only give preference to films that have not screened anywhere else, they may demand it.

A world premiere means exactly that. It is the first time your film screens publicly. World premieres are of paramount importance in the festival environment. Know that the more prestigious festivals will not want your film if you've been around. Do not submit your film to festivals wildly. Don't be promiscuous. Don't be wanton. Be strategic.

* * *

It's odd, but while this book was being written, Laura spoke to a filmmaker with whom she had last spoken to months before, who had told her he wanted to make a documentary about his aunt, an immigrant from Asia who moved to the American South, and as an elderly woman won a beauty title. As a human interest story and/or examination of culture, race, and age, the idea seemed a good one.

So he finished his film, and planned a big screening with the film's subject in Los Angeles. And he invited Laura. He had submitted his work to its first festival (a regional one that focused on ethnic films) and had made an application to enter his film in a market.

Laura may not have seen the film. But the alarm bells were going off big time because she knew that filmmakers have an urge to get their work out there without the least bit of planning for a best-case scenario. In truth, he and Laura agreed the chances were slim that the film would get any sort of theatrical release. But why not try at least? Then, if he should find there was really no distributor interest in the film, it could be submitted wherever he wanted—throw it out there to see what happens. (The filmmaker *had* in fact hoped for a theatrical release, but could have lessened his chances significantly.)

Laura asked: What about applying for a festival where there are buyers present? Or setting up a screening for buyers? Why not save your big premiere-type event for if and when your film is going to be released. And if you don't get distribution, you can have your big event after all other possibilities have been exhausted. The fellow in question agreed to set up some small screenings for crew and family, get some honest feedback, and fine-tune his movie until he was absolutely certain that it was ready to be shown to people who could change his future for the better.

"This should probably be off the record," said producer Christine Vachon, "because I don't want to tell a story . . . but it's just kind of interesting in context." (We have opted to use the story to illustrate a point that could be useful, but will not name the film.)

Vachon said she was talking to one of the producers of a movie that had just gotten into a Cannes sidebar (subsection), which they were very happy about. But when she asked about the international sales, it turns out that the company selling the film took it—after it hadn't gotten accepted into the Berlin Film Festival proper—to the Berlin Film Festival Market, where the film was strictly a product for sale.

"So every international buyer had already seen it," Vachon said. "And they saw it in a market context. And it's a film that really needs an audience's love to survive, because it's a very sweet movie.

"So now they're going to Cannes, and I'm like, 'You guys are screwed. Why did you let them do that?' They didn't make one sale in Berlin. You'll never get those people back. The only real thing that people have to remember is people only get to see a movie for the first time once. And you can't blow that."

Geoff Gilmore, director of the Sundance Film Festival, said it's never too early to think about your strategy. In fact, "Consider festivals before the start-to-shoot stage. Certainly, when you're in post you're developing a strategy. But the strategy about what you do at a festival has a lot to do with what kind of film you've got. And a lot of that is just very detail-oriented, and may affect your post schedule."

* * *

Festival strategy for films that already have distribution will be navigated by the distributor. For films that don't have distribution, consider the following:

If you want buyers and press to see your film, you must go to festivals attended by buyers and press.

If you want media attention, go to festivals covered by media. Most festivals are covered by the local press to some extent, but only a few are covered by national press, critics, and the trades. The majority of festivals are not covered by buyers.

Then, answer these questions:

What kinds of film does the festival normally screen? Are they the kinds of films your film should be in the company of? Will your film screen well there in comparison? Will your film play the way it should there? Broad comedies, for instance, might not find Sundance hospitable, but could do better in Toronto.

"An important thing," said producer Matthew Greenfield, "is to take a very hard look at your movie, and really judge what is the best possible festival to begin in, what would be the ideal: Is it Sundance, New York, Los Angeles, Venice? Pick and keep going. Target them with a realistic eye, and don't give up. There are movies that have been rejected by ten festivals, and on the eleventh got in, and got picked up. And then there are also some movies that are not festival material, that are good movies, but are not just the kind of movies that are going to play at a festival. And it's important to know that."

What kinds of films seem to do well there? Are they edgy, dark films? Do crowd-pleasers work there? Is there a section or sidebar that makes sense for your film? Have films like yours played well there? There are films that may play better in Seattle than at Sundance.

What's the festival's signature? In other words, its tone, its aims? Is it about generating audience attendance or commercial tremors? Each festival has a character, so to speak, and a film that could screen well in Seattle might differ from a film that will screen well at the New York Film Festival.

"Once you've gotten all this money from your relatives, and you've made the film, you're bursting at the seams to show it," said James Schamus, copresident of Focus Features and cofounder of now-defunct Good Machine. He said that in unspooling one's film and getting the measure of one's movie, discretion is the better part of valor. And ego.

"As a filmmaker, you're kind of playing to an audience of two or three initially—although it happens a few times," said consultant to independent filmmakers Jeff Dowd. What he means is that the various decisions that affect a film's destiny at any stage are often made by one or two people.

"How do you get into a film festival?" he asked. "One programmer loves the picture. That's all you need. One Henry Fonda in *Twelve Angry Men*. One advocate in the jury room. And then the other people say, 'OK, if you're so passionate, I kinda liked it, too.' And then Gilmore says, 'I like it, too.' Believe me, for a lot of films, whether it's Cannes, or it's Noah Cowan in Toronto, it's about one or two people."

In North America, the festivals that are highest in profile and that attract the greatest attention are Toronto, Sundance, the New York Film Festival, the

Los Angeles Film Festival, Telluride, Tribeca, Seattle, SXSW, and the AFI. There are certainly many other festivals, such as OutFest, New Directors, etc., among hundreds that cater to specific audiences or ideals.

"Oftentimes with people, I say, 'There's lots of other places you can go,'" said Geoff Gilmore of Sundance, which turns away thousands each year. "And I do mean lots of places. There are hundreds of film festivals out there, festivals that can help filmmakers figure out their strategies for them.

"One of these strategies has to be, 'What am I trying to do? Am I trying to get attention for my documentary? Am I trying to sell my feature film?' The answer depends on what their goals are. 'What kind of a film do I have?' 'What level of response do I need?'"

"Filmmakers have a way of thinking about things," said entertainment lawyer Sue Bodine. "They often go into this process with the idea that there's a 'right' way to go about it, and if you do this the 'right' way, you will get this really fantastic extraordinary result. If you don't, then you won't.

"It's hard for them to realize that there are all these different unknown factors," she added. "What other films are there, for instance. There really isn't any formula for how to do it, and there's no rule that says you have to be at Sundance. I think, with young filmmakers, they really want someone to tell them the answer of how to do it, and then do it. Of course, while there are things they should know, I find that when they get into that mindset, sometimes it's a mistake, because they make choices based on somebody else's certainty— instead of really thinking through all of the different realities of their own film, and the marketplace."

Justin Lin, director of *Better Luck Tomorrow* (2002), had very low expecta-tions, which is probably not a bad idea with his type of film—dark and starring an all-unknown Asian-American cast. "If you're going to go on this journey, you can't predict anything," he said. "We didn't even think about getting bought. I was just hoping to get maybe a couple of good reviews and so maybe I could make my next movie for $500,000. That was my realistic goal."

So then the question becomes, What are you dealing with? An unknown, calling-card movie that is simply about getting a filmmaker's career to the next stage? Or, as Gilmore puts it, "a film that needs to be sold in order to make sure that you don't lose your house"?

* * *

Which festivals are festivals where films can get picked up?

"Sundance, Cannes, or Toronto, for American independent films," said

James Schamus. "A little bit now in Berlin, by the way, because of the timing of various things, including the movement of the American Film Market out of the winter and into the fall, so Berlin may well take that place. But wherever films are being screened for the first time, and where there's a critical mass of buyers.

"But," he added, "Every year, there are only going to be two or three films that fit into the category of 'bidding war.' Only two or three." Picturehouse president Bob Berney says, "Sundance, Cannes, and Toronto are the ones where we've probably bought ninety-nine percent of our films."

Where else?

"*Slacker* was in Seattle," said Michael Barker of Sony Classics. "We've bought a number of films in Toronto, Cannes, Telluride. We've certainly pursued films that came out of San Francisco, New York for sure. New York chooses very few films—it's a very elite group so it's pretty privileged, and high profile, if you're in New York, and are still for sale. Usually by then you're already sold. But I remember we got *Crumb* out of New York. The New Directors series—there's always a jewel or two in all of these festivals. If there were good films in Tribeca this year that we didn't pursue, it was just about the moment in time."

"Toronto is right before the fall season for the Oscar campaigns," said agent Cassian Elwes, "so it can be a great launching point. And a lot of studio people are there with the movies that they've just bought earlier in the year. They're already there with their own movies; they can easily see other films."

Christine Vachon added, "Regional film festivals are good for whatever their region is, especially for gay-themed films, but really, as far as film festivals are concerned, unless you count Sundance, there are really only four: Berlin, Cannes, Venice, and Toronto. With all the others, it's different. . . . I just think with all the other film festivals, you have to have a different agenda for going there. You're not going to get discovered, you're not necessarily even going to get picked up.

"If you don't get into Sundance," she said, "Go to SXSW, which is clearly a contender."

"Over the past couple years the attendance has just sort of gone through the roof," said SXSW's (South by Southwest Film Conference and Festival's) program director Matt Dentler. "Both in a consumer sense and in an industry sense." He said the quality of the films they're getting now has greatly risen, as has the quality of the premieres, and that more filmmakers are coming.

"A lot of it has to do with Austin," he said, "and it's become a great place to foster film relationships. The film business here is really booming, and we've really benefited from that. The film festival is not just a side effect of the music festival—we're getting so big in attendance that some people think we should split the two."

One thing that filmmakers should know about SXSW, Dentler says, "If you play SXSW, it does not mean that you did not get into Sundance. That assumption is wrong. At times we have films like *Napoleon Dynamite* and *Super Size Me* and we actually accepted them before they premiered at Sundance. That was one of our tipping points."

"Telluride's one of the funnest festivals there is," said filmmaker Shari Springer Berman (codirector of the acclaimed *American Splendor*). "It's wonderful. I wouldn't say it would necessarily help get your film sold, but as a film lover, it's a great festival to go to."

"We think our mission is to celebrate the art of film in all its dimensions, and throughout history," said Telluride director Tom Luddy. "We also present approximately twenty-two new films each year, but we try to show them in the context of an ongoing celebration of films from the past. We have people like Pierre Rissient, who specialize in bringing us revivals of unappreciated films from all over the world. We always have silent films with live music, too, so we try to show new films in the context of the history of cinema."

Luddy is a longtime figure on the art-film scene—a scene he's seen change.

"We started before Sundance or Toronto," he said. "There was just New York, us, Chicago, and San Francisco. Now there's hundreds and hundreds and thousands of festivals, so the festival map has changed, but we're always on Labor Day weekend and always only four days.

"Our goal," he added, "is to get people out of cities and into a very beautiful space where immediately you forget about phone calls you have to return and scripts you have to read, you're just so knocked out by the environment— we wanted it to feel further away from home than Cannes if you came from L.A.—and even in Cannes, you can still feel like you're wheeling and dealing in the L.A. world. Something about the magic of the environment that loosens people up—it's a special magical place. We've gotten much bigger, in terms of number of venues and number of people, but I would like to think we've still retained the kind of intimacy and environment that mountain valley gives us."

And yet . . . and yet . . . even Luddy's unassuming Colorado festival has been a crucible of commercial success!

"*Roger and Me* came straight from the lab," Luddy said, "and nobody knew who Michael Moore was, and Roger Ebert was there, and people really liked it, and because we have empty slots, we ended up repeating it seven or eight times and by the time he was in Toronto, everybody was already talking about it.

"*El Mariachi* was a totally unknown film that we world-premiered, and Robert Rodriguez came. David Siegel and Scott McGeehee came with *Suture,* which Pierre Rissient saw and brought to Cannes the next year for *Un Certain Regard. Happiness, Eve's Bayou, Swingers* were shown first in Telluride. *Lost in Translation.* We look at lots and lots of them—we can't show all of them, we're not like Sundance, but the good ones—usually two or three."

"It depends on what you want," Vachon continued. "If you're a film-maker who understands, for example, that your film is inherently not terribly commercial, but what you really want is to get as much exposure as possible, then I think the kind of festival you'd be looking for is different from the [one you'd pick] if you really just want to get your film bought. I think it really depends on your objectives."

"Aim for the bigger festivals—Toronto, Cannes, Sundance," said Magnolia's Eamonn Bowles. "You can always submit to the other fests if you don't get in. But if you accept a smaller fest, it often will nix your chance of being at the bigger fest. But, most importantly, don't compromise your film in order to meet a festival deadline. A great film trumps a great opportunity."

Marcus Hu, copresident of Strand Releasing, does the circuit. "The festivals that I attend every year without fail would be Sundance, Rotterdam, Berlin, Cannes, Toronto. These are festivals that function as both great festivals as well as a marketplace for an independent distributor such as Strand. AFM, MIFED, and other self-proclaimed markets generally shoot for more commercial product, but gems still appear at those places as well.

"It's a really an odd situation with all these festivals that keep popping up. Tribeca, Los Angeles Film Festival, Sundance—of course, the holy grail of them all is Sundance, at least for American independents," Hu added. "The second might be New Directors, the third may be Tribeca, the fourth might be the Los Angeles Film Festival."

In Hu's opinion, "In terms of importance in North America, of course, Sundance and Toronto are almost equal, although the real big American indie sales happen at Sundance and that's where they're really covered, too. Toronto is more for cinephiles and not so much known for its business as it is for being a real festival. It just happens that business gets done at that festival."

But he warned, "As a filmmaker you can really get lost at a place like Sundance—how does anyone find a voice there if you're not in one of the competition slots? If you're in American Spectrum, what's the chance you're gonna get lost there? There's only so much attention a journalist or a buyer can expend. You're trying to get all of their attention, but they can only concentrate on so many things. So know that they're going to concentrate on all the world premieres that haven't been seen before, and are available for them to either buy or write about, because writers are looking for that discovery, something to write about."

"That's something that I always argue, that people have to be careful about when they go into a big festival," said Geoff Gilmore. "Even when they go into Cannes—not so much the official selection, but you can get lost in the mass of 1,600 features inside the marketplace, and the ninety films in the official section. How do you find visibility in all of that? That's one of the reasons why the idea of a smaller festival may be a good place to go. Telluride and the New York Film Festival, for instance. One of the reasons they're great places for launches is that they're so focused in terms of what they do, that the film will get attention no matter what."

Peter Scarlet will warn filmmakers of some of the dangers of Tribeca. "Because it's a big festival, filmmakers need to be armed with strategies as to how to reach those folks because even the most curious journalists and the most curious buyers are not going to be able to see everything. And I'm not speaking about just Tribeca but many festivals. I've seen young talent go off with work to Berlin or Venice or Cannes and come back kind of looking a little worse for the wear and a little ragged because they hadn't provided themselves the service of a publicist or didn't have the materials needed. Who knew they would go and find themselves facing a press corps of thousands.

"New York, as a launch festival—less so as a place to sell a movie—is focused," Gilmore said. "Telluride, the same thing. You have that focus on a program of twenty-eight or so films and that's what you're dealing with. And, obviously, the message that has always been sent is that if it's in one of those programs, it's quality.

"But I will tell you," he added, "I've had filmmakers come out of the New York Film Festival who didn't sell their film and come to me immediately after and say, 'Will you please take our film?' Sometimes we did, and sometimes we didn't. But it almost always was based on the fact that they viewed New York as a place to sell the work, and I'm not so sure that's the right strategy. It was a big honor for them, but it sure didn't help them find their market."

The Los Angeles Film Festival is a good one for many reasons. The size is really manageable. More importantly, for filmmakers, it's in a city where a lot of buyers live, and which has a lot of journalists covering the industry. While it's also true that it's probably harder to get people excited about film there—since they are steeped in it every day—it is in Hollywood, after all. Plus, everyone knows someone in Los Angeles who has a sofa they can crash on. It is a much more affordable festival than many.

The New York Film Festival, on the other hand, is not only in an expensive city, it's a city with the liability of *The New York Times*.

"When I was on the New York Film Festival selection committee," said *New York Times* critic Manohla Dargis, then with *LA Weekly*, "Christine Vachon would not show us *Far from Heaven*. She refused to, because she didn't want to chance a negative *Times* review in September when they weren't opening for months. And nobody blamed her."

"The New York Film Festival has had movies play there," said David Ansen of *Newsweek*, "that were then reviewed by *The New York Times*, and then lost their distributors."

"*The Woman Chaser*," said Dargis. "A lovely little movie that should have found an audience, but got slaughtered in *The New York Times*. It died an unceremonious death."

It's not the paper, it's not necessarily the critic—sometimes it's just the luck of the draw. Richard Peña, respected program director of the New York Film Festival, has often said that films that would get lost in the shuffle of Sundance (especially foreign films) get far more attention in New York, either at the festival or in the regular programming schedule of Lincoln Center's Walter Reade Theater. And he's right. The question is, Do you want all that attention? And that particular attention?

"You don't want an acquisitions atmosphere that's so public," advised Gilmore. "*The New York Times* review is part of the reason."

A bad *Times* review—assuming, quite soundly, that the paper's readership and the foreign/indie film audience are one and the same—may as well have "RIP" at the end of its last paragraph. It may indicate mob-think, it may be a sign of intellectual constipation, but there it is.

But Peña, quite rightly, takes pride in the gravity given the New York Film Festival.

"They take it seriously," he said of its critics, "and that's something to be proud of. It's a festival that really selects films. It's not an encyclopedia; it's not a panorama. The films are here because somebody chose them. People on our board asked me about Tribeca, and I have to explain that Tribeca is much more like festivals all over the United States. We're the unique ones, in a certain way. Tribeca has presented itself, in their minds, as a new formula, a new style of festival, and, frankly, it's just the opposite. That's what festivals are like everywhere. It's we who are weird and unique and an anachronism, and hopefully we'll remain that way."

Peña compares the New York Film Festival to theatrical Broadway, as opposed to out-of-town tryouts.

"Very, very often," he said, "when we've shown a film that came out of Sundance, that film has been significantly changed. It's been shortened, music's been added, voiceover has been added. All kinds of things. You can do that when you show at Sundance and then go out into the world, because people are there seeing it first and whatever; you don't get your major reviews. At the New York Film Festival, it's very very difficult to change your film after it's been shown there. You've been seen by major critics, you've received major reviews. In a certain way, it's showtime.

"The New York Film Festival," he added, "is essentially a public festival for people who are interested in film—in some cases, intensely interested in film—and because we're in New York and have more people in the industry, in that way, we take on a certain air of a professional festival. But we're quintessentially a public festival. Sundance is a professional festival. And each one has its place."

Tribeca Film Festival's executive director Peter Scarlet would describe his festival as "International in the best sense of the word. Our prizewinners for the past several years have been primarily our international entries and some may say that's because we're in the wake of Sundance, and it probably has something to do with it.

"New York is an international city, and we're really at the crossroads of the world here. At a lot of festivals, the foreign films are often a sidebar. I really think it's important to strip away the flags and show the best films we can." A fairly new festival, Tribeca has had some success with buyers picking up films like *Roger Dodger, Interview with an Assassin*, and *Transamerica*.

Carl Spence, Seattle Film Festival's director of programming, said of his festival's program, "It's always been eclectic. It's always had a broad range of films from high-profile studio films to arthouse fare to American independents, its highlights being American and international cinema. It has changed over the last ten years to be honest, because there's been a lot of competition that's popped up. It used to be and still is to some extent, the summer launching pad for American independent films and we show probably thirty to forty American independent films each year, twelve of those in competition."

Of Seattle, Spence added, "It's always been an audience festival, but over the years, we have gotten more national press up here. Films do get reviewed by the trades here, we do have press here, and we have buyers, but it's not a Sundance/Toronto feeding frenzy, but films are discovered and then thought about. It's not a buyers' market. Not every film should be positioned as they are in Sundance or Toronto, because it may just get lost or slaughtered."

While Seattle is widely regarded as primarily an audience festival, writer-director Richard Linklater said, "My experiences have generally been great, but I guess there's nothing quite like that first time. For me, it was at the Seattle Film Festival in 1990. It was there that, out of complete obscurity, *Slacker* was initially embraced not only by the festival staff, but by the audience and local critics. It set the tone for what was to come."

And any festival director—be it Peña, Gilmore, Rosen, Luddy, Dentler, Spence, Scarlet, Christian Gaines (AFI Fest) or Thierry Fremaux (Cannes)—will get proprietary about his or her festival and the way people think the submission process works.

"Sometimes you hear or read people saying something like, 'I decided to put the film in Toronto,'" Peña said. "And you're like, 'You really decided that?' You mean you submitted, and they accepted it? Or you just sent it to them and said, 'Show this'? It sounds like the latter, doesn't it? And maybe for certain distributors, that's their relationship. I don't know."

It could simply be bad manners.

"Or assumptions," Peña said. "People assume they have power and they don't. But if anybody made that comment about the New York Film Festival, I'd go nuts. Nobody decides to put their film in the New York Film Festival."

What are the secrets in submitting to festivals? Does having people call on your behalf help?

Gilmore said the basic truth is that people submit their films "and it really is about that process of submission and discovery. I have no problem with people sending us messages, notes, having people who could influence my decision call me and talk to me about it. Just because it brings a film to my attention. But boy, so much is misunderstood.

"It's always presumed that if someone brings something to your attention they're telling you what to do, and even in the *New York Times* article," he said, referring to a piece that ran in January 2005, "the article with John [Sloss], the assumption that somehow I was talking with John leads to a presumption that somehow he was telling me what to do. Of course, he doesn't tell me what to do. It's the opposite. And yet, the fact of the matter is I have no problem talking to John—or a hundred other people—about what's out there. I call Laura, I call everybody I can, or Cooper will, and say 'What's out there?'"

Stories are abundant about how Sundance was pressured into showing this film, or coerced into showing that film, or strong-armed into NOT showing some other film entirely. Gilmore knows it.

"But it just doesn't work that way," he said. "Not simply because we get a lot of choices, which is, of course, part of the issue. It's because I've learned my lesson about what I used to call the 'damage of doing favors for people.' You can never do a favor for someone that doesn't turn around and bite you in the ass—which is what constantly happens.

"You think you're actually extending yourself to help a company—'OK, we'll show this film for you'—and again and again the company bites you back if the film doesn't perform—as if you were somehow responsible for that. Somehow, you slotted it wrong. Or you didn't program it as opening night. Or whatever they expected you to do. So we don't do it. I've learned my lesson. Favors almost never pay off. They almost never get you anything. And they basically put you in a situation where they create expectations that, for the most part, aren't deliverable. You can't be expected to make a film work."

He said people are free to call him. "I'm not saying I don't take phone calls," he said. "I take phone calls from a lot of people. I'm not bragging when I say this, but three studio heads called me this last Sundance, two heads of agencies. Not one of the films they were talking about made it into the festival.

"And that's just normal. The reason I don't bring that up in interviews usually is because it makes us sound arrogant. I'm just saying that the ways in which independent film have now crept into the business means that a studio head will call about something, usually not their big picture—he's got his vice presidents to do that—it's usually always something personal, on a level that has to do with a son's film, or an executive's son's film, a personal favor. Or sometimes it has to do with something a little slicker than that. But it's just the nature of the beast that you get those kinds of phone calls."

Gilmore says he's gotten calls from Howard Schultz, the head of Starbucks; from the heads of technology companies "and you can't imagine why.

I've gotten calls from Mark McGwire and from Evander Holyfield. I've gotten phone calls from, y'know, the world about a film one or more of them were in, or were involved with. Again, you take their phone calls, say 'Thank you very much' and go on."

Seattle's Carl Spence said, "It does not help to have people bombard the programming staff with recommendations for a film, though it doesn't hurt to have someone who has an association with the festival send an e-mail or something. Every film that's submitted, we do look at."

* * *

Regardless of what has been stated above, the plaintive cry of many an independent filmmaker will always be, What if I don't get into Sundance?

"I was once on a panel during the IFP [Independent Feature Project] Market in New York," said publicity veteran Jeremy Walker, "and a Sundance programmer was sitting on the other end of the dais when this very question came up. Now, I have had many great successes at Sundance, and the festival is, and I think for many years to come shall remain, the best event on the planet at which to put an independent film on the market.

"But the market is just that—a market, just like any other, driven by supply and demand," he said. "Like any other, the independent film market may be influenced somewhat by outside forces like the press, and the weather, and geopolitical conflict, and even the current occupant of the White House. When I suggested on the IFP panel that the Tribeca Film Festival, which takes place a few months after Sundance, was also becoming a great place to put a movie on the market, the Sundance programmer took issue and made a pointed defense of their turf. Her message to the audience of aspiring filmmakers was clear: If you're thinking about Tribeca, show us your movie first."

But only so many films can get into Sundance, Walker said, and like any festival, a good percentage of those films will fail. "Conversely, I have been utterly shocked that at least one film I was affiliated with early on did not get into Sundance—'But it's the ultimate Sundance movie!!!' was the chorus sung by the producers and me upon getting the news. But this film went on to enjoy its world premiere at Tribeca and won a key award, Oscar buzz, and a distribution deal with a hot company."

"I do think that there are other festivals out there that one can go to," said Sundance's Geoff Gilmore. "I just don't necessarily believe—and I'm not saying this out of ego, of course—I'm just saying the industry doesn't necessarily attend them en masse the way they do Toronto, Cannes, and Sundance. There are festivals in which there are at least some industry participation and I think those should be looked at, whether it's Tribeca, LAFF, or even Seattle. SXSW has programs that are very carefully considered and well done, and the AFI Fest–AFM combination may prove to be interesting in the future.

"The thing that people have to realize is that really good films surface no matter where they are."

Carl Spence, Seattle Film Festival's director of programming, said, "If you don't get into Sundance—and I'm the first one to say that for American independent films, that's the best place with the most opportunities to have your film sold, *if* it's in competition and *if* it's favorably received—if that doesn't happen, there are other festivals that can push a film along in its life and help it find its home in one way or another."

Acquisitions Screenings

Many filmmakers opt to set screenings for the acquisition community, and don't necessarily tie them to a festival. Going to a festival with your film can be very expensive and one can never predict the outcome. While most films go to festivals with hope of getting noticed and bought, such is the exception and not the rule. Most, in fact, do not. *Swingers*, which did not get into Sundance, was screened for buyers and got bought by Miramax. *Slingblade* screened simultaneously in New York and Los Angeles and was bought before the end of the evening by Miramax as well. *P.S.*, the Dylan Kidd follow-up to *Roger Dodger*, was bought after serial screenings to buyers. Nicole Holofcener's *Lovely & Amazing* screened for acquisitions folks in Los Angeles, went to Telluride, got good reviews, then was bought out of the Toronto International Film Festival.

It can be difficult because the perception—whether or not it's true—will be that your film did not get into the festivals. "I remember at IFC," said Berney, "we bought *Together*, the Lukas Moodysson film, which we really loved, and Toronto didn't include it, even though they'd done his first film, and it was a favorite there—they just didn't like it. And the producers actually screened it at a private screening at Toronto while distributors were in town, and got everybody in. And we bought it."

But it was risky for the filmmakers, because screening close to the dates of a festival reinforces the fact that the film didn't get into the festival. And priorities are out of whack. "It's hard to get people out," said Berney, "and you get the assistants to show up, not the people who can actually decide. And then if the assistant doesn't like it and says something, then you never get a chance. It'll just be dead."

So festivals, by default, become the best filtering system for people who buy movies. "It's not perfect by any means," he said. "There are politics—the director of the festival hates the producer, or something happened they didn't get their last great film—and they're just excluding them. There can be such horrifying exceptions, but for us, for a small company, it's a filter system that we sort of accept."

"We cut a trailer for *Chasen's* on a Steenbeck in our apartment," said codirector [with Robert Pulcini] Shari Springer Berman. "Bob cut it. So we set a screening of the fifteen-minute piece and we kind of invited a lot of people who were in town for the IFP market. We sent out cards, we got a lot of RSVPs.

"And by the way, we weren't even part of the market but we utilized the fact that these people would all be in town," she said. "First of all, we were too late to even get in the market, and there was also a fee and we were just so bare bones that we just basically used the fact that everybody was in town. So we got a list and invited all the people that you would have invited to a market screening. We had the screening and there was a person there, Alicia Sams, who was working for Deandra Douglas at the time and they were looking to do documentaries and we got the money to finish the film. Once the film was finished, we started screening it at festivals for distributors."

Recruited Screenings

An alternative to doing a standard acquisitions screening is having a recruited screening—a National Research Group (NRG) screening or Online Testing Exchange (OTX) or some other recruited screening. (NRG, a major Hollywood research and testing outfit, is part of Nielsen Entertainment.) Recruited screenings are better suited for big studio films, but can be used for indies, too.

"I've seen a lot of that," said Picturehouse president Bob Berney. "They invite a distributor to go down to the NRG screening and look at the research, look at the cards, if you feel you have a broad comedy that's not a typical independent film—like *My Big Fat Greek Wedding*. But there's that occasion where you have an independent film that is such a 'tweener,' and you really think it's got a broader commercial audience. That's one way you could do it, but it's expensive for a filmmaker or a producer to hire them to do it . . . and, of course, it can backfire. If you go down there and if for some reason they've had test screenings before, and that one flops, it can be a disaster."

Then there's the problem of people who are being paid to be part of a focus group, and who really think they want to be film critics. Or think they're being paid specifically to eviscerate the film.

"Yeah, it's risky," said Berney. "The festivals are an imperfect system, but . . ."

Prefestival Screenings

And just when it seemed it couldn't get any thicker, there rises the question of screening *before* a festival.

"Generally," said entertainment attorney Sue Bodine, "I would say screening for a distributor before a premiere at a festival is a mistake, unless there's a compelling reason to do it, and sometimes there is. That's the common pressure that will be brought on to filmmakers. 'Let us see it first, we really want to see it. . . .' There's a lot of flattery involved, and it's very hard for filmmakers to resist."

But it's often a case of bait-and-switch: Show it to us first. We want it. Or at least, if you show it to us first, we might be more inclined to want it. . . . Oh, and, by the way, now that we've seen it? We don't want it.

Two of our sources, asked what the biggest mistake an upcoming filmmaker can make, answered as follows:

"To succumb to the line from a distributor that if you show it to them first, there's a greater likelihood that they'll buy it," said sales agent John Sloss of Cinetic.

"To think that he has multiple chances to get distributors' attention," said Required Viewing's producers rep Steven Raphael. "Your film is only HOT when no one has seen it. Don't expect the 'little engine that could' story to happen to you."

"If you're considering screening for the press before a festival," said PR vet Mark Pogachefsky of L.A.'s mPRm Public Relations, "you have to be pretty sure you've got the goods. Or you have to have decided you have nothing to lose either way. For Sundance, I find sometimes that it's worthwhile to screen documentaries in advance. People tend to be more forgiving of that genre; it's a category that everybody's really interested in at Sundance, but everybody doesn't really have the time. So sometimes I find that screening the docs helps give them a leg up."

But otherwise, the risks outweigh the advantages. "If I had an available title, that had name talent in it," Pogachefsky said, "I would most likely not screen it for press ahead of time. Generally, the circumstances involved in screening a dramatic film before a festival like Sundance are probably not conducive. For Cannes, if I had something that was smaller, or in a sidebar, I may take the chance, because I know that major press is going to have a hard time getting to it, with the competition movies and everything else."

Blind Submissions

The filmmaker can always go another route—blind submissions to distributors. Or even exhibitors. While no one in distribution or exhibition wants to encourage filmmakers to send their unintroduced tape or DVD, they can't, at the same time, say no: One never knows when a real gem might show up in the mail, and they don't want it to slip through the cracks. Not theirs, anyway.

The hazards are obvious, though. When we talked to him, Greg Laemmle, president of the Laemmle Theatres chain in southern California, had just started Laemmle/Zeller Films with Steven Zeller and released *Up for Grabs*, a doc about the legal fight over Barry Bonds 73rd home run ball.

"We go to the usual festivals," said Laemmle, "and tend to really seek out the films that might otherwise slip through the cracks, like the film that won the grand prize in Sundance in 2004, *Down to the Bone*."

And he agreed that he is open to blind submissions from filmmakers. With qualifications.

"We have a very open-door policy both at Laemmle and therefore at Laemmle/Zeller," he said. "But, that said, if I've got a stack of films on my desk—and I do—I'm probably going to look first at the ones that have been recommended by people I know, and whose taste I appreciate. I look first at the ones that come from a producers rep, because they're not going to be repping films they don't think they can make money on. They work on commission, so they're not going to want to handle a film they don't think has any potential.

"And you're going to look at what festivals something's been at and maybe some of the early reviews and get a sense of what's important to look at. And other films just keep getting moved to the bottom of the stack."

Karen Cooper, director of Film Forum in New York, was asked what she needs to see in an undistributed film to make her want to play it.

"The same thing I see in a distributed film," she said. "I must say here that programming at Film Forum is shared here by Mike Maggiori and me. And Mike sees as many films at festivals all over the world throughout the year as do I, and together we call in work by reading *Variety* as well as a variety of different film magazines. We call in work just as it's completed, or after it's won prizes at festivals, so we quite aggressively look for work. We don't wait for work to just come over the transom. Although more comes over the transom than ever before, because over a period of time you obviously develop a reputation."

And how much of it do they actually play?

"Very little," she said. "Mike has pointed this out to me that maybe we should stop accepting stuff unless we've asked for it. But I still remain hesitant about it, not at least seeing a few minutes of a movie, because there's always the possibility of some gem."

An example?

"It's tough," she said with a laugh.

"Honestly?" asked Strand Releasing's Marcus Hu. "It's not a great idea. That said, over the past sixteen years, I think we've picked up two or three films that way."

Cooper said most of those unsolicited films that have really played well have come from people who are themselves "curatorial by nature."

"For instance, Fortissimo Film Sales," she said. "They have a great reputation. They themselves turn down a great number of films and only represent ones they think are strong. So if they send me something, even if I haven't asked for it, I'm going to look at it. So there's *that* kind of unsolicited. But then there's also the kind from the filmmaker who just got out of NYU, and I get that, too. And I just find it hard to turn it away without looking at least at a few minutes. Part of that impulse is because we are so exclusive. We show so few of the films we look at, I feel at the same time I have an obligation to look at as much as possible."

Has there been an example recently where someone sent you a film, and it actually played?

"Sure," she said. "Let's see. But is it somebody? Or a professional?"

No, like somebody.

"An actual person?" She looked through some calendars. "An actual person . . . OK, here's an actual person: *Let's Get Frank*. I ran into the editor of the film, or maybe he was the cinematographer. I'm not sure. The director of the film is Bart Everly and it wasn't Bart I met, but it was at a party given by Mira Nair, and I said, 'What are you doing?' And he told me about *Let's Get Frank*, that it was a new documentary about [Congressman] Barney Frank, and it captured all the hearings at which Frank was a great supporter of President Clinton, and about the whole circus that existed then in Washington. And I immediately called the director and said, 'Send over a tape.' And we took the film, and we played it."

For most independent filmmakers, a theatrical release is the ultimate. The brass ring. The dream date. The all-expense-paid trip to Paris complete with room at the Georges V, free meals at Café de Flore, and your personal tour guide, Johnny Depp.

But the opportunities have changed for filmmakers and there are more options. "Don't be so quick to dismiss television," producer Christine Vachon advised. "If HBO comes knocking on your door, don't turn up your nose. Or Showtime or Lifetime or any of those."

HBO Films has made films like *Real Women Have Curves, American Splendor*, and *Maria Full of Grace*. While it may be called HBO Films, they have released films theatrically. In the past they've released films in conjunction with Newmarket, or with Fine Line, but with the newly formed Picturehouse, the company headed up by Bob Berney, they are in the distribution business as well.

What HBO Films offers is the ability to provide resources and a machinery so that a filmmaker can just concentrate on making his or her film. Maud Nadler, SVP Independent Productions, HBO Films, describes the process.

"I'm not trying to make a ten million dollar movie for three million dollars," she said. "What I do is take what I think is a project or script that in the real indie world, if I got a million dollars in equity money, I could go make the movie. So instead, I'm asking HBO for three million so I can make that million-dollar movie the right way. So I just kind of reversed it all, but it's really important that I don't try to make something that should really cost more for a little."

She adds, "At the core, a good film is a good film, and we try to figure out where we are going to reach the largest audience. It's not about, and it shouldn't be about, 'This film is so good it should be theatrical.' There are very fabulous films that you can get a bigger audience to see on television than the hundred people that are going to show up at the theater. You need to do what's best for a film and not what's best for an ego."

It's a very sensitive subject, television vs. theatrical. "I can't be the one to say, 'Theatrical is not what it's trumped up to be,'" said John Sloss. "That's an emotional, subjective thing. I can tell clients they'll make less money. Unless their film really hits theatrically, which is a huge risk, they're doubling down on their investment in essence. They're taking a huge risk. I can tell them that more people will see their film on TV, assuming they get a good deal with a major pay buyer, than will ever see it in a theater, no matter how successful it is. I also have to tell them there are a different set of critics for television than there are for film. There remains a completely irrational, although not unfounded, just irrational emotional connection in most filmmakers' minds to the big screen."

"On one film we made, *Joe the King*," said Forensic Films' Scott Macaulay, "we were offered a pay cable premiere for more money than the theatrical distribution offer. The director, the other producers who were also investors in the film, and myself, we all took the lower money offer, because of the prestige of theatrical. I remember the cable guy said to me, 'You may find yourself regretting this one day.'

"It was a really beautiful movie," he said, "and, in retrospect, given the promotion that cable companies are able to do, I think more people might have seen the film. It goes back to the concept of figuring out how to define success on your own terms. I think that film would have been perceived as more successful had it gone that route than it did going small-scale theatrical, which wasn't as successful even though the distributor did a great job."

* * *

"I think knowledge is always good, although I do believe that a little knowledge is dangerous, too," said Christine Vachon. "I think a lot of filmmakers put the cart before the horse, and are trying to get me involved in a discussion, before they take their first film to Sundance, about whether Sony Classics would be a better place than say Warner Independent. And it's a little like, 'You should be so lucky that either place would want your crummy little movie.'

"It is true. I feel like independent filmmakers certainly get screwed enough that it's not a bad thing for them to want to educate themselves. At the end of the day, for most independent filmmakers, the Holy Grail to them is theatrical distribution. And they'll pretty much do anything to get it."

But in educating themselves, filmmakers might also look into some of the newer options out there and create more strategic distribution schemes for their films. Independent industry veteran, new-media expert and consultant Peter Broderick is working in these new models—hybrids of the old and new. (See Chapter 12, "The Marketplace.")

There are new models, like Laemmle/Zeller Films, that will acquire and release your film in fairly conventional ways, but with an unconventional setup that eliminates costly overhead.

And there are new opportunities created by organizations like IFP, FIND (Film Independent), and companies like Netflix and IndieFlix.

Self-Distribution

If and when you still believe you deserve a theatrical release, there is the last outpost, the Fort Apache of cinema: self-distribution and the service deal. There are some classic examples of films that were self-distributed: *Brother's Keeper, Licensed to Kill, Maya Lin: A Strong Clear Vision, I'm the One That I Want*, and *The Debut*, among others.

What one does via self-distribution generally is called four-walling: You book the theater, and, with a little luck, the grosses will cover the costs.

"What's showing at theaters is mostly what's brought to us through our distribution relationships," said Greg Laemmle. "Outside of that, it's largely done on a four-wall basis. People send me their films because they want me to look at them, but at the end of the day, because I'm working directly with the filmmakers, it's usually going to be done as a four-wall. Unless it's really something that has an appropriate level of cachet, and I understand why."

But someone like John Sloss takes a dim view of four-walling. "I rarely recommend that," he said, "because most of the time it feels like a vanity situation. And also, that kind of theatrical release, where nobody wants your movie, and you just say 'I'm going to go to the public, I'm going to prove everyone wrong,' that's a risky thing.

"On the other hand, I would absolutely agree with a service deal—if you feel you've got the goods, and if there's no risk in the P&A, and you don't need the advance. Then you could make deals where the distributor takes the lowest percentage and you make the most money. In a way, that was the approach we took with *Super Size Me*. We took less money up front in order to have a better deal on the back end. And that's the idea behind those service deals, especially *The Passion of the Christ*."

Service deals are partnerships you can enter with smaller distributors in which you basically pay a fee for use of a distribution apparatus, where the distributor hired will arrange the theaters, the print shipping, the advertising, all for a fee.

There are also extraordinary examples of how a service deal can be more profitable than, and preferable to, a standard distribution deal: *My Big Fat Greek Wedding, The Passion of the Christ*, and *Monster*.

If a distributor has not come on board, before you resort to either self-distribution or a service deal, ask yourself honestly: Do people really want or need to see my film? Who is my core audience? Is there a good reason why nobody bought it? Is there a place for it out there?

"If a film is good, but doesn't seem to be achieving traction," said publicist Jeremy Walker of Jeremy Walker & Associates, "it may simply need to ripen. Either the culture will change and make the film more relevant or the filmmaker will realize how to make the film work in the culture. If neither of these things comes to pass, the lesson to be learned is that perhaps the film may not, indeed, be any good. At some point it's important to move on."

IndieFlix

There's another stop on the Indie Express that only recently, as of fall 2005, was providing filmmakers an alternative, supremely inexpensive system of self-distribution: IndieFlix. Founded in Seattle by directors Gian-Carlo Scandiuzzi and Scilla Andreen, it is a Web-based, no-risk method of getting films out there—maybe after all other avenues have been exhausted.

"First and foremost, we're filmmakers," said Andreen. "He's made more than I have; we've made two together, several shorts, I've directed some music videos, and some shorts that did really well at Sundance and stuff. And Carlo did really well in the eighties in foreign distribution, when videos cost ninety-five dollars a unit and people would buy like forty thousands units. It was like crack."

But the "game" as she called it, was the same "whether you're making art, schlock, or crap."

They made what they called "artful" movies that got good reviews and several awards and grand jury prizes "and we had distribution offers from Artisan and Lions Gate and various other 'name' companies, and realized that the terms were so horrible—they wanted the rights for twenty years; we got them down to seven. Our list of deliverables was so high we could have made another movie; the terms were just ridiculous. You'd have to make ten million dollars before you saw a penny, and then they still wanted you to go out and do this grassroots campaign and marketing and publicity for our own movies, even after we had to do all that other stuff. And that was a *good* deal."

So Scandiuzzi and Andreen said "forget it," figuring, on the model of Bob Berney and such films as *Memento*, that they'd be better off getting the money together and doing it themselves. But, of course, they were still in theatrical mode.

"Of course," Andreen said. "We're filmmakers, diehards, artists. That's our art—we think it needs to be bigger than life, on the screen, the group experience in the dark. All filmmakers want that. You never seem to give up the dream, that's the weird thing about filmmakers. It just repeats itself. It doesn't evolve. So we just said, 'It's time to evolve.'"

The IndieFlix deal is that a filmmaker submits his or her work—on virtually any format—and signs a deal memo stating that the rights have been cleared, and that IndieFlix is allowed to sell the work, and then—IndieFlix sells it. They burn DVDs to order, give the filmmakers 30 percent off the top, and the IndieFlix bookkeeping, Andreen promised, is "transparent."

Unlike CustomFlix, which was purchased by Amazon.com, the filmmakers don't have to lay out any money, or produce the DVDs themselves—something more like a traditional service deal. IndieFlix creates the product, the filmmaker supplies info on the film for the Web site, and sales are tracked. The smallest filmmaker could be IndieFlix's biggest seller, which will only make them bigger.

"We might be the last stop on the track," said Andreen, "but our goal is that eventually filmmakers will go out with their little mini-DVD cams and make a movie for practically nothing *specifically* to sell it on IndieFlix because it costs them *nothing*. And we give them the publicity tools, the marketing tools, and we make it for them, and deliver it in a timely manner.

"We feel every film has an audience, and it's all relative—some people love crap!" she laughed. "You know what I mean?"

Sundance

The Holy Grail

High up in the oxygen-free, euphoniously christened Wasatch Mountains lies that combination Xanadu, El Dorado, and Death Star known as the Sundance Film Festival—a phenomenon of such widespread and disproportionate influence it really deserves a chapter all its own.

FIRST, A FEW FACTS: The festival is a program of the Sundance Institute, a nonprofit entity begun by Robert Redford in 1981 that celebrates its twenty-fifth anniversary in 2006. When Redford started the Institute, there already was a festival taking place in nearby Park City—the United States Film Festival, which was founded in 1978 and would remain independent (there's that word again) until Redford's Institute took it over in 1984. And it would keep the name U.S. Film Fest until 1989, when it was renamed Sundance.

This background is pertinent if only for the reason that it's wise for a would-be player to know the ground rules, the cast, the lay of the land. The Institute, for instance, isn't subordinate to the festival; the festival is a program of the Institute—as are the producer's conference, and the directing, documentary, theater, composer, and screenwriting labs that go on throughout the year. The Institute is based in Salt Lake City and in Beverly Hills.

Sundance has become so large in the public imagination and the sweaty dreams of filmmakers that it's become a do-or-die proposition. Production schedules on individual films are routinely arranged to meet the festival's late fall deadline; directors have been known to hold their movies back a year on the off chance they might be accepted. People who would never, in a million years, intentionally pay money to see an independent film, or a subtitled film, or— God help us—a documentary, know what Sundance is, partly because they know it's associated with Redford, and partly because the word "Sundance" has evolved to mean many things to many people. Each year, the successes of such films as *Mysterious Skin, Me and You and Everyone We Know, Rize,* and *Junbug,* as well as older titles such as *In the Bedroom, The Motorcycle Diaries, Maria Full of Grace, Born into Brothels, Napoleon Dynamite, Garden State, The Station Agent*, and *Super Size Me*, help to cultivate a taste among audiences for independent film.

But at the same time, it remains a struggle for many independent films that don't have stars, or a sexy hook, to find a spotlight. And now that more and more celebrities are involved with independent film, some independent films are just more equal than others. Casting stars in your film doesn't make your film a better film, but in an extremely crowded marketplace, it can be seen as a safety net. It is in fact, the product of many things, most visibly the ever-evolving economics of getting an independent film financed.

Sundance is criticized sometimes for selecting films with recognizable names. But take a look at those names: Many of them have their roots in independent film, and grew up and out of indie film. Many of them choose to keep one foot in each world. And as independent film is often a place where roles and stories can be more interesting, allowing actors to really show their stuff, stars are more open, even seeking roles in them, more than ever before. The way movies are put together now, and with more money coming from overseas—and generated from casting "names"—Sundance is neither immune to nor the cause of this.

At the same time, though, all of those independent films without stars seem to become a little bit smaller by contrast, and their challenges a little more difficult in terms of distribution, or as lures for the media. For television journalists, the film without stars becomes an even tinier blip on the radar. Most top television entertainment programs don't cover films like *Mean Creek, Capturing the Friedmans, Me and You and Everyone We Know*, and *Junebug*. This is partly why most people across mid-America never hear of films like this. And why we simultaneously resent them for not turning up at the box office. With more stars present at Sundance, taking up the precious spotlight, it's no surprise that it irks people.

Shows like *Entertainment Tonight* certainly aren't in Park City covering these little independent films without stars. Britney Spears (or whatever megawatt celebrity du jour is creating a traffic jam on Main Street) could not care less about what's going on in the theaters once the cameras outside stop popping. The official sponsors may have their capitalist hearts in the right place, but the so-called "ambushers"—the corporate entities who come, set up camp, and feed off the Sundance "aura" for all its hipster nourishment—couldn't care less.

However, for the lean, mean filmmaking machines who rightly see Sundance as their prime chance at the brass ring (envision it, instead, as a golden DVD), there's a ten-day window in January that's the size of a mail slot.

How do you get in? There are no hard-and-fast rules and no tips that can assure anyone of anything. Every film is different, and every year the climate is different. And then there's personal taste. The first step: You start by submitting the film and sending a tape. And as you've probably heard, the programmers get several thousand a year.

"Years ago, I was in the same building as the Sundance guys on Santa Monica Boulevard, for a few years, one floor below," said Jeff Dowd, consultant to independent filmmakers. "We'd go home at night, they'd be leaving with backpacks of ten, fifteen movies; Gilmore would have a suitcase. Let's assume these guys are crack-addict vampires who never sleep. Do the math. You take twenty movies home at eight o'clock, you're back at work at nine in the morning."

Lesson for filmmaker? "Your first ten minutes better be really good, that's all I can tell you."

Let's for the moment look at the festival itself. There are those who would argue that if Sundance had never been a competitive film festival—there are sixteen-film lineups in U.S. documentary and feature competitions and, as of 2005, similar contests in world cinema—then the entire movie industry today might look different.

"Without question, it's always been an issue," said program director Geoff Gilmore. "Redford views it as, I think, the wrong thing to do for films, generally, and I view it as a necessary evil. And I view it as a necessary evil in a very simple way: It is what gets these films visibility. It gets the program visibility with media, and it gets kind of a visibility with general audiences, even. A critic wrote an article in a magazine that I read a couple of days ago that decries the fact that a film like *Police Beat* didn't get an award. She makes it seem as though it's our fault, and I'm trying to say that I don't sit with my juries and tell them what to do, even though I put that film at the top of the list, with every critic I talked to beforehand, as a film they should see. I'm not in disagreement, but we don't think that the jury awards are an accurate specific reflection of the best films at Sundance. They're one of those standards."

What are the others?

"There are usually three of them," he said. "Critical appraisal, audience reaction or buzz, whatever you want to call it, and jury reaction. Since all three of those are simultaneous at the festival, it oftentimes takes weeks afterward before people begin to look at films and say, 'Wait a second.' Films like *In the Bedroom* and *Napoleon Dynamite*, which were not considered to be wonderful films in the festival context, became much more interesting films because of their market success later on."

Competition provides narrative. The media love a narrative (it gives them a beginning, middle, and end), and while competition might be antithetical to the entire Sundance ethos, it both draws more attention to a select group of films and draws incredible media attention not only to the films but to the independent film landscape in general.

Why do filmmakers, distributors, and exhibitors care and want to be a part of the event? Because not only is it where some of the most interesting filmmakers have been discovered, but for those films that will open soon thereafter, it means great exposure, as well as a certain cachet.

On the selection of films, the people who pick the Sundance program—John Cooper, Shari Frilot, Caroline Libresco, Trevor Groth, and of course Gilmore—they can only pick from what's available, and what comes in.

"Film festivals like Sundance are only as good as the crop that's out there," said Marcus Hu, copresident of Strand Releasing. "I have to say I admire that festival so much for having established and found so much great talent. That festival is one that really nurtures talent, through the Institute and labs. And as much criticism as we can dish out about it, it really is outweighed by all the good they do. And Redford—who else is out there helping filmmakers get their dreams realized, with workshops and all these kinds of things, flying these poor filmmakers out and discussing their scripts—who else is doing that? I'm in awe of what they do."

What they do, and have done, is provide a conduit not just for talent into the Greater Indieworld, but into Hollywood as well. Film director Bryan Singer's a good example. Having split the grand jury prize for features in 1993 with *Public Access*, he made *The Usual Suspects*, then went on to make *X-Men* movies for Fox, with his crowning achievement set to be *Superman Returns*. Another competition filmmaker, Justin Lin, has made studio movies—*Annapolis, The Fast and the Furious 3* and is prepping the remake of *Oldboy*—since his Park City outing with *Better Luck Tomorrow*. Tommy O'Haver has gone on to make *Get Over It* and *Ella Enchanted* since his *Billy's Hollywood Screen Kiss* premiered in Park City.

Lin described a conversation. "I was talking to this exec, and he said to me, 'We strive to work with the A list—Spielberg or Scorsese, or to work with the indie A list—the next Spielberg or Scorsese.' That's why they go to Sundance. It's kind of strange to hear, but that's why."

When one considers the success of the Sundance Film Festival—with the sold-out screenings, the pushing, the shoving, the shortage of hotel rooms, the cutthroat competition for restaurant reservations—one can't help but think the programmers can do precisely what they want; that they are immune to the economics of the film world, and can program only the finest, most artistic cinema available, box office be damned. So why do so many lackluster films—and Gilmore will admit they're not all spectacular—get into this place?

"I've never viewed festivals—and this is what I think a lot of people are only beginning to understand about me—I've never viewed Sundance as a platform simply for art," Gilmore said. "I never have."

He said what Sundance changed were the two popular and dominant images of what film festivals should be. One was the high-style, auteur-heavy event that, like Cannes, was symbolized by gowned women in high heels walking down a red carpet; it was the kind of festival emulated by director Richard Roud and the New York Film Festival in the sixties, seventies, and eighties, with New Yorkers in their stoles and tuxes awaiting the big art film that was coming from Cannes.

The other was the high-brow-bordering-on-ethereal art event that could double as a séance.

"Sundance is neither of those," Gilmore said. "Diversity of storytelling is much more interesting to me. There are ways of storytelling—some of which might be very much about art, some of which might not be about art, but might be about genre—and there are people that would look at those works and say those films don't belong in a film festival. I have critics who did that to me this year, did it last year, and will do it to me every year, who will always come to me every year, saying that what a film festival should be about is art. I view it as one of the poles in the circus tent. And I believe that part of what Sundance has helped to develop is an appreciation for work which is outside the context of art."

Films "outside the context of art" may seem like a strange category for a film festival program to embrace, but it certainly clarifies the Sundance Mission According to Gilmore. Knowing that he eschews what some critics and audiences would consider "fine" film in favor of eclecticism and genre work says a lot about a lot of Sundance lineups. Although there's another catch.

One of the conflicts between the critical community and Sundance has long been the festival's insistence on "diversity"—as in a racially, sexually, ethnically, and otherwise demographically even-handed overview of the independent year in film. Films that come out of the labs often face being dismissed for being "Sundance" projects.

"Why has Sundance Fest become known for diversity issues—which is what we've become known for over a decade?" Gilmore asked. "Because that's one of the things that we focus on. Diversity, personal storytelling, stories that weren't focused on auteur definitions. And I'm not suggesting—and I really won't, in fact, I get very angry about it with certain critics; I shouldn't, but I do—that independent film isn't artistic. I think it is. But I also believe that first-time filmmakers, a lot of them, may not have the level of aesthetic achievement that you'll get in those auteur films." And comparing the two, he said, isn't really fair.

Gilmore's affection for genre and willingness to push the indie envelope, can be, he said, a decided boon to fledgling filmmakers. "When a *Saw* comes to Sundance," he said of the 2005 horror film, "gets bought out of Sundance, and roars to a fifty million dollar gross, you have that sense of 'Oh, well, wait a second, there's a spectrum of films. . . . I can be in that corner of it over there. . . . I'm not the high-art documentary' or 'I'm not the esthetically complicated diversity tale. I can play at midnight and still do very very well.' And that range of work at Sundance, or at other platforms, is something people are very much dealing with, just as they are at the international markets.

"Kenneth Turan argues consistently," Gilmore said of *The Los Angeles Times*'s critic, "that what Sundance should be focusing on is not discovery work, because it puts too much pressure on the filmmakers in that context, but that we should be bringing the 'masters of independent film' and having a competition the way Cannes does. That we should be having the masters of reinvented film. He said it again this year, with the idea being that we put Hal Hartley and we put Rebecca Miller and Jim Jarmusch and Robert Altman in the competition, not discovery work. It's a different point of view.

"My point of view is that the discovery work is actually fresher and more interesting to have in a competition—not always successful, but fresher and more interesting than some of those auteur films. And again, the argument as to what people look at and what they think about when they deal with independent films is something we could talk for a long time about."

Sundance exists on two very disparate planes: It is very much a celebration of personal cinema. And it is also the green room for your Hollywood audition. Resume films are all over the place at Sundance. They're like bacteria; they infect the whole atmosphere. They are also a fact of Park City life. Fortunately, the audiences (and even sometimes the juries) are smarter than the festival or the media.

The media can cause more problems than they solve, or even observe, at

Sundance. In a feverish race to detect heat and buzz and predict what's going to win before the festival has barely started, the various press outlets will anoint certain films at the expense of others. This is also fairly unavoidable—no one, even if he or she were to spend the entire ten days in screenings, can see the entire festival before it ends. Buzz detection becomes buzz creation.

How to avail oneself of this phenomenon? Not all of it is under one's control, but certain things are. Insist, particularly if your film is available (for sale), that your film has its public screening before its press screening (most happen this way, but not always). This ensures that the first buyers and journalists to see the film will see it in a public setting. Second, make sure your publicist has tickets for reporters and critics—of course, you want the right reporters and critics (see the next chapter, "The Media: Friends or Foes"), and you want to make access as simple as possible for key people. Make sure that you or your sales rep also has tickets for buyers who might not have badges.

Most importantly, make sure your film is as good as it can be.

Laura's view: "In the interest of disclosure, I have worked with Sundance for a few years as a media consultant. But I have also worked on dozens of films there for the past fifteen years or so and have seen it grow incredibly, both in terms of size and in influence. I believe most journalists have a love/hate relationship with Sundance because it is, simply, so much work in a really intense and emotional short period of time. But the feeling of discovering new filmmakers and their new work and the ability to discover them and actually change their lives is invigorating. It also works as a place we go once a year to recharge our interest in film, remind ourselves of why we do it, and to reunite with old friends.

"That the festival has grown so much, and that there is so much corporate support, are good things for independent film, though that may feel and sound counterintuitive. Remember, at its core, Sundance is a nonprofit arts organization. And the more attention the media, corporations, and people in general pay to independent film, however annoying, the better, so long as the creative process stays intact.

"I've seen so many lives changed by Sundance. And I've seen filmmakers become far more educated about the business and its machinations than they used to be. They are much more savvy to the process and while it's disheartening, I understand. The stakes have gotten much higher and the potential to really be plucked out of nowhere and have your film seen and career launched is real. It does happen."

Which probably explains why filmmakers treat getting into Sundance like a life-or-death proposition.

Just the announcement of the lineup can turn industry folk rabid. *Better Luck Tomorrow*'s Justin Lin remembers being accepted into competition. "The Monday after Thanksgiving in 2001 my phone was just going off the hook," he said. "My answering machine was filling up every hour. Everyone was calling—publicists, studio people, managers and agents—*everyone*, and I didn't know who was who, and no one had even seen the film. And these are the same people who would have not returned my calls three days earlier."

Asked to describe how he felt after his world premiere screening, Lin laughed and said, "It wasn't the end of the screening—it was when the movie started, twenty or thirty seconds into the movie. It was the first laugh. People laughed and all of a sudden you realize that people were actually connecting on a certain level. I remember right after the screening, too, you could feel an energy, like people felt like they were the first to see something.

"We got an offer right away," he said. "Agents were coming down and giving me their cards. And I felt like my life was different. It changed right at that moment. It really did at many levels."

He had driven to Utah with $200 in his bank account. "At the end of that first screening, I thought about all of us," he said of his cast and crew. "We had a cabin and everyone went—there were about twenty-five of us. And it was great."

"That's what's so exciting. Even if nobody's heard of your film," *The New York Times*'s Sharon Waxman said. "If you're in the festival, people will go see your film. If it's good, people will find out about it, even if it's a film that nobody has been talking about."

Miguel Arteta, whose first film, *Star Maps*, sold to Fox Searchlight, said, "Definitely aim for Sundance. It's where the Filmmaker-from-Out-of-Nowhere-Can-Rule bar none. And there's no feeling like it when you unspool your film there for the first time."

Arteta's producer Matthew Greenfield explained, "In 1996, we submitted *Star Maps*, and at that time it was, as it is now, the best place to premiere an American independent film. And we thought that the film was good, but we also knew it wasn't really for a general audience, and that as an independent film for specialized audiences, we felt like Sundance was a place where that was actually prized, where that was a good thing. So we felt like that was the best place to give it a shot." Greenfield's *Star Maps, Chuck & Buck*, and *The Good Girl*—all got bought after their Sundance premieres—and his fourth film, *The Motel*, premiered there.

"Sundance is the destination for independent cinema," said agent Cassian Elwes. "I think the reason for that is because their taste level is fantastic. They've been right so often. There are so few films that became independent successes that didn't play at Sundance."

For Kirby Dick, the festival legitimized his films. "I've done Sundance a number of times. Two of my films *Derrida* [2002] and *Sick* [1997] could have really been considered fairly marginal, but I really think because they were presented at Sundance and were well received there, that really moved them much more into the indie-doc mainstream, if there's such a thing. Sundance has been great. With the exception of two films—one of which played at SXSW, *The End* [2004], which was never supposed to be theatrical and which was made for Cinemax, and my first film, *Private Practices*, which premiered at Filmex, all of my other films have premiered at Sundance—*Sick, Derrida, Chain Camera* [2001], and *Twist of Faith* [2005]. All I can say is that Sundance has been very helpful."

"That's one of the best things about Sundance," said Waxman. "Seeing what has happened to people like Richard Kelly who made *Donnie Darko*—to see what happened to his movie and his career. Or with *Super Size Me*. I had seen the film early on and had interviewed Morgan Spurlock standing on Main Street in front of the Egyptian; he was freezing. In the next couple days, people started circling. It was interesting to see what happened to that film."

For some films and filmmakers, Sundance will make a huge difference in the trajectory of the film and their career and the trajectory of all kinds of films, not just *Napoleon Dynamite* and *Garden State*. That *Born into Brothels* got a distributor in ThinkFilm is not necessarily something that just happened because they went to Sundance; the film would most likely have gotten distribution one way or the other. But that the film made it this far, and won an Academy Award for Best Documentary, is due to the critical body of support that was conceived at Sundance, as well as the good will that came from those who saw the film and met the filmmakers. It was a springboard that enabled the filmakers to jump higher.

There's only so much planning one can do, and at some point, your film will be judged, it will speak for itself and there's *nothing* you can do. And it can be excruciating. Todd Field, before his film *In the Bedroom* screened, said that this was perhaps the best and worst time of his life, a moment of complete anxiety, excitement, and fear. He probably lost eight pounds in the weeks leading up to the festival.

That all said, it's not the be-all and end-all, and there are a hundred ways to get to the same place.

"Sundance is a really rarified, weird audience," said Robert Pulcini (*American Splendor*). Just because a film doesn't hit there, doesn't mean that it's not going to connect with audiences sometime in the future."

"Every film has a different life, a different legend to it," said Sony Classics' Michael Barker. "There have been films discovered in many different places. Sundance is a very special place, just like Toronto is a special place, because everybody's there. Exhibitors, distributors, critics, journalists. Those are the Meccas—Cannes, Toronto, and Sundance. But the fact is, in those places, people are distracted, because they are also great places to launch films. So maybe they're not the best place for your film to be, and it can be a blessing in disguise to be turned down by those places because you could be one of the few American independent films in Telluride and be noticed in a major way. Or in San Francisco. Or in Seattle or SXSW. There are so many places where a picture can be discovered. I think this idea of wanting to go to Sundance at all costs because you're going to win the lottery and get thirteen million dollars—which doesn't seem to be paid anymore for films—that's kind of silly. . . . Sundance is very important, but it is not by any means the only place."

"Don't put all your eggs in one basket," said Pulcini. "We've had so many projects that failed. We may have won at Sundance, but we've gotten rejected so many times, probably more than anyone else in history. Our short films, our screenplays, even the screenplay for *American Splendor* was rejected by the labs, and that was basically the shooting script. It's so easy to get discouraged, but we always try to have more than one pot on the stove. I've met so many people who have this one script, and it's the focus of their lives for years. It's all they talk about and do. We were never like that. It was kind of like the way we made documentaries; we decided to make a documentary when we were out there trying to break in as screenwriters. I think you have to really diversify your career plan."

While Sundance can change the course of a film's life, there are other viable paths, explained producer Scott Macaulay. "If you screen there, everybody sees your film. You make an immediate impression on people. The road is sometimes a little bit longer at some of these other festivals, and you have to work them in a different way. But the industry is really rapacious when it comes to looking for new talent and that talent can be found in any number of places. You really only need one person at a screening who's in a position to do something to react meaningfully to your film."

Geoff Gilmore pointed out that Sundance is "one of the places where you can trust you're getting a very high level of scrutiny, a level of scrutiny that oftentimes involves decision-makers who can walk out of the room and buy the movie if they like it, then and there, who don't have to wait to send the film to Los Angeles for the next person—although that happens too, depending on what the issues are. We have to go through a long list of different buyer strategies now about the idea of simultaneous screenings in Sundance, buyer screenings in New York and Los Angeles, where buyers are being shown a movie in order to facilitate sales that start with a Sundance screening, but are also being backed up by a print being shown to a studio executive or a major company executive."

Despite filmmakers' hunger to get in, do Gilmore and his team still actively go out and look for films to show?

"Well, we do, and we don't," he said. "The international stuff, absolutely; we're out there scouring the world for international work, and there's no question we do that. Some of the premieres? Sometimes. But I'm very cautious about that. I tend not to call a company up and say, 'Send your film to me,' and then reject it. Because it tends to build up bad relationships with the company.

"I may do it the other way around. I may have someone send a message to someone, 'Hey could you ask so-and-so if they're interested,' but it doesn't usually work. Again, the idea of trying to make companies think about festivals? They do think about them now. Years ago, they didn't, and you had to call to put that idea in their heads that 'Maybe this could play at a festival?' Now, it's not something you have to put in there."

Enough about the festival. The festival is not the only thing that Sundance does.

* * *

Miranda July, writer-director of *Me and You and Everyone We Know*, is probably the least typical of Sundance lab graduates. A performance and installation artist, her work was once better known to museum goers than filmgoers. But she found the experience invaluable.

"I found out about the lab from Tommy Pallotta, who's an independent producer [*A Scanner Darkly*]," July said. "He suggested I apply, having known my work from performing in Austin. So I applied."

She had started writing her script in June of 2001. "I applied that fall, it wasn't that developed, and I didn't get in," she said. "In 2002, I applied for the next round, and again, didn't get in. But I got encouraging notes. I applied again, and got into the January 2003 Screenwriting Lab.

"The week of the lab," she said, was "life-changing. I remember describing it as a positive trauma because even though I was a professional, and had been supporting myself as an artist, doing what I wanted to do, I never put myself in a position where I could be helped. And in some ways, getting helped is the way you're taken most seriously.

"There's something that just changes you on a molecular level, and how you think of yourself," she said, "when you have people engaging with what you consider really personal work, in a really deep way. I had conversations with people that were more or less like therapy sessions. I remember my first meeting with Alice Arlen, the woman who wrote *Silkwood*. I was completely intimidated. I wasn't sure what she thought of my script. I remember asking her whether something I was doing seemed like a device. And she looked me dead in the eyes and said, 'Don't use that word, my dear. You're much better than that.' And that kind of says it all."

July said that the Sundance people knew that "I hadn't gone about this in a very traditional way, and that I wasn't that interested in three-act structure, or even arc in some degree, and then I rewrote like crazy."

But July waited to make her film until she was ready, because Michelle Satter, the director of the Screenwriters Lab, "is pretty ruthless about that. I was incredibly impressed by her—not by a lot of others—but I took her word quite seriously. She's so subtle and soft-spoken. I applied to the Filmmakers Lab and got into that. That was another kind of trauma. It's not as rigorous as actually shooting your movie, but for me it was much, much more rigorous than anything I had ever done, and it kind of hinted at the really grueling physical and emotional labor of making a movie, which was great to have. It was like getting beat up ahead of time so you know what to expect when you got your ass kicked later on.

"I had some of my advisors there: Miguel Arteta, who really stayed with the project, and Mary Kay Place, who was really more of an advocate for the project, which is also so important, at every stage. She told everyone she knew.

"I did so much rewriting after the lab, but I think it just brought me deeper into what I was actually doing, so that I was in a place to work very hard for about six months after and really make good changes. I was confident, and had the intimacy of what it was really going to be like to shoot it. I never looked at the notes I took down, though they seemed so important at the time. The problems were clear."

After the Filmmakers Lab, July's project got into No Borders, which is a program of the IFP Market, which lets in two Sundance projects a year. She went to No Borders, had a screenplay reading in L.A., and then was invited to Cinemart in Rotterdam and met with people there, some of whom had interest. "And all along the way we're sending the script to everybody," she said. "And people are even reading multiple drafts, like HBO reads many drafts, and we were never completely sure that [an HBO deal] was never gonna happen. One of my advisors had been involved with *The Motorcycle Diaries*, and out of the lab they were really keen on doing the film. But that was a case where they wanted stars, like many others.

"One big thing about the lab," she said. "In one of my meetings with all the advisers—people like Ed Harris and big-name actors like that—there I am saying I'm not going to cast stars. I'm not going to attach anyone. I'm going to get this made without doing that. Because that seemed intrinsic to the story. And that group of people at the lab, the Sundance people and advisors, all said, 'We think you're right. Stick to that.'

"I just know now," she said. "The hardest thing about each of those steps is that you don't have any sense of scale. You don't know what's a make-or-break thing, or what's important. I had such good advice. Miguel would often tell me—'This matters and this doesn't.' That was invaluable. Having an introduction to the industry through a group of people like at Sundance, who have no other interest other than for you to see your vision through, kind of sets the bar really high in terms of your expectations of people in an industry that's really not like that. I got to keep my values, and I worked with a company [IFC] that gave me final cut, which was perfectly in keeping with my Sundance education, and now the combination of that and Sundance has put me in a place where I sort of feel like I have very little to gain by compromising in any way.

"I feel like I am the biggest brat, and I must sound like it," she said, "but the truth is, it's so much work that I don't think anyone should do it. If you want to make yourself miserable, there are so many other ways you could do it. You should only do this if it's straight out of your heart."

6

The Media

Friends or Foes?

The Critic, still fresh after a day of intellectual jousting with what the "industry" presumes to call feature filmmaking, returns to his stately home. He returns James's greeting at the door (while surrendering his hat) and promptly repairs to his study—that sanctuary from the work-a-day world, that fortress of solitude, that womblike refuge from the pedestrian and trite.

Sliding a white-gloved finger along the beveled edge of his Louis XVI giltwood buffet (just to check the new girl's progress), he settles, satisfied, into his green leather Georgian wingback chair, ready to take on another poseur, another undernourished talent, another escapee from the pits of film school hell.

James has, as is his habit, decanted a snifter of Godet 1940 Grand Champagne—not enough to dull the senses, just excite them—and the Critic feels the rising anticipation of his own analytic process. Dipping quill in ink (some in his "trade," as he likes to call it, have surrendered to the tug of technology, but the Critic insists on the tactile sensation of transferring profundity to parchment), he leans his head back, considers the universe, and applies the first words to paper: "Cinema is . . ."

WHATEVER CINEMA IS, the preceding is total hogwash. Most film critics—or any members of the entertainment media, for that matter—are far more likely to be underpaid, overworked, stressed-out creatures who don't exactly scuttle across the floor of Hollywood's ocean, but aren't dining on lobster and fois gras either. They are much like the people they are writing about—people who do what they do because they can't imagine doing anything else (although running a small island nation would be just fine).

It might not be unusual for a reviewer to have spent the day at two or three—or four, or five—films, grabbing a hot dog here, a seventeenth cup of coffee there, and finding only in the late of night or early morning the time necessary to give a particular movie its due. And at a film festival—isn't "festival" a rather blissful word for what generally goes on?—it's even worse. The conditions are more pressured, the menu of films is more crammed, the deadlines are cruel and the attempt to get a meaningful grasp of what's on the menu, much less absorbing what it all means on some grander scale, is a Sisyphean task at best.

Knowing this, the filmmaker has to brace her- or himself for being treated like dirt. Not that he or she will be—but lowered expectations are always healthier, particularly in the realm of independent film.

The entertainment media may seem to be populated by many specialists doing many special things. In actuality, the people who write about film can very often be the wearers of multiple hats—critic and reporter, perhaps, or someone who splits his or her time as an industry reporter and/or film-market analyst, jobs that have much more to do with the commercial prospects of movies than their artistic value.

The reporter may also have to cover the entire entertainment beat, so knowing all of Hollywood's comings and goings may leave little energy for having a full understanding of the indie film biz. In addition, he or she might be responsible for capturing the response to a given film, both critical and popular. (This summons up the old cynic's formulation for how to assess the credibility of unnamed sources in an opinion piece: If the writer says "many say" it's because everyone at lunch shared the same opinion. "Some say" means they didn't. "It has been said" can be construed to mean that the writer said it to himself.)

The point is, a filmmaker is dancing in a minefield. There is no way of dealing with critical response, or preparing for it, and any attempt to cater to it—should one be crazy or cynical enough to try and pander to some abstract critical sensibility—would only backfire. The only thing to do is make an honest film, because that's ultimately what has the best chance of being well reviewed—and if it isn't, it's what you're left to live with.

But there are some things you can do to ameliorate the toxic effects of the press, one of which is taking advantage of serendipity.

Personally, the memory of David O. Russell, director of such films as *Three Kings* and *Flirting with Disaster*, giving John a ride in his SUV through the snowy roads of Sundance—and he wasn't even going to see Russell's then-current movie, *Spanking the Monkey* —has always made John think kindly of him. Actress Michelle Rodriguez's willingness to sit for an impromptu interview about *Girlfight* on a beach at Cannes was endearing, just because she was so hungry to promote her movie. And Judith Helfand's hustler spirit, getting people out to see her moving documentary *Healthy Baby Girl* back in 1997—a film that provoked the kind of interactive Q&As that make the film festival experience so unique—engendered a deep admiration for how the entrepreneurial and artistic instincts have always walked hand in hand.

But a lot of critics are under intense pressure, and don't care, out of principle or out of self-protection, to deal on a personal level with filmmakers whose work they have to review. This doesn't mean, of course, that there aren't ways of massaging the press.

One way is to remember that people have egos. It's human nature. If you're at a film festival, let's say, there may be dozens of journalists who want to interview you. It's most likely not because you're the new Fellini. It could be because your movie is about a cross-dressing member of the Royal Order of Raccoons with a Liza Minnelli obsession, in which case be grateful. It could also be that a journalist thinks your film shows actual promise, in which case be very grateful. John still remembers his interview of first-time filmmaker Christopher Scott Cherot, director of the comedy *Hav Plenty*, which seemed a very promising debut. Cherot must have thought so too, since he read a magazine all during the interview. That we have not heard his name since is probably coincidental. (See Chapter 10, "Manners and Mis-manners.")

Once you become the head of a studio, you can treat the media any way you want. Certain U.S. film companies have developed a penchant for showing their, shall we say, less desirable films, or "product," to critics on Wednesday nights—Wednesday afternoon being the deadline for most Friday reviews in most daily papers. This technique serves one primary purpose: keeping negative reviews out of the weeklies (*People, US*, etc.). Since those publications can't run a review until well after the film has opened, the predicted damage can be kept at a minimum—without anyone being able to say the studio didn't screen the film at all, which is suicide (or homicide, if you take the filmmaker's point of view.) At the same time, what you've done is made the daily critic, who *can* get a review into the pre-opening-weekend editions, extend his or her work day—not only until the end of the film, but well after (since the review will have to be written that night, for an early-morning, last-ditch effort to make Friday's paper). This does not, it goes without saying, endear a critic to the film in question, especially if the film is far removed from being a cinematic masterpiece, or even watchable, and he or she is passing up a good meal, a hot date, or a relaxing and well-deserved evening at home.

The point is, you can't go wrong making life easier for the critic: If your film is at Sundance, and your mother is there, too, and you have only one ticket for your film, and you happen to see *People* magazine's Leah Rozen walking down the street, and she doesn't have a ticket—stiff your mother.

This is especially true if you have a film with heat. Tickets will be at a premium; the critic might look at the program and say, "I'll never get into this screening of Film A. I'll be wasting my time. I may as well go see Film B; at least I'll be sure to get in." If you're the director of Film A, you generally want to make sure that critic has a ticket.

* * *

Most buyers really listen to what the media think.

"You listen to the buzz," said Strand Releasing's Marcus Hu. "And that's how we make a lot of our decisions when we're choosing a critically driven film. Because with a company like Strand, where we can't afford to buy huge ads, what we really do is rely on critical response and the support it will get and the feature space we'll get. That feature in *The New York Times* IS our double-truck ad. For us, that is far more important, especially with the smarter audience we're looking for—the one that reads the article in the *Times* or *The Village Voice* or *Time Out* or *The Los Angeles Times* or *LA Weekly*. They're more likely to pay attention to that feature article and that good review than look at a one-page ad for a movie. And I think that's how for sixteen years we've been able to stay alive, by going by what we, at least, perceive the critics will think."

But it can backfire, too. "We've picked up films we thought the critics would get behind, and they totally didn't. I am sometimes devastated by a bad review. Others roll off my back. But when you're really passionate about one, and the critic just doesn't get it, you go 'Aaaarrgh!!!!'"

"If it's an independent film," said Bob Berney, president of Picturehouse, "and if it's different, you really need a supporter, a critic, maybe an early review at a festival. Because for the exhibitors, it just makes it rise up out of the hundreds of films that they're looking at, the fact that it was in a festival, and the fact that it got some kind of review notice out of Toronto, let's say, it makes all the exhibitors at least go look at it first."

Something national or broader is even better. "Something like a quote can really make a difference to people following the film," Berney said. "Or the local critics at least saying, 'I'll review that one.' Because I think outside of New York and Los Angeles, the papers are really limited. They'll only review two independent films that week—not like here [in New York], where you have ten a week, fifteen, or twenty. So I think it does make a difference."

Berney, while at Newmarket, distributed *Monster*, the film about serial killer Aileen Wuornos, a role that won Charlize Theron an Academy Award.

"We had an early Roger Ebert quote that was pretty wild," he said [chuckling], "'the best performance in the history of cinema' and first we were thinking 'It's kind of over the top,' but we used it anyway."

"I have been told," Ebert said, "but am not positive, that when Roeper and I reviewed *Monster* three weeks early, and praised Charlize Theron's performance, the studio decided to release it theatrically when it was headed for video. It went on to win an Oscar. We went so early with it because we thought it was important that it not get lost in the crush of holiday openings."

"It really made a difference on *The Woodsman*," Berney said of the 2004 film about a paroled child molester, "because you need not only the quote, but you've got to have some kind of background on a movie with the subject of a pedophile. Even with Kevin Bacon and Kyra Sedgwick, and the fact that it was in Sundance, and all the festivals, you have to have someone qualifying it, saying there's more to it than tabloid subject matter. That was really tough. Really taboo. It was one of those things where we fell for the movie and then made the deal and then went, 'Uh oh.'"

Kenneth Turan, film critic for *The Los Angeles Times*, told us this story about *Mad Hot Ballroom*.

"This is a film that played at Slamdance, a documentary that Sundance had turned down, for reasons I'm still kind of baffled by. You can't trust that festivals put their best films in prominent places, and you can't trust good festivals to always take the good films.

"The publicist for the film, Winston Emano, of TCDM, who worked on this film, I have a relationship with, and if they tell me to look at something, I will look at it. And he said, yes, it is at Slamdance, but you should see it. I looked at the film, and I really liked it, I thought it was a completely charming film. Another thing the publicist did which was really effective, he got stills from the film to the paper. When the paper is going to run an overview story, they don't go out on a search to go find photos for all the films, they use what's been sent.

"Because the publicists had done their job, I had seen *Mad Hot Ballroom* and I wrote good things about it, and it ran with a photo, in my opening story about Sundance and Slamdance. When you have a piece of art with a story, it's an added bonus. It makes the story more interesting, it gets the film more attention.

"And the publicist told me later that although Slamdance is not a stop that buyers necessarily make all the time, people went to see it because of what I had written, and it got acquired by Paramount Classics, and it went on to be fairly successful. This is one of those rare times, where everything works the way it's supposed to. Again, it has to be the right film, and this is an audience film. Had it been at Sundance, probably all kinds of people would have been all over it.

"I want to really emphasize, because it's a really important point to make, it's not me, it's the paper. This is not the strength of my opinion, or what I know, but that I work for a major newspaper in a film-intensive city like Los Angeles, so what I say has an impact. *The Los Angeles Times* is the morning paper for a lot of people who work in the movie business. If I went to work somewhere else, no one would care what I might say. Whatever influence I have is because of where I work."

* * *

Following are some good pointers to remember when you are talking to members of the press corps.

Know enough about the film and create a few sentences you can roll off your tongue that make the film intriguing without giving away too much. This is the so-called "elevator pitch" (imagine you're stuck in an elevator with Harvey Weinstein. Or maybe not). Though you may be asked, "What's your film about," nobody really wants to sit and hear you tell the story in detail, scene for scene. How fun is seeing a film when you know what's going to happen? An intriguing three or four sentences will do.

Have all information handy if they ask—screening dates, times, director's name, cast, and a compelling reason why they should see it. Can you get them a ticket if they need one? Create as little resistance as possible—if you want someone to see your film, make it as easy as you can for him or her.

Do not exaggerate. Too many times, expectations for a film are raised, and then the film is judged by them. We've all had experiences where films have *not* benefited from overblown expectations. When talking to press about the film, less is more. Let them discover it—they like doing that—or at least let them feel like they did, as opposed to being given the hard sell. Desperation is unattractive, and repellant in most cases, and in this one, too. If you plan on being in the business for a while, remember the boy who cried wolf. This is about credibility.

Low-pressure tactics are the best. If you're desperate, or if you push too much, it'll backfire. Most critics want to choose what they see, and if they feel like they *have* to see it, going in, they may already be in a mood to not like it, particularly if it's not their type of film. Or if they've been harassed about it. It's human nature.

When talking about your film at festivals, Miguel Arteta—director of *Star Maps, Chuck & Buck*, and *The Good Girl*—recommends the following: "Be enigmatic and have a little sense of humor when you talk about your film at the festivals. Don't tell people exactly what it is and means to you. You gotta let the film do that.

"And whatever you do, do not go on and on about how hard you worked on it, and how hard everybody worked on it."

Tell the truth. "A neophyte but very intelligent producer had one of the hottest films at Sundance a couple of years ago," said publicity vet Jeremy Walker, "a film he had financed out of his own pocket. And the night of the film's premiere I had put him together with one of journalism's most savvy industry reporters as the deal was going down. The access, I figured, would result in major coverage that would make my client happy and, in a very real sense, put this movie on the map and would set it up to become the hit that it indeed became. As it turned out, I was right about everything except the happiness of the client: Indeed, the producer, when pressed by the reporter to reveal the budget of the film, did not politely decline to do so, but for some reason lied about the figure instead. The reporter, also very intelligent, learned the true budget figure, and then chronicled the discrepancy, and the producer's mendaciousness, in print. If your world view allows lying to fall under the umbrella of misbehaving with the media, then the lesson all filmmakers should take from this story is never, ever lie to a reporter: You will be found out."

Be real. Or at least act like you're being real. Good press for your film should not feel orchestrated. Nobody wants to feel like they're part of a machine. Don't be a pusher or an operator; understand the importance of being sincere and accessible.

Read between the lines. "When you throw your film out to the world, the press are going to look at it and critique it," said RJ Millard, former marketing VP at IDP Films. "If you're not getting press coverage, it's more often the case that they don't like it. That's the hard truth. If they like the movie, the press that cover independent film will do what they can to write about it. If they don't like the movie, they won't."

Be brief. A pet peeve? "The lengthy novella e-mail pitches I get," said *Good Morning America*'s Karen Rhee. "I prefer highlights and then, if it's something I'm interested in, I'll review all of the information, do more research, or ask for more. And also, sometimes, people will just send me an EPK [electronic press kit] without any information. No note, no production information—nothing. Am I supposed to watch the whole thing, and try to figure out why it's been sent to me?"

Understand the built-in time constraints. To get a picture of how journalists "cover" Sundance and literally how one might schedule his time, we turned to Roger Ebert.

"When I arrive at a festival like Toronto faced with hundreds of films, and can see at most three to five a day, I begin filling in the calendar on my computer," he said. "I put in major premieres, major directors, prize winners from other festivals, movies generating lots of publicity, movies with big stars, and other movies I may have heard about. But that is only stage one. Then I talk to the key publicists for indie films and distributors. There aren't that many of them. They are pretty honest in pitching what they think is worth seeing. I'll discover films that way. By the third day of the festival, I am way 'off the calendar' because the buzz, the conversations on line, my fellow critics, and the publicists have all been part of the process by which I select my three to five films a day. After a while you develop a sixth sense. Somebody will tell you about a doc about an old man who walked into the Amazon and lived with cannibals, and you skip some big Hollywood studio picture to see it, and you're glad you did."

Know your journalists. At festivals, press can be found anywhere. Find out what a press badge looks like. Don't be afraid to strike up conversation with a journalist—they are people, too. Most of them, anyway. A greeting, some basic human conversation before going in for the kill, would not be a bad idea. Laura's old boss, Mark Pogachefsky, used the term "publicity by collision" to describe festival work. It's true that being out and about is where and how this happens. Most journalists at festivals are running from screening to screening, or getting a quick bite and not sitting in their rooms, and if they are, they're busy writing or catching much needed sleep. (Others, of course, nap at screenings.) At a festival, you shouldn't call them in their rooms—they won't be able to put a face with the call, and you'll most likely catch them off guard or on a deadline.

It also never hurts to know who writes about what. Read some reviews, and get a sense of individual writers' tastes. Seems fair enough—if they're going to see your film, you should read their writing. Once you have a sense of what kinds of films appeal to their tastes, you can compile a list of the critics or writers who might be inclined to like yours. Sometimes it's hard to remember, in all the excitement of getting accepted into a festival, that critics may very well hate your film, and that your chances could be blown by a couple of bad reviews. Why cast a wide net and catch opinions that might be dangerous to your film?

Most journalists are pleased when they're aware that people read their work and know its content. Reaching out to them either through a representative or directly is okay, but know what you're doing. Public relations veteran Fredell Pogodin recommended this, but added, "If you can't do that, hire someone who can." You can choose either to send a letter with info about the film, or you can choose to send a copy of the film, but first read the chapter on tapes.

An example that might be useful: There have been many times that Laura has worked on films that were about youth—angry, nihilistic, sometimes good, and sometimes not. Knowing that Kenneth Turan of *The Los Angeles Times*, in many cases, doesn't like these films led to her telling him that *Teen Movie X* was probably not his thing. Feeling out the vibes first, and sensing a lack of interest, she said, "It's going to get bought, so you can see it later. I'll let you know when it's screening in L.A."

This is not because she was trying to do a disservice to the film—quite the contrary. For buyers, seeing Turan walk out of a film can be damaging. Also, she knows that if he is likely to dislike a film, his *not* seeing it is better for the film, as buyers will ask him his thoughts. Films like *Better Luck Tomorrow* and *The Virgin Suicides* benefited from this. This is not to say they aren't good films, but the risk was not worth it.

Sometimes there is nothing you can do to control the situation. Imagine your film is in competition at a prestigious film festival—in that case, most press are going to go and see it. (If their paper has spent money for them to attend the festival, they will be inclined to see anything that might win, so they can report on it.) If you are in one of the many sidebars, or subsections, that some festivals have, knowing in advance who might like the film will allow you to personally court them to come and see it. Temper your strategy depending on what section of a festival you're in. In other words, you may need to be more tenacious if you're not in one of the main competitions. Whatever your situation, there are things you can do to make things better.

Have good materials. See Chapter 7, "Materials," on this subject.

Don't trap anyone. If you want to ask critics what they think, don't get up in their faces and beg, "Did you like Film X?" Ask in more general ways: "Have you seen anything you've liked?" "Anything worth catching?" Don't corner them and put them in that spot. Let them share what they want to share. Or not. Many critics make it a policy not to give reactions, or do not care to share their opinion until after they've written the review, so be diplomatic.

"You have to be careful in terms of how you approach or deal with journalists in terms of soliciting their opinions," said publicist Mark Pogachefsky. "You have to understand that looking like an eager puppy and going, 'What did you think? What did you think?' is probably not the best way to approach it, though I do know some eager and enthusiastic young people who have been guilty of that, myself included.

"But you should know when the proper time to approach a journalist is, and how to factor the nature of your movie into that process," he said. "If you have the lighthearted, musical, guilty pleasure of the festival, feeling people out after a screening is probably not the worst thing. But if you have a more challenging film that needs some time and distance, then you may want to let the film sink in for a day or two before asking their thoughts."

It can be not only really irritating to critics, to be asked what they think, but you may be crossing a line. "I was working on *Blue* for Miramax, back when they were really aggressive about getting reactions from critics," Laura said. "So I call the guy, who it turned out was an intern assigned by *LA Weekly* to review the film, the day after he came to see it. I was friendly and asked, and he said 'I loved it.' I relayed the information, and sure enough, the paper comes out, and he calls the film a 'phlegmatic piece of shit.' I'll never forget that—it was his way of saying 'Don't ever call me to ask what I think.' Another time, many years ago, I called David Ansen from *Newsweek* to get his thoughts on a film, and he said, 'I don't give reactions. Don't call me to ask me what I think.' I was apologetic and stammering, and he said, 'Look, it's because of Miramax that I stopped giving reactions.'"

Don't overprepare. Know that there's only a certain amount of preparation you can do. The press are the press, and they can't be predicted. If they like a film, they can make it successful, but publicity can't *make* them like it.

Finally, and perhaps most importantly, don't obsess. Don't preoccupy yourself with press. Have fun. Or at least try to look like you're having fun. Patrick Scott, a young filmmaker *(The Migration of Clouds)* spoke on a panel once and said something really simple and meaningful, after agents, reps, and publicists had gone on and on about what to do and what not to do. "Have fun and spend lots of time with other filmmakers," he said. "Enjoy being at the festival and don't think too much about the other stuff. We've all gotten more work from each other than from anyone else."

* * *

As was pointed out in Chapter 2, "The Delegation," a lot of the principals in Indie World know each other and socialize with each other, not only because they might want to, but because they have to. Consequently, they know a lot about each other. This familiarity extends to the critics and film writers, too. Frankly, they've often seen each other—well, not always at their best. There are a lot of skeletons in a lot of closets. While we can't imagine anyone ever taking advantage of the situation, people do get to know each other fairly well, especially when they're thrust together so often and, as it happens, in so many places where they would be lonely strangers, if not for the other film people in the room.

So friendships develop, as do grudges. But it can sometimes make for a dialogue—keeping one side or the other from existing in some kind of hermetically sealed terrarium.

"I've actually argued with David Ansen from *Newsweek* for hours on end," said Strand's Marcus Hu. "There are arguments about movies that literally have gone on for years. But as I say that, David was responsible for John and I picking up two movies for us—*Wild Reeds* and *The Delta*—two films that were really, really critically acclaimed, much more so on *Wild Reeds*. But *The Delta* marked the discovery of Ira Sachs as a really strong, independent American voice." Sachs went on to win the Sundance Film Festival Jury Prize for Dramatic Feature in 2005 for *Forty Shades of Blue*.

"Marcus always credits me with *Wild Reeds*," said Ansen. "And Harvey Weinstein credits me with turning him on to Zhang Yimou with *Ju Dou* at Cannes."

"David has an incredible sense of being able to discover these films and really push as a critic to get them bought," said Hu. "Amy Taubin has pushed me to buy films; Manohla [Dargis] will sometimes say, 'Y'know, you should pick up that movie.' Because critics know we handle difficult pictures, we often get recommendations from critics. Godfrey Cheshire, I remember coming up and saying, '*You got to buy that movie!!!*'"

"It's so tricky," said Taubin. "Ethically, it's so tricky. I'm a person who's very open about what I like. So if a buyer comes up to me—I talk to Eamonn [Bowles, president of Magnolia Pictures] constantly, and others, and we share notes—and it's a film I really like, I'll say, 'You have to go see this film.' I don't have a problem with that. So that's why you want journalists to see your film, and you might want to have journalists see your film before the festival. I know everyone wants to have their film seen on the screen. But it's more likely that I'll watch a DVD of a film at Sundance before Sundance than I'm going to get to their movie."

"Basically," said Kenny Turan, "what happens at festivals, when I run into these people [buyers] on the street, we chat. I'm curious about what they're liking, and they're curious about what I'm liking. I have told buyers to see a film, but frankly they don't necessarily listen to me. It is really just like an exchange of information, it's not pronouncements or anything. There's a whole list of films that critics like, that either were not acquired or were acquired and did dismal business. In some ways, critics, while they can be important to films like these, they're not infallible."

Sony Pictures Classics copresident Michael Barker said that the films he looks at are usually found "through someone we recognize or someone whose taste we respect. Someone recently said, 'Mike, I saw this movie in Sarajevo'—I think it was [journalist and programmer] Howard Feinstein—'I think you should look at it.' So I had somebody track it down, and looked at it. This happens all the time. A producer. Or a critic." In Cannes one year, Barker ran into Turan at a black-tie event and Turan told him of a film he had just seen and really liked. Barker left the event and ran to the screening, eventually buying the film, *The Dream Life of Angels*.

"Listen," said Taubin, "you have to know that 50 percent of this is luck. It's going to be luck that some lunatic who isn't part of the system, but who has some power, sees your film, and there's just some chemistry. That is luck. I always love the Kevin Smith story. That was such a great thing. His movie, *Clerks*, screened at the IFP market the last morning, and there were only ten people there. But Bob Hawk was there, and Bob called Peter Broderick and Peter called me. And they said, 'You have to look at this film.' And so I did, and I wrote about it, and that helped a lot. And certainly Bob and Peter helped a lot. And the three of us banged on [producers rep] John Pierson's door. We kind of wore him down and finally, John took it. That made the big difference. And you would never think that I would like this movie about these guys working in a convenience store, that has absolutely no visual style. But it had a great script. And while it was really crude in every way, that really worked for it, because it was about crude guys. It was great. One of the things you should not do is to pigeonhole what you think we might like. You just never know."

* * *

"One movie that I really loved a lot was *Show Me Love*," said Strand's Marcus Hu, referring to a Swedish dramedy originally titled *Fucking Amal*. "Oh man, it was just dismissed in *The New York Times* as a piece of fluff, and that really hurt the movie.

"But you know, what's very odd is that when Lukas Moodysson's next movie came out the critics were saying ' . . . and the incredibly great *Show Me Love*.' Why didn't they support it when it came out?"

The answer is, critics can—excuse our Swedish—fuck up. The revisionist tack on *Show Me Love* is a way of apologizing without apologizing. There are very few times that a critic can come back and correct him- or herself and say, "I was wrong about this movie, here's why and I'm sorry." Part of it has to do with the curious position that a critic occupies. Although a critic's personal taste is a prime factor in how a film gets reviewed, the critic is also the voice of his or her publication; in a way, they are speaking for an institution, not just themselves. *The New York Times* and *The New Yorker* are extreme examples. Pauline Kael, who's been dead for years, is still the last word on a lot of movies that she reviewed and which are now reissued, restored, or rescreened in a repertory cinema. *The New York Times* will rerun a festival review when a film opens theatrically, because—and the paper is right—there should be only one judgment on a film from a particular publication. Otherwise, you might as well have people write in and then publish their reviews. And make it like the Internet.

There are many kinds of press—there are feature writers who write big stories, there are columnists, there are critics or reviewers, and there are reporters. There are many kinds of media outlets, too, and they all cover news differently. When thinking about the media, in general, it helps to think about who their audiences are. Also, if you can imagine how the editorial process works, and how a journalist works within his or her paper or television show, and put yourself in their shoes—empathy!—it can help you.

Knowing as much as you can about the editorial process, respecting it, and not trying to control it, will serve you well. "Effective press outreach is hinged on at least a cursory understanding of how media organizations work, the roles and/or beats of various editors and writers, and how individual journalists prefer to receive pitches," said B|W|R's Chris Libby. "Generic pitches designed for anyone and everyone will undoubtedly yield generic results."

"I learned a lesson once dealing with *The New York Times*," said Jeremy Walker, "a lesson about the limits to which a publicist should attempt to insert him- or herself into the relationship between a reporter and the reporter's editor. I was pitching an L.A.-based *Times* correspondent on writing about an L.A.-based director, and seemed to have gotten the reporter's attention and interest. The reporter had just come off of covering the Clinton White House and was himself a newsmaker, and I was very excited to be talking with him. After we completed our conversation I realized that I'd failed to share a bit of history about the film and the editor at *Arts & Leisure* that the reporter would presumably be working with on the story, should it come to fruition, and I called him back to say, 'By the way, the editor at *Arts & Leisure* has already . . .' and the reporter went ballistic and slammed down the phone on me. I was shocked and not a little frightened. The next day I faxed a note of apology that also explained that I did not understand what I had done wrong, and a day or so later I got a fax back. The reporter also apologized, then explained his anger by relating a truly harrowing tale about how, the previous year, he'd been assigned to write a feature on Gwyneth Paltrow, but had to reschedule his interview with the actress because Clinton had given him access at the same time. When he called the publicist at Miramax to reschedule, the publicist had apparently, and rather snottily, said something to the effect that they would just have to find another writer, *as if the publicist were the editor of the story*. Clearly this bugged the shit out of him, but thanks to the nasty Miramax publicist, whoever that was, I ended up learning a valuable lesson."

It's often been said that the way to someone's heart is through their stomach, and this can be true of journalists too, though if done with sensitivity and only when the right opportunity arises.

"On certain films, the party is obvious," producer's rep Jeff Dowd said, referring to strategic festival hospitality. "For something like *Scratch*, we had a situation where we had to educate people about this art form. So one of the things we wanted to do was have a party so they could see how good these people were."

And on other films, it's all about the pure schmooze.

"I'll give you a good example," Dowd said. "*Goat on Fire and Smiling Fish*. We're in Toronto. The director's father happens to run a lobster thing out of New York. On Monday, we sat in Michelle Mahieux's office and pulled the trigger to have, on Thursday afternoon, a party where we'd give out free lobster to people. Beer and lobster. It cost us almost nothing.

"Basically, two or three hundred journalists were there. As much lobster as you wanted to eat. Beer, music. Guess what film won the Discovery Award voted on by journalists at the Toronto International Film Festival. *Goat on Fire and Smiling Fish*. Coincidence? Yeah, maaaaaybe. . . ."

Sometimes, it just helps put filmmakers on their radar. Dowd said everything he did with those filmmakers—"they even went to press screenings, which you're not supposed to do, and they worked the room"—was about ingratiating themselves with the media. "The thing is how you present yourself at a film festival. Those guys wound up in Roger Ebert's first column because they ran into Ebert, and they were winning guys. It helps, very often, to be able to introduce the cast members and the director and people like that to journalists before they see the movie. You may not agree with that. . . ."

No, not necessarily. And neither do others. "I don't really want to know filmmakers that way. It's too much," said *New York Times* film critic Manohla Dargis." I don't want to be the filmmaker's bitch."

Lisa Schwarzbaum of *Entertainment Weekly* feels similarly, albeit more gently, "To be honest, I don't want filmmakers to pitch their films to me at all. It's probably awkward for them," she said, "it's certainly uncomfortable for me, and to my way of thinking it's just wrong—a PR line that shouldn't be crossed. I want to know a filmmaker's work, not the filmmaker! I know that there are in fact some perfectly ethical colleagues of mine who enjoy the contact, and that's fine, but I'd rather keep the relationship 'clean' and respectfully distant."

These things must be done delicately because it can be a double-edged sword. It may put the critic in a difficult situation—it takes what should be business, to paraphrase Don Corleone, and makes it personal. A film should be judged on its merits, not by the charisma, or by the abundant seafood, of its director at a party. The results of a one-on-one encounter between filmmakers and critic, prior to the screening of a film, can work two ways: Yes, it might make one critic more inclined to favorably review a film, but it might push another one to go the opposite way—he knows he's been schmoozed and will challenge himself, bending in the contrary direction to prove that he is totally objective. No one is, of course. But it's a pretty idea.

"Somehow," Dargis said, "having an event with a group is a very different kind of thing. Individually, it's too much pressure. There's a way that you can manipulate critical groups very nicely, and I would say that the smart movie companies do that all the time, by having filmmakers come and introducing them."

"There's something to be said about direct contact," *Good Morning America*'s entertainment producer Karen Rhee said, "if they're charismatic. They could win me over—you feel closer to that project if you're talking to the filmmakers. Those filmmaker meet 'n' greets can be very effective."

But she added, "Don't show desperation, though. Don't show those colors. I don't want to see them."

"It's like dating," said Dargis. "Never show that you're desperate. The surest way to never get a date is to look desperate.

"Letting the work speak for itself works a lot better for people like us. We are constantly being barraged with stuff, so it's about how you sell yourself. People can get on my nerves very quickly, and it's really important to try not to do that."

When you are introducing yourself and your film, Dargis said, "It's like resumes—you don't make them five pages, you make a resume one page. Make it quick and clear. Everyone's time is really special, and you are just one of many special people.

"And don't make me feel like I have a stalker. If I don't call you back, don't continue to leave a bunch of messages. I will think you are some sort of freak, and that is the biggest way to turn me off. Begging and badgering is an instant turnoff."

Sharon Waxman, who writes about Hollywood for *The New York Times*, does appreciate a little contact. "At festivals specifically, everything you do to remind people like me to see your movie helps," she said. "You put a last-minute flyer in my mailbox, it helps. I get a phone call saying, 'The screening is at this time and I think you're going to love this movie,' it helps. Now saying that as a journalist, it's annoying as all get-out, because you're running from thing to thing, and you're crazed anyway, but there are times when somebody will call you up and I'll think, I totally forgot about that, and I really want to see it. 'Oh good, it's showing across the street, I'll go.' You can overdo that, too. You can turn a journalist off by calling them too much too. It is a fine line."

Journalists, according to filmmaker Bill Condon, whose *Gods and Monsters* played Sundance in 1998, can give you "a very real sense of where you are in the pecking order. I'm supposed to have breakfast with [one-time *New York Times* reporter] Bernie Weinraub, two days after our first screening, and I get that call late at night saying he can't make it. And because everyone's in the same place, you go in for breakfast, and he's there eating with another director. So you literally have been bumped for someone else."

Condon benefited enormously, however, from the critical reaction to *Gods and Monsters*, which is precisely the type of film to which good reviews are essential. No amount of critical flak is going to bring down a major studio's big-budget mall movie—those types of films are immune to bad reviews, as are certain stars. But smaller, more cerebral movies need good reviews—because their intended audiences read them. And steering audiences toward cinema that a critic thinks is genuinely worthwhile is the reason why so many of them do what they do.

"You spend your life as a critic looking for films that you think are good," said Kenneth Turan of *The Los Angeles Times*, "and you do it because you love films, and you want to help other people who love films to find films that they will really enjoy. So it's such a treat to find something that you like and are able to champion just because you think other people will like it.

"People are so hungry for good films. They really are. People love movies, but it's so hard for them to pick out which ones are good."

"I think we do champion these movies," said Dargis, "and we do make a difference. And I really do try to believe that a movie's going to be good, and we really try to go in with open eyes, open mind."

Publicist Fredell Pogodin said that critics can really lift a film they love and "can be very generous and will champion and support a film if they feel they can make a difference in terms of its success." She added, "They will go out of their way to ask their editors for extra editorial space for interviews, think pieces, etc."

"I love movies," said Amy Taubin. "And not everyone is like this, but I like finding things. I like being there when you can do something for someone, or you can say, 'This is a really good movie.'"

"Actually," said Roger Ebert, "from my end it feels like I turn down so many more opportunities than I take. But it's true I look for unheralded films and get really excited when I love one. I think that started at my first Chicago Film Festival, in 1967, when I saw a film named *Who's That Knocking at My Door?* by Martin Scorsese. He was a completely unknown NYU student, this was the film's first showing anywhere, and my review was the first one he ever received. I knew—I just knew—that this was a great filmmaker. I felt the same after seeing the first film of Mike Leigh [*Bleak Moments*, 1967] and giving him his first review. And I wrote the first review of a Gregory Nava film [*The Confessions of Amans*]. At Sundance this year I was so excited to see *Me and You and Everyone We Know*, which was unheralded. A year ago, it was *Tarnation*.

"Because I have the great gift of the TV show," Ebert said, "I know I can actually help some of these films in a meaningful way. There is so much publicity for big releases that I'm happy when I can tell people about a smaller film they should see." He continues, "I have also supported a lot of films through my Overlooked Film Festival, like *Tully, Kwik Stop, Diamond Men, Innocence, Sidewalk Stories, Songs from the Second Floor, Surrender Dorothy, The Terrorist, Two Women*, and *Thirteen*."

But even if a critic really likes a film, there are things you should know.

"There's this misconception among filmmakers," Turan said. "They basically want me to write a blurb for the film, 'See the film and help it out.' But that's just outside of my job description. But on the other hand, if filmmakers just want me to see their film, and they send me a copy, I will look at anything that anyone sends me. I feel I owe it to people to do that. I will put it on, and watch it as long as I'm interested, but I cannot publicly comment on these films. I am happy to look at them but that's as far as I go. It's just a question of time and a question of what the paper would want."

"Sometimes I'll get a DVD in the mail," said Ebert, "or be handed one at a festival, and I'll be asked to view it, and sometimes I will. The ratio is about fifty to one."

Most daily critics already have their hands full. "The problem is that I'm already viewing an incredibly large number of movies in the daily performance of my job," said Ebert, who is a syndicated critic for *The Chicago Sun-Times*. "I write more than three-hundred full-length reviews a year, plus festival films, my film class, etc. I don't have the actual time at two hours a pop to view dozens of additional films. My position basically is that festivals and distributors exist as the viewers of first opportunity, and when a film actually gains some kind of distribution, then it is reviewable."

"Sometimes filmmakers don't understand the editorial process or the ethics of journalism," said Amy Taubin. "Half the people who contact me ask me to write something they can use in their press kit. I'm a journalist, not a press agent. I do not write about movies for public consumption because you need it. But it's a funny thing. They do it all the time; they think that that's what you do. They think we provide them with quotes. 'I saw the piece you did on Andrew Bujalski, and I was wondering if you could do a piece like that on my movie.' These are big no-nos."

Can you predict how the press will react, or what the critics will think? "Although individual writers routinely surprise, publicists regularly predict in broad strokes what will resonate with the critics," said B|W|R's Chris Libby. "That being said, we struggle to determine to what extent critics will rally behind a movie, and how the critical reception might evolve from festival through release months or years later."

"As for being able to predict what critics will like, no," said Jeremy Walker. "Critics are people, and people are unpredictable. But people also have distinct world views, and a good publicist reads critics' reviews all the time and will know, for example, which critics view films (and probably life) through the prism of gender and, for another example, which critics historically hate movies featuring adorable children. *My Life As a Dog* was a universally loved movie back in the day, except by Vincent Canby of *The New York Times*, who panned it. He hated movies about adorable kids.

"I find myself telling filmmakers and clients over and over that any time you expose a film to a critic you are taking a risk, but by proactively showing a film to critics before a festival you send the tacit message that the publicist and the filmmaker are confident in the film. By showing a film early, you can also control certain things that you cannot always control at a festival: that the critic is seeing the film at a time of his or her choosing, ideally at a time of day when he or she has not seen three other movies; in a quality screening room with good projection and sound; and at an altitude that is not known to precipitate headaches, nausea, and general spaciness. And though one can never be responsible for the personal habits and proclivities of another, film festivals are chock full of parties. Show your movie to the critics before they go to a film festival, unless of course it's a surefire crowd-pleasing comedy, which always work best with an audience that is psyched to be there."

* * *

Thus far, the assumption has been that filmmakers and/or their representatives are seeking out journalists. Sometimes the shoe is on the other foot, in which case, counseled *Good Morning America*'s Karen Rhee, "Rule number one is: Call the journalist back. Because there will come a time when you need them. Especially if it's someone that you will most likely work with again."

Be mindful of deadlines. When journalists call, they are normally in need of information. And fast. It's best to assume that they are on deadline because in most cases, they are.

To get your film featured on television is a whole different animal; for entertainment television—for shows like *Entertainment Tonight, Access Hollywood, Extra, E!,* and the like, it is by and large about talent, or "stars." For other television programming, filmmakers have a better chance if the subject matter is timely or controversial. *Fahrenheit 9/11* and *Super Size Me,* for example, got a lot of broadcast attention.

Not all films have news angles built in, but you can always work to build interest, getting one print story at a time until you have a handful that can help you in supporting your pitch. Also, a build-up of favorable critical responses, awards, or word of mouth can help.

"It's very important who's working on the movie," Rhee said. "What publicists are working on the movie, and how early they get to me and how convincing they are and how accommodating they are. Sometimes you get convinced to do things you wouldn't, otherwise."

An example?

"When I was working at E!, I had just landed in Toronto, and literally my phone rang as I was getting off the plane. And it was Laura saying that if I didn't come see this *Better Luck Tomorrow*, I'd be a bad Asian. I can't live with that kind of guilt. I was only in Toronto for twenty-four hours, and I went to see the movie; it was the first thing that I did. Then she brought me to the cast dinner, and I ended up doing a piece on the movie because I saw it and there was a good story to tell. We did a really big piece, and that would normally have never happened.

"The film wasn't necessarily relatable to my audience," she said, "but the way a film is presented to a journalist really makes a difference. We're all salespeople in this business. It's both the way you sell it to me *and* whether I think there's an interesting piece I can build around it."

"Over the years," said mPRm's Mark Pogachefsky, "you can get a sense of what you think people will respond to—it's more a question of what someone won't like, versus what they will like. Because people always surprise you. I think, over the years, you get a better sense of what someone won't respond to. One of the things about a festival is, there's a lot of movies all in a limited amount of time. It comes down to encourage or discourage; chase or don't chase.

"Harry Clein [PR Veteran with a capital V] always used to say, 'There are three hats that you need to wear when you're watching a movie,'" said Pogachefsky. "'One is what you think. One is what the audience will think. And the other is what the press will think. And those three hats are not necessarily the same.'

"Ultimately, I've learned that there is not a direct correlation between publicity and box office. You can do a fantastic job on a movie that no one goes to see. There are so many other factors involved. Or the critics can all love a movie that no one goes to see. So it's all kind of relative because there are forces in the marketplace that have nothing to do with you."

Materials

The Right Stuff

There's an old joke among musicians:
Question: **What's the definition of an optimist?**
Answer: **A trombonist with a pager.**

The definition of an optimist in Indieville? A director who films a "making of" documentary on the set of his first film. Stick to the simple, the persuasive, and the truthful, and your press materials will serve you well.

IF WE CAN CONSIDER a movie a guided missile for the mind (although some, as we know, are actually unguided missiles for misguided minds) then the press kit may be considered the booster rocket that helps it attain the proper trajectory. In less Goddardian terms—that would be Robert, not Jean-Luc—filmmakers want their films to take off and press kits help them do just that.

How? Because they contain the fuel of information—the information necessary to suckle from the stars that very precious mother's Milky Way of public attention—ink. A press kit is a tool, essentially, by which filmmakers not only inform the media about their film but set the tone by which those films will be received. Later, the press can sell them on e-Bay. Some people will buy anything.

Although a press kit is, in fact, just a bunch of information about a film, when creating it, consider a kit and photos an aperitif: They should be heady, bright, but full of clear information about the film, and its text should whet the appetite, in a way, preparing the palette of the viewer to receive the experience in the best possible way.

Unfortunately, you can't get anyone drunk on a press kit; those who see it will like it or not. But it can only help to make sure the materials are accurate, available and clear.

Following is a bare-bones, do-it-yourself guide to assembling press materials for your film.

Preliminary Production Notes

✍ *Cover page.* Provide the title of the film; key cast/crew info; running time; print and sound format information; where to find photography if online; sales and local press contact information.

✍ *Cast and crew lists.* Make your list as complete as possible, and certainly include no less than key cast and crew. Make sure your cast list identifies character names. If the credits are not final, say so.

✍ *Synopsis.* Create both a short synopsis (two or three paragraphs) and a long one (one to two pages). Do not spell out literally what happens in the film scene for scene, and if there's a twist or an intriguing plot turn at the end, speak more thematically about it rather than giving it away. Some members of the press may sit and read the material before the screening starts, and you don't want them waiting to re-experience the same story they've just read to themselves.

✍ *Director's statement or Q&A.* Produce a one- or two-pager that explains the inspiration and goals of the director in his or her own words, or a question-and-answer interview with the filmmaker that queries him or her about the movie.

✍ *Biographical information.* Assemble career summaries—laudatory, but not fawning—about the key cast, and key crew.

Remember that contact information is very important. If someone liked the film, how would they contact you, if they wanted to ask you questions, interview you, or—praise the Lord!—buy your film? If you are at a festival, or somewhere off your home turf, be sure to include a local number where you can be reached.

If you have the time for more, include a short bit about how the production went, the casting, etc. If and when someone buys your film, they will more than likely spend much more time on your press kit, so don't worry too much about this, especially if your time is limited.

John notes: "There is often crucial information missing from press notes that can delay, and possibly prevent, a critic from reviewing a film. Sometimes it's also harmful to your cast. If an actor or actress gives a standout performance in a supporting role, and the role isn't adequately identified, the critic has a hard time figuring out who the performer is. Example: In the indie *Shackles*, which played at Tribeca Film Festival in 2005, there was a brief but gripping performance given by Cynthia Martell, whom I didn't know at the time, but who made a huge impression. Her character was so minor she wasn't even referred to in the film by name, so the regular cast list was useless. Ideally, there should have been an explanation of who Martell was included among the cast bios—she and I would both have appreciated it. You expect subordinate actors to get short shrift in studio press kits, but in indie films credit shouldn't be so difficult to hand out."

It is important to know that press kits do not need to be fancy or expensive. Photocopies, stapled, will suffice. Most press kits will end up in the garbage anyway. Spend your money where it matters—on your film. Folders, elaborate covers, slides, stickers, photographs—imagine if you were a journalist carrying a dozen or so of these around with you. These things add up and just make their load heavier. It's about the information: It should be accurate, clear, and well written.

Rachel Rosen, program director of the Los Angeles Film Festival, said, "Good things come in small plain packages—I like things nicely presented, but simple. You want to be able to look at it and get the picture."

"Don't waste too much time on the press kit," said RJ Millard, former marketing and publicity VP for IDP Films. "Nobody cares. A great one-line synopsis and full main and end credits. You have no idea, but critics want that, and some critics can be irritated just going into your screening if they don't have the information they need. And you don't want them crabby going in to see your film. Keep your IMDB thing updated," he said of the encyclopedic movie Web site, imdb.com. "Everyone uses it."

Manohla Dargis of *The New York Times* just wants information. "Not fancy, but neat, professional, and make sure everything is spelled right. Nothing gimmicky."

Dargis's *Times* colleague Sharon Waxman likes to know a little bit, but likes it kept short. "The back-story is always interesting, particularly when you're talking about people we've never met before or heard of. We want to know who you are and where you come from and the basic story of how a movie comes to be made and put it on one page. But don't give me a whole book. You can have a book written, if we see the movie, and we like it, then we might be more interested in the rest of the information, but be prepared to give it to us on a single page." She adds, "It doesn't have to be polished and glossy."

Strand Releasing's copresident Marcus Hu said, "Your press kits should help journalists and critics understand an understated art film—'spell it out for them,' so to speak. Also, make sure the talent that may be doing interviews gets a copy and reads it. It will help them speak about the film."

Should you put other reviews in your press kit? "I don't read other people's reviews if I'm going to write about a film," said critic Amy Taubin of *Film Comment*. "But that doesn't mean it doesn't help if you stick them in, probably more so for foreign films than American films. For smaller films, in particular, it could be really helpful. Or even small pieces of reviews.

"I must say, I don't pay much attention to press kits," she added, "though I always look to see if I recognize any of the crew—the DP or any of the other below-the-line crew. That might convince me to go see it. I do want full cast and crew lists for when I start to write."

Photography

Do not include photos with press kits intended for writers; they do not, generally, need them. Writers may, however, need to let their photo editors know where they can access pictures to accompany a story or review. Where exactly he or she can find them on-line should be clearly marked.

Have your photographs available digitally, on a Web site, with the ability to download hi-res images, or available on disc. As an aside: If your actors have the right to approve them, get them approved by your actors.

Many festivals have their own press material sites—make sure your photography, and, if possible, broadcast materials are available there, too.

Make sure each festival press office has a stash of both production information and photography, as well as clips in case they are requested.

For festival purposes, you don't need reams of photographs. Pick four to six images that best convey the feeling of the film—clear, striking images taken during production. Be sure to include two shots of the director—one alone and one where he or she is working, perhaps with one of the actors.

For your release campaign, you'll want at least twenty images from the film for photo editors to choose from.

Important! Caption your photos. Provide reference numbers for each image, as well as the title of the film, the subjects, and a photo credit. (Be sure to identify the photographer.)

If and when you sell your film, you will need, contractually, to fulfill the distributor's delivery requirements, which normally ask for many more usable captioned images. It may make sense for you to take care of these all at the same time; that will make it easier later.

Good photography is crucial. "Oh, my God, that's the number one most important thing—the photos," said Dargis. "This is an absolute true story: I used to work for a glossy magazine, and I have many friends that work at glossy magazines, and often our reviews have been killed because the photos were bad. You can have a reviewer love a movie, but if the photos suck they may not run the review. That has happened to me. It can make or break your movie. You could have a review that can take your film to the next level, but the photography can be a deal-breaker. And sorry to say, but pick the most beautiful photos of women. Those tend to run more."

"Imagine," said Rosen. "The photo editors have just gotten a stack of three hundred photos and they don't know the films, so they are just going to run the prettiest or most interesting photo. Look at the Tribeca Festival—for a movie that no one's heard of, you could get a quarter page in *The New York Times*. That's huge. You can't buy that."

Millard goes even further. "The film can be bad, but if you have good photographs, the photos will run. But if you've only got two shots, they're going to be played out, then people are going to be done with it."

Asked what were the biggest mistakes made by first-time filmmakers, even Andrew Herwitz, lawyer-turned-sales rep, answered, "They don't take stills on the set. It's a real problem."

Strand's Marcus Hu explained that a well-taken, well-chosen photograph can become the symbol for your film. "One of the key things is to make sure you do really great set photography during your film, because ultimately that becomes the major tool for selling the film—it's the picture that appears in the festival catalog.

"You know that still from the *Blair Witch Project?*" he asked, referring to the 1999 film's ubiquitous shot of a frightened character's face illuminated by an upturned flashlight. "That still was in the festival catalog and it became like an icon. And really, whether they took good set photography or not, that became the image. So you have to think ahead—if you've got this indie film, take a really great image because that's what people are going to look at and decide, 'Oh, I want to see that movie.'"

During production, take as many hi-res photos as you can and shoot a good variety of them—singles of the actors, actors together, a few behind-the-scenes images of key crew members. Get these all approved (if needed) during or shortly after production to save yourself the headache of doing it later. Identify and caption the images so they are clear. And do it before you forget anything.

"Take an abundance of production stills," said Eamonn Bowles, president of Magnolia Pictures. "Include simple direct shots of the main members of the cast, individually and interacting with others."

Trying to do this after you've wrapped can be difficult. "Arranging set photography after the film has wrapped is a nightmare," said Hu. "The actors have changed their appearances for their next jobs, wardrobe is hard to find, sets can never be fully arranged again without going through expensive costs, flying talent in to assemble a photo shoot is costly and hard to negotiate with their agents, etc.

"This is one thing that should not be ignored, since those key images will be selling the film in the marketplace and can really affect the perception in the marketplace—as well as making it easier for your publicists to help promote your picture. Remember that if you have a good, attractive photograph that has interesting content, the chances are that you'll get good placement over a boring headshot, so choose photographers who understand the material they're working with."

"If you can afford it," Millard added, "get a great still photographer. If you've got bad art, not only are publications less likely to run the photographs, but the distributor won't be able to make a decent poster. We run into the same problem every time: We don't have good enough art. You don't have the leads together, you don't have them smiling, you don't have anyone interacting with each other. You don't have them in the signature outfit they wear in the entire film. If there's something that's indicative of these characters, you need to get that on film. That's one of the biggest things I tell filmmakers before they start shooting."

"Even just one great still," Rosen added. "It's one of those things—people don't understand how necessary an expense it is, but it's one of the most important things. There's so much that happens going into production, so people don't think about it. They want to deal with it later, but then it's too late."

Electronic Materials

What's on an electronic press kit (EPK)? A variety of short clips from your film, interviews with key cast, director, and possibly key crew, and behind-the-scenes footage (b-roll). Make sure you include the film's name on the tape cards between segments, identify the clip, and list the running time. Remember that the clips from your film will be used the most by the media. Use only a couple of short pieces of b-roll (they hardly ever run) and save the rest for the DVD. For festival purposes, you do not need a full EPK.

It may seem for many like pie in the sky to even be worrying about this, but for broadcast, press clips are extremely important (radio can extract audio clips from them if necessary, too). Let's say CNN wants to do a story on your film and interview you (wheee!!!). Let's say they do not have a clip to support their story (boooooo!). This means they will most likely not run either a story on your film or an interview (waaaah!!!).

Pick three to five clips that do a good job of capturing key moments in your film, and they can range from thirty seconds to two minutes. Pick scenes that are emotional, scenic, visually interesting. (If your film has a twist or surprise, you will probably want to avoid anything that gives it away). Make sure that your EPK includes cards that provide the film's name, identifies each clip, and lists the running time. Include a menu on your EPK case as well. You do not need a trailer, a b-roll, or interviews for your festival outing.

Although the industry is moving toward HD, Beta is still the format used most, and while a festival will request a specific quantity, we suggest making a few more than that, keeping two on hand and two with someone who works in an office in New York or Los Angeles, so that if you need to FedEx them somewhere, you can ask your friend to do it. Remember, trying to send a FedEx from Utah (Sundance) or Cannes can be difficult, unreliable, and costly. Also, once you're done with a festival, hold on to your EPKs and ask the festival press office to return any that are left over. They can be expensive and you can use them for upcoming festivals.

Laura once went to Sundance without clips for a 1996 film called *Care of the Spitfire Grill* (changed to simply *Spitfire Grill*). "I knew better, but it was just due to timing and the fact that the print was going straight from the lab to Utah. So we had no choice but to forego the clips. Once the film screened in Utah, and people began to talk about it, you can imagine my chagrin and stress level when an *ABC World News Tonight* producer called and asked for clips. I had to have them pulled from L.A., FedExed to me in Utah, and sent to his office in New York, and all remotely. They would have chosen another film to highlight if I had not supplied them with clips."

Good Morning America entertainment producer Karen Rhee said, "I need material on HD. Any clips, b-roll, additional sound bites from the cast members, filmmakers—the more material the better and I need the materials at least a week in advance. If it's a piece that requires storytelling and not an interview segment, then I need it earlier."

For your EPK, interview key cast, and key crew (director, writer, producer), using a DV camera, shooting Digi-Beta or Beta SP. Interview each separately, rather than in groups or pairs. These can be short takes—fifteen to thirty minutes each. Also, be sure the sound quality of these is really good, and that the camera is fixed and steady, or they may be unusable later. The sound quality is very important—no airplanes, no air-conditioning, no cars passing by, no wind. These segments may be used further down the line for your DVD as well. If you have an extra pair of hands, have these interview segments transcribed and save the transcripts. The text can be used for various aspects of your production notes.

Shoot behind-the-scenes footage during production. Pick the days that will show the most interesting scenes, the most unusual locations—days you are able to catch the director interacting with the actors. You do not need hours of this, just a few minutes of some good scenes. Log accurately what is on each tape for easy reference later.

Hold on to all of this raw footage for when you have a theatrical distribution plan. The footage can then be assembled into a full EPK, and eventually for your DVD as well. If you end up with a distributor, the studio that will be releasing your film can pay to finish it.

Other items that you may (or may not) need are trailers, posters, postcards, and giveaways.

- ◆ *Trailer.* Do not spend a lot of money on a trailer for festival use. Most distributors will want to create their own.
- ◆ *Posters*. Create a few posters for festival use.
- ◆ *Postcards*. Your postcard should have a compelling image and title on one side, and all pertinent info on the back, including screening dates, location and times, local and regular contact info, key cast, key crew. It may make sense for you to make thousands, and just sticker the backs for each festival outing. Use them in industry mailboxes and in common areas with high traffic.
- ◆ *Giveaways.* Unless a giveaway is really clever and well suited to the film, and most importantly, unless it is something people will want to carry home with them, save your money. It will most likely get thrown away. Nobody is buying a film because it has great promo items. Sharon Waxman of *The New York Times* said, "What we're looking for are interesting voices, something different that we haven't seen, or just a well-told story and well-made film. I don't need a hat or pen or T-shirt."

8

Screeners
To Give or Not to Give

Listen closely . . . in de night . . . when de moon is full . . . and you can hear the plaintive howl of the independent filmmaker:

"My film was made to be seen on a screen! Not on a TV! Not in a living room, with people getting up to make sandwiches, but in a theater! With hundreds, perchance thousands, of people watching it together, in a community of love and art and admiration for what I've given my life's blood to give them!"

THE QUESTION OF SCREENERS—prerelease copies of the movie on DVD or tape—is a charged one, and for the purposes of this book, let's think about them for two types of audiences—(1) press: critics and feature writers and (2) buyers—and for two types of films: (1) films that do not have distribution and (2) films that do have a distributor.

The decision to make screeners available really depends on a variety of factors. What are your objectives? To get publicity? Is the publicity in line with your acquisition strategy? Is anyone going to buy your film because *The Village Voice* wrote a blurb about it? To whom are you giving them and why? To buyers or to the press? How much of the viewing experience will change if it is seen on a TV? What would I have to lose if this journalist sees the film on tape? Is the amount of exposure worth it? Is your film available? Do you have a release date for which this publicity is serving? Should you think about screening your film before the festival instead?

For films that do not have distribution, if a journalist or critic says he or she doesn't have time to see your film, and would like to have tape, really consider the pros and the cons.

If your film is not a high priority for press or buyers, screening the film before the festival for press or sending tapes or DVDs could get you exposure where otherwise you'd be excluded. But you need to ask yourself whether yours is a film where a viewer's experience will change drastically if seen alone, or at home with their family, and not with a public audience. Critical opinion of your film during this stage is extremely important, so screening under optimal conditions is the ideal.

Most films look better on the big screen, but if you've come to the decision that the majority of the press are not going to make it to your screening because you're in an armpit sidebar of your festival, and your cast and crew are all relatively unknown, seriously consider using tapes or DVDs, and give a few to the festival press office, which will be fielding such requests. For higher-profile films, in competition or with cast, hold on to the screeners so you can control who sees them rather than making them available through the press office to anyone who asks.

"I would never suggest providing festivals with screeners for random, uncontrollable industry and press purposes," publicist Chris Libby warned. "Screeners should be used on a case-by-case basis, if at all, based on broader issues like legitimate piracy concerns, the level of media interest, and the impact of potentially missed media opportunities."

Let's say, for example, that a Big Important Newspaper is doing a story on films that deal with issues of infidelity as told by women filmmakers. Your film has this theme, and you are a woman. The story is being written by a reporter and not a critic. In that case, the screener risk is one you should take, particularly if your film has a low profile, is in a sidebar, is a foreign film, or is a documentary.

Picturehouse president Bob Berney added, "I think if you were advised by the right publicist on some key article then, yes, just to get some notice of your film out of the hundreds. Yes, but only on the advice of someone who really knows where to put it and [with a journalist] who might respond to the film and with the understanding if it's the right journalist for the independent film, maybe he won't write about it if he doesn't respond favorably."

Berney said you have to trust that the journalist has an interest in independent cinema, and isn't interested only in getting some kind of scoop. The journalist has to realize the chance that the filmmaker is taking. But sometimes the risk is worth the gamble.

"Before Sundance, a lot of times, *The Los Angeles Times* will do some highlights and it does focus distributors on which films they might go to first," Berney said. "The audience, too. I think it's a good idea, but you can't just do it yourself unless you really know the media. I think you could make a really bad move. Just as I caution against showing a tape to any distributors, the same risk is there. Showing it to a critic early just may not work, but I think showing it to a critic is safer than showing it to a distributor."

But don't send tapes to journalists if they haven't asked for them, or if you haven't had a conversation about the film during which they've shown interest. It just doesn't make the film seem that important, and, in the end, the tape will probably go unwatched. We walked behind a reporter from *The New York Times* as he was leaving a festival press office once, and his hands were full of paper and tapes. He walked down the hall, stood next to a garbage can, rifled through the tapes, kept one, and tossed all of the others in the garbage.

"Send me an e-mail," said critic Amy Taubin. "And explain a little bit about what your film is, in the first person, and offer to send a screener or additional materials. Make the offer. Most likely, I'll write back, saying, 'If you'd like, send a screener. There are a hundred screeners on my floor, but I will try to get to it.'

"There *are* a hundred screeners on my floor, but I put them on for five minutes," she said. "Filmmakers never realize how important the first scene of their movie is. I can count on the fingers of one hand the times I've been wrong about a film after the first five minutes, you know? Especially with young filmmakers. If there's someone there who really has been specific and has some sense about what movies do, and how what they do relates to whatever story they're trying to tell, the advice is that the first five minutes of your film better work. After five minutes, you do know at least if you want to get to the next five."

"There are members of the press who are reliable," said John Sloss, "and will say to you, 'Show me the movie, and, if I like it, I'll write about it. And if I don't, I won't.' And if you have a way to get to them, that could be a really valuable asset in the process of selling your movie because, as we know, more and more distributors are relying on the word of the press before they are willing to take a leap and go for a film at all."

"I always tell people, fine, but don't expect me to watch it," said *The New York Times*'s Manohla Dargis. "And I don't make any promises. But I've had people contact me directly, and they'll say, 'I just want to make a special appeal to you,' and I'll say, 'Fine, send it to me. I don't want to talk to you about it, but send it.' But if you're going to send something to me, do not spell my name wrong. Take the time to spell it right. That's a peeve of mine and I'm sorry to say, if you spell my name wrong, it's going in the trash."

Kenneth Turan of *The Los Angeles Times* feels similarly about tapes. "Just send by mail to the paper, and put a note in, and I will look at it. I do this regularly, but (A) they should not expect to hear from me, and (B) they should not follow up. If for any reason I see something, and I want to contact them, I will do it myself.

"The one reason why I work this way," he explained, "is because I understand everyone can't afford a publicist. But working with publicists makes it smoother, because they understand the constraints I'm under, they understand what I can do and what I can't do, and filmmakers, because they're understandably so personally involved with their film, don't understand those constraints.

"What filmmakers don't understand, and what I'd like them to understand, is that it's not possible for me to write about a film unless it's (A) at a film festival, or (B) in release. I don't do blurbs for films that are just out there and need the help, no matter how worthy they might be."

Another option for filmmakers to think about is screening their films for the press before festivals. "Because there are so many films at a festival," Turan said, "my goal is to discover the films that are really worthwhile, that I feel are really worth writing about. My drive as a critic is to get people to see the best films that I can find. And film festivals don't make that easy, because they program hundreds of films in a two-week period. You can't see them all. In theory, the festival would put all the good films in the most important sections, but they often don't do that. I remember *Gods and Monsters*, which went on to win an Oscar, was not good enough to get into competition at Sundance, so you cannot count on the festival. . . . You have to look at all the sections. So in the context of festivals, I use screeners really as kind of a screening device to help me decide ahead of time, because it's so time-consuming to go back and forth to screenings; it saves time to just have a look. Often, if I really like a film, I will turn it off and set up a screening, or make sure I see it at a festival. It limits the number of films I can see at a festival if I don't work with screeners before.

"I've seen major films before festivals, and I have not. It really depends on the prerogatives of the people whose film it is, how savvy they are. I would highly recommend it."

Why don't more people do this?

"What happens, unfortunately, is that producers have a fantasy of how Sundance works that does not really click with the reality of how any festival works," said Turan. "They fantasize about a big crowded screening, and that the critic is in there with hundreds of people who are wild for the film, and they're all screaming like crazy, and the critic gets swept off his or her feet and just falls in love with the film. So they're reluctant to let a critic see a film ahead of the festival because they fantasize that that's going to happen.

"In my experience, and I've been going to festivals for about fifteen years, it almost never happens. What is more likely to happen is the reverse. This film that the producers and filmmakers have worked so hard on, because of the quirkiness of scheduling, is the fiftieth film you'll see at Sundance, it's the last film you'll see on the last day, the fifth film you'll see on a very long day at the end of a very long festival. And you are so exhausted that it doesn't matter what the audience does, how crazy the audience goes, you don't like the film.

"If I was a filmmaker, I would show my film to key critics before a festival without any doubt—because of the experience I've had, and seeing how critics work, and seeing how festivals work. You are way better off doing that. But film-makers, especially producers in particular, really like to dream, and they like to fantasize, and they like to feel like they know better. When you're dealing with independent films you may be dealing with first-time producers or relatively new producers, but even with major films, the smarter producers will understand and some will show the film earlier. It's really the smart thing to do. If I had a child who made a film, or anyone close to me, I would really recommend it. Don't show it to everybody, but pick three or four key critics and show it to them."

There are cases where screeners have really worked well for a film. "The obvious case is *Hoop Dreams*," TV and *Chicago Sun-Times* film critic Roger Ebert said of the 1994 doc, "which Gene Siskel and I saw in Chicago some weeks before the Sundance festival and reviewed on the show [*Sneak Previews*] before it even played Sundance, because we thought it was so good. We saw that in a screening room, however, not on video.

"Recently," he added, "I asked for a DVD of Carroll Ballard's *Duma* [2005] and liked it, and showed it to Roeper, and we decided we wanted to do it on the show, and that got it a trial run in Chicago when the studio was think-ing of going straight to video. *One False Move* [1992] I saw on a "floating film fes-tival" where Sheila Benson introduced it, and after Siskel and I did it on the show, it got distribution.

"Of course, people would argue that films are meant to be seen on the big screen. But the truth is that it is impossible to see everything that you're inter-ested in."

"I prefer to see everything on a big screen," said *Newsweek*'s David Ansen. "But there are certain exceptions—like a documentary that was shot on video. That's probably the only time it's a good idea."

"I prefer to get a screener copy of the movie right away," said *Good Morning America*'s Karen Rhee. "If I get a chance to actually see the movie, then I'll at least consider it. But if I just get a press kit in the mail, chances are that I will never even get to it."

Concerning the practice of handing out discs or tapes on the free Sundance shuttles that move people from screening to screening, Sharon Waxman said, "That method is good. But I personally don't look at their movies because I don't have time. There has to be a screening mechanism and getting into the festival is one."

In most cases, it is not wise to send tapes to the trades *(Variety, The Hollywood Reporter)*, as film industry people make a lot of decisions based on what those publications say. Know that the trades don't cover every festival, and that they cover them differently. *Variety* will send someone to review as many films as possible that have public screenings. *The Hollywood Reporter* will cover higher-profile films, or films that have a release date.

Greg Mottola's *The Daytrippers* was a film that almost slipped through the cracks. It was a film that was said to have been bought by Miramax, but when that deal didn't work out, other buyers shied away from it. Then, to make matters worse, a tape of a nonfinal version made its way to one of the trades and a mediocre review was published. So the film went to a few festivals and slowly gained what was really almost unanimous positive critical response. Finally, CFP (Cinepix Film Properties; now Lions Gate) bought the film, and it played in theaters for months.

For the journalist covering films that have distribution and are opening in theaters, there often are simply too many movies—and often too many editorial powers that be wondering why they're giving precious ink or airtime to films that are going to play just one theater when instead they could be running a story on some aging megastar and his latest constipated epic, which could, unfortunately, be on multiple screens at each multiplex it plays.

And what about piracy?

Public relations veteran Jeremy Walker described the catch 22, saying, "The use of screeners as a marketing tool is, of course, only one practice that is threatened by Hollywood's antipiracy efforts, but it is also emblematic of the industry's inherent mistrust of anything it sees as outside of, or other than, itself."

Walker went on. "We live today in a climate where the vast majority of people who control the movies—the people at the major Hollywood studios and their specialty divisions—are watching in horror as fewer and fewer people are going to see them while technology is aiding those who pirate them. . . . Recently we watched in horror as security people employed by the studio used metal-detection wands on nationally recognized film critics as the critics were going into a screening of a film for which their support would be vitally important. The contradiction served as a metaphor for what is going wrong in the industry in general: In a shortsighted attempt to protect the commodity they are trying to sell, the merchants are making the very experience of their commodity increasingly unpleasant.

"Critics should see films the way audiences see them: on the big screen, so that bad sound and photography can be damned and technical excellence can be praised. Comedies should be screened in a room full of people. But if a marketer and a filmmaker want a publicist to leave no stone unturned in their fight to gain as much exposure for a gem of a movie in the face of substantial competition, the publicist must be allowed to make it very easy for editors, feature writers, TV bookers, talk-show hosts, Internet bloggers, shock jocks, and anyone else with an influential audience to actually see this marvelous little movie, and those people who cover the industry must be trusted not to contribute to its destruction."

The truth is that during the course of a film's theatrical release campaign, sometimes screeners are the only way you can get press to see a film. Films like *The Daytrippers* (1996), *Our Song* (2000), *Slam* (1998), *Girlfight* (2000), *Raising Victor Vargas* (2002), *Better Luck Tomorrow* (2002), and *Real Women Have Curves* (2002), as depressing as this might sound, wouldn't have had the campaigns they did without screeners, sometimes hundreds of them. With all of the films opening every week, and with all of the competition, how do you expect audiences to come see the film when you can't even get film journalists to come to screenings? In cases like those, it will be a decision made by your distributor and publicist. For these films, and many others that fall in this category of independent film, we would tell you that approximately ninety percent of their radio and television pieces and twenty-five percent of the print stories were generated by journalists who had seen these films on tape.

For those who have just completed their film and are beginning their road to distribution, the question of screeners gets divergent responses, depending on which end of the business one is in.

Competition among buyers to get the tapes of available films before the festival can be fierce. And festivals have learned how desperate buyers are to nab them. Sundance Film Festival director Geoff Gilmore says, "We are absolutely scrupulous, [John] Cooper and his guys, about locking stuff up, because we know the idea that a film would come from Sundance out into the market would be a terrible thing. But yet, there are examples where arguably that happened. And some examples where we're still confused as to how that happened.

"This one tape actually had a burn-in on it that located it with us, and to this day the only thing we can suggest is that someone got paid off among our lower-level staff and sold it. I still don't know how else that would have happened."

Focus Features copresident James Schamus said, "You don't want to be sending cassettes around. Generally speaking, unless the cassettes are being sent around under very specific circles, where the relationship is solid between the sales agent and the buyer, and there's a measure of trust already, a lot of things can go on while a tape is playing on a television set, you know? And if you're not dealing with people who are respectful—and it's hard to tell who those are—you can simply sit around and imagine all the things that are happening— on the couch, and in the bathroom, and in the kitchen, and on the phone— while the tape is playing.

"But, that said, under most circumstances when a legitimate buyer says they'll watch a tape, they'll watch the tape," Schamus said. "They will. But you know how that is: It's putting the agenda on their time, under their control. On the other hand, cassettes are good if you don't have a lot of money, and can't set up multiple screenings—aren't in New York or L.A. and Sundance at the same time. I sketch these things out not as practical reasons, but just as mind-sets, the two ends of the continuum."

"I think it helps us," said Bob Berney, "but I'm not sure that it's a great idea for the filmmakers. In fairness, if we see something early on tape, I think I can evaluate stuff. But even I could really miss it. I could miss the reaction. I think other distributors do, too. Everybody fights to get these tapes, and all of a sudden there's a whole series of tapes of every Sundance movie. I think it does a disservice. If you have a legitimate screening where it's good quality, it's still risky, especially if the film is a word-of-mouth film, a really emotional film, or a comedy."

A good screening can make a filmmaker overconfident, and more apt to distribute copies. "And I think it's risky to do that," Berney said. A distributor wants to make sure of a film's worth, digest it a little, make sure it's not an impulse buy or predicated on "festival fever." A conversation between distributor and filmmaker is better had after a screening, and after checking the responses of "the critics, and the audience reaction and your gut instinct.

I think it's really risky unless you have the goods" to send tapes or DVDs, he said.

"I wouldn't send screeners out to buyers until you've had your round of screenings for them," said Eamonn Bowles of Magnolia Pictures. "At that point if you haven't had bites, send out tapes. Don't be too precious about it. I've bought more films from tape viewing than screenings, and it can often be annoying when you've expressed a desire to see a film that's been around and you have to go out of your way to make a screening."

"If the film's already played at some festival, already world-premiered somewhere, absolutely send out tapes," said RJ Millard, former marketing and publicity VP at IDP Films. "There's no reason not to. But not for the first time. If you are playing SXSW and you think there's a distributor that's perfect, that's another thing. Do your research: Find out which ones are interested in documentaries, find out which ones release horror films. And target those people. Don't waste your time—Zeitgeist is not going to pick up a horror film, for instance. If you are going to SXSW and the distributor you're interested in is not there—say your film is screening on Thursday—give them a tape on Friday so they can get into the game.

"I would say thirty percent of the films we ended up buying we've seen on tape," said Millard. "And that doesn't mean that we wouldn't have bought the other seventy percent had we seen them on tape. It just so happened that we saw them at a screening somewhere."

"There are a lot of issues that come off this point," said consultant John Sloss, who as a sales agent–lawyer has been essential to a lot of deal-making in the independent realm. "There's the issue of whether or not your film plays well on a small screen. There's the issue of someone watching the film from start to finish if you're not controlling the environment in which they see it. The trade-off is, it's your chance to get decision-makers to see the film, as opposed to a distributor screening, to which most of the decision-makers won't come unless you have some real juice."

Agent Cassian Elwes said, "The biggest mistake I've seen made is filmmakers sending DVDs to agents, reps, lawyers. Once the movie's out there on DVD, if it turns out to be something that's interesting enough for the studios, people will exchange DVDs for other favors, and things like that, and that's hurt films in the past, to have their movies being handed around."

"I got really bad advice," said Justin Lin, director of *Better Luck Tomorrow*. "I was in the rough-cut stage and we ran out of money. Someone told me to just send out the rough cut to some producers reps in hopes that they'd help find financing to finish the movie. That could have killed us. We sent it out and no one would return our calls. Because the movie was nothing to anyone, it was worthless. But as soon as people noticed we got into Sundance, that tape got circulated. This was an AVR 3—low res, rough cut, temp music, and rough sound. And it got circulated to a lot of the distributors and stuff. It literally almost killed any chance we had. People were seeing this on their TVs, low res, without an audience, and it's not even a movie yet. I actually saw a fourth-generation copy of that rough cut later on—a producer I met with had it."

"It's not about trying to keep things from people," he said, "but really, at the end of the day, you're just trying to get people who could be interested in your movie to watch it in the best environment, with an audience, the way it should be. That was my big lesson, on the business side—it's all about presentation, and you want to put people in the best environment possible to judge your movie."

Writer-director Richard Linklater said, "I would not have been flattered by any distributor who wanted to see *Slacker* on video. It's usually some underling covering their ass so they can feel they didn't get scooped, but fundamentally they want to fast-forward through it before they reject it. Better for them to see it with an audience in the right environment."

Documentary filmmaker Kirby Dick had thought his film *Sick* was too marginal to get a theatrical distribution deal and said, "With *Sick*, I knew it played really well on video and my films have all been shot on video. I really didn't think anyone would buy it, so anybody who wanted to see it, I sent it. Because I did this, by the time the film got to Sundance the film already had some buzz."

But with a few years of experience since 1997's *Sick*, Dick said, "In general I try not to send screeners to buyers. That's a tricky situation. I never thought anyone would ever be interested in distributing *Sick*; I was really interested in just having it not overlooked because it might have been seen as marginal." (CFP bought the film after its Los Angeles Film Festival premiere.)

Here are some general guidelines for sending screeners to buyers (with the caveat that all films and their circumstances are different):

❏ Have a strategy in place for both buyers and for press before the issue of screeners comes up, because once you get into a festival many people are going to ask you this question, and the tendency is to be so excited that someone wants to see your film you may want to send tapes to anyone who asks. Which would be a big mistake.

❑ If your film is available and you are working with a sales rep or producers rep, consult with them. If they have a lot of experience, they will give you guidance in this. There is probably nothing more discouraging than going to the world premiere of your film, and finding that no buyers attended because they had already gotten their hands on a copy of your film—perhaps it's even been circulated. In any event, word of your film is out there. Remember that the movie business is a very small community, and word travels fast, even among competitors.

❑ If you are not working with a sales agent or rep, determine if your film is a high priority for buyers and/or press. Are they going to scramble to see it or not? How do you know whether your film is important enough for buyers to want to see? If you are in competition; if it's a world premiere; if you or any of the other creative folks involved had a very well-received previous film; if you have producers that people respect; or if you have recognizable cast names. In those cases, rule out screeners. Buyers will turn up when you show the film.

❑ Create a few tapes and/or DVDs to have on hand, but don't pass them out freely. Wait until after your first public screening to assess your situation. Did it screen really well and are you getting little hints at interest? Then don't pass out tapes or DVDs—buyers will make it to your next screening, either sending more of their troops for second opinions or to get another read on how it plays. Use the screeners as needed, with discernment and deliberation.

Buzz

The Hum of Life . . . Or Death

"**B**uzz." Boy, do we hate that word. Sure, on occasion, it can be very advantageous to have a lot of *good* noise being made about your movie. But for some reason, to us, "buzz" has come to mean undeserved, unwarranted clatter. Cacophony. Pandemonium. Din. And, ultimately, disharmony. Because when people talk about "hype" and "buzz," they are usually talking about something that has percolated beyond the point of salvation before anyone has even had a chance to see the film and decide for themselves. And in those instances, it is never good for the film at hand.

Buzz at film festivals is generated by a number of dubious sources:

* It comes from the acquisitions community, and centers around those films that are available, and have a high "want-to-see" factor. This anticipation creates excitement and is generated by a film with a big cast, which gives it the perception of being marketable, or by a film that has never been seen but is highly anticipated because of various names involved—the writer, director, or producers. And if it's available, of course, then the buzz accelerates quicker, because it's what all the buyers are trying to see.
* From publicists who talk a film up.
* From programmers who mention, maybe just once or twice, the films they are excited about to two friends—and they tell two friends, and they tell two friends. And so on.
* From reporters who have to write in advance about a festival that features films they haven't had a chance to see. They have to write

about something. So they speak to buyers and programmers—see above—and the noise grows.

All of this combined does of course raise the awareness of such films, but it also raises the expectations—and no film, no matter how well it screens, can live up to those expectations. For films that are for sale, this kind of noise is not only distracting, but also dangerous.

It's a phenomenon that has to do with eagerness, optimism and . . . uh, optimism. But how many times has that deafening hum of anticipation completely dissipated by the first reel change? We remember all too well. Buzz that happens before your film screens can be, and almost always is, a bad thing. It heightens expectations unfairly. It doesn't allow a film to be discovered. It doesn't motivate people to champion the film—it can, in fact, make a negative reaction more negative because of the nosebleed-inducing heights from which expectations have fallen. It usually has nothing to do with the merits of the movie.

"There are legion of examples of films that got overhyped, either by programmers of festivals, or by agents, by the press, that created a negative motivation in the audience and in the press to want to dislike a movie," said sales agent John Sloss. "It's either because they were told it was great—and because, inherently, when you're told something is great, it's usually disappointing—or because, when people are told something is great too many times, they simply want to debunk it."

"The hype and buzz that's created by the festival itself is something that you can't control," said agent Cassian Elwes, "and if the movie's really good, the festival jumps up and down and says how great it is. I'm a big proponent of not overhyping films, and not manufacturing hype and buzz, because I think that films can never live up to the expectations. By and large, we're dealing with small films with low budgets, mostly with actors that you haven't heard of, so the studios are going to be disappointed when they see the film if they think in advance that 'this is the greatest film ever.' They're hard to market, hard to sell. It's so much more fun for a studio—a distribution person, actually—to discover a film, rather than being told how great a film is before they see it."

"Programmers can also do a disservice in their introductions," said Rachel Rosen of the Los Angeles Film Festival, who also said prescreening cheerleading can backfire, especially by people trying to promote their own festival. "People clap at every single credit on the screen, and by the time the first frame of the film starts, it just makes you sit there and think: 'OK, show me. Rock my world. Don't just show me a movie, change my life.'

"Of course, the movie can never live up to that."

"Overhyping is one of the worst things that can happen," said *New York Times* film critic Manohla Dargis. "There's a big bull-shit detector that most good critics have. . . . All hype does is work against a movie's favor. Really profoundly."

A little bit of buzz—or excitement or curiosity—about a film is a good thing. But weigh it against all of the factors involved. What section of a festival is your film in? Will it survive the expectations or, even better, exceed them? Very few films can do that. In truth, the lower the expectations, the better a film will play.

Some films manage to have their cake and eat it, too, and once in a while buzz will serve both the critics and the buying community.

"The buyers and critics do exactly the same thing," said Dargis. "They work themselves into states of frenzy about stuff. The *Hustle & Flow* screening [at Sundance 2005] was the most interesting thing I have seen for a long time. People had pumped themselves into thinking it was the second coming—they were almost shaking with excitement. And I was thinking, 'okay. . . . '

"Sometimes," Dargis said, "I like to sit away from people, not with my pals, because there's such a weird peer-pack thing."

"It happens with buyers, too," said Paul Federbush.

While to downplay a film's virtues can help a film, a balance, of course, still has to be reached: There has to be enough excitement to get the right people in, without getting them there expecting the next best thing to sliced bread. Moderation is key. And positioning is crucial.

"One of the easiest mistakes a filmmaker can make," said Sloss, "is to assume that all hype is good—when the likelihood, more often, is that the opposite is true. It is often true that the best circumstance under which to screen a movie is with the lowest expectation possible, while still getting people into the theater."

"Clients who instinctually fixate on kick-starting 'The Buzz' give me angina," said publicist Chris Libby. "The media and industry scour Sundance and similar festivals for the next potent cinematic voice, or the next big sale. The frenzied festival setting creates unfair, unrealistic expectations for most films, particularly for for-sale titles with name cast and pedigree."

Here's an example of such a film that was handled in an exquisite way: *The Motorcycle Diaries*. Before its world premiere at Sundance, the film was about to burst its seams with buzz. The film had pedigree. The names involved included Walter Salles, Robert Redford, producers who were highly regarded, and an extraordinary up-and-comer in actor Gael Garcia Bernal; plus a screenplay that was based on a beloved memoir by Ernesto "Che" Guevara. And nobody in the world had seen it. Knowing how the resulting expectations might damage the film, the publicists repping it, Mark Pogachefsky and Michael Lawson, met with the producers, who saw the impending dangers, and a game plan was laid out that they all agreed on.

The film was positioned as "A quiet adventure—more of an awakening . . . a turn in one's being." For all of those who had read the book, and knew who Che was—in other words, those who were expecting a road movie about a revolutionary—it was really important that the story's action be downplayed.

When the publicists were asked about the film, their response was one of quiet enthusiasm. "It's good," they said. "You should try to see it." Nothing exclamatory or exaggerated. For those that saw the film under this spell, it worked. The handlers were really careful to cultivate the idea that this was Ernesto Guevara in his pre-"Che" days, and in doing so allowed the film a chance to speak for itself. It really helped in the way the film was absorbed and appreciated.

"It's one of the most difficult things to manage," said Pogachefsky. "Things tend to take on a life of their own. Where all of a sudden a movie no one has seen becomes what everyone's talking about. There's also a difference between hype and buzz. Hype is almost a fallacy, and buzz seems more organic. You want people to be talking about the movie, but at the same time you want them to be talking about the movie in the way you want them to be talking about the movie. Movies are fragile, and you don't want to add more weight than they can bear."

Don't get us wrong. There's only so much you can do to influence anything, in film or in life. In an ideal world, the cream rises to the top. There are a few examples that make us happy, even if they didn't make tons of money. The filmmakers got good reviews, and some of the actors are busy today.

There was a film in Directors' Fortnight at Cannes a few years ago—it was called *Long Way Home*, directed by Peter Sollett, and it had no pulse in Cannes, no pulse whatsoever. Laura remembers her gratitude when, after leaving France, she read *The New York Times*'s final column about the festival by A. O. Scott that said really beautiful things about the film. Later retitled *Raising Victor Vargas* and released by IDP/Goldwyn, this little urban dramedy might never have had a chance in the world without him. It was a brief mention, but Tony gave that film journalistic CPR.

Another film Laura loved was *Our Song*. "Sometimes people just don't go see good movies—in fact, it happens all the time. But *Our Song* was a movie that [publicists] Reid Rosefelt, Jessica Uzzan [of the defunct Magic Lantern in New York], and I all loved, and though nobody went to see it, it's one that had as strong a campaign as any, and really great reviews. These are the films that I'd call the 'begging movies.' There are so many ways that PR work can be thankless and degrading that one really grows to appreciate the films that really make you realize 'This is why I'm here; this is why I chose this life for myself.'"

If a lot of filmmakers ever knew how dogged the attempts were *just to get press to watch their movie*, they might well be humbled about how difficult PR can be—even for their films. In the case of *Our Song*, the film made a few critics' Top Ten lists at year's end, and director Jim McKay is still making movies.

An example of a film resurrected by buzz is *I Love You, Don't Touch Me*. It screened to buyers before Sundance, and as no interest came from this screening, the people behind it decided to screen it for Kenneth Turan of *The Los Angeles Times* prior to the festival. Laura remembered that Kenny liked *Ed's Next Move* and other films of that vein. So though it was a gamble, there was also very little to lose: This was a way to resuscitate a film that had very little chance of going anywhere. Kenny liked the film and sat down with the director Julie Davis, and they hit it off. He wrote about her and it piqued the interest of buyers who had passed earlier. The film got bought by Goldwyn.

The best kind of buzz is the kind that happens after a film screens, when the room goes dark and the audience is thinking, "I'm not sure what just happened, but I loved it. What was that, and where did it come from!?" When you can feel that vibe in the room—well, it's exciting, because it's based on some kind of truth.

For films like these, the buzz comes from the critics and the audiences, who have been won over by storytelling, plain and simple—not by the presence of big stars or fanfare. And while it has become harder and harder to find champions for these films, they are out there. And remember. They want to see films they'll love, too. Building that support is the groundwork you need to build on, and sometimes it can help a film that might otherwise have gone nowhere.

Independent distributors rely on the buzz that comes from critics. "When Jon [Gerrans, copresident, Strand Releasing] and I go pick up films at a festival," said Strand's Marcus Hu, "for instance *Nenette et Boni*; *Clean, Shaven*; or *Head-On*, sometimes we'll kind of go around and say, 'Hey Manohla, what did you think of that movie?' and while critics may not say anything, you can see it on their faces."

There's nothing that critics like better than the surprise and the element of discovery—it can make them feel like the film world's Archimedes. And that can lead to advance word of mouth, or critical buzz. And that is what will help you build the momentum you need to get E! or *USA Today* to do something about those little gems, the ones that would otherwise go unnoticed.

And this is what we mean by building.

Laura was in love with a documentary called *The Cruise*, directed by Bennett Miller, which was bought by Artisan (see "Case Studies," page 181) and she set herself the private goal of getting the film's subject, Timothy "Speed" Levitch, onto the *Tonight Show with Jay Leno*. A month and a half before the film would open, she started conversations with Tracey Fiss at the *Tonight Show*.

"She must have thought I was crazy, but once a week, I sent her a few great clips, reviews, and stories about this eccentric New York City tour-bus guide. I'm not sure what finally made her say yes—maybe the full-page *USA Today* story in the Travel section (we got declined by the film editors) helped. Finally, Timothy "Speed" Levitch was a guest on the show, and with Robin Williams, no less. Tracey may not think back fondly of those days, but I do."

Publicist Michele Robertson did the same with *The Full Monty*, and another lesson to be learned here is *no* doesn't always mean *no*, but it could just mean *no* for this moment—a *yes* sometimes needs to be cultivated. Just remember: Don't be an annoying stalker, but be persistent.

In building critical response—a.k.a. benevolent buzz—setting a tone is important. *In the Bedroom* was a film that needed good positioning before it went to Sundance because Sundance, with all of the edgy fare, is a place where this film could have suffered just for being more of a classically made drama. To help people along with it, publicists would promote it as a real old-fashioned movie, well-paced and deliberate, with great performances. Just a few words to describe the film, to set expectations in line. The festival catalog text on the film also helped in setting the tone. It's common sense—imagine when you've seen a film and then imagine what you would tell someone in your recommendation that might help them appreciate it differently. We're in no way saying that a film will work or not because of the way you talk about it—in the end, the film has to work on its own. But setting the proper tone—so expectations aren't out of whack—helps a film to be appreciated in the best way possible. That is the goal.

Another film that was built by critical support is *Tarnation*, a film that L.A. publicist Mickey Cottrell was working on. Once in a while, a film comes along that you must be a part of. Filmmakers should take this to heart, because for those of you who absolutely and truly have no money to spend on something like publicity but have made a film that can serve as someone's *raison d'être*, you can find someone to help you because they love the film. A lot of people in this particular part of the business are not in it to make tons of money, but choose to do it because they love film. Something about this film touched Mickey, and rumor has it he offered to work on it for nothing. This does not happen. But then, neither do films like *Tarnation*.

Buzz can hurt you if it's not managed, that is, if it *can* be managed. Focus Films copresident James Schamus told us, "It means the following, and it's happened so many times. Everybody lines up, and it's not the film they lined up to see. So they assume that somebody else in the room will have bought the hype, and they just walk out. They just leave. They don't even start to discuss the film; they don't even begin the bidding. They don't want to participate—they've been disincentive-ized. And it might have been a really interesting film that had its problems, and you might have motivated yourself to kind of invest something into it—but you've been motivated to step away. So when you do the hype thing, you'd better have the goods. And it's hard to tell what the goods are until you screen it publicly and get some context."

There are famous examples of films that sold for a lot of money: *Spitfire Grill* (1996), *The Castle, Happy, Texas* (1999), and *Tadpole* (2002). They are painful examples of buyers overpaying for films, who continued to pay for it when those films opened in theaters. They are the reason for the term "festival head"— something that happens at festivals, where the lack of oxygen at Sundance, for instance, affects your mind and judgment and makes you see things that aren't there. And miss the things that are.

However, "those films," buyer Paul Federbush said of *The Castle, Happy, Texas,* and *Tadpole*, "had Harvey Weinstein in common. Every year, more as a corporate publicity strategy than anything else, he'd go around and throw around a lot of money. That was a strategy, to keep an edge, so he could be shown films first. It's sort of an investment in the perception that [Miramax] were big buyers, they paid the most, and when they asked to see your film and see your film first, you should consider it, because nobody paid as much as they do. None of those films actually worked and made as much as they paid for them. But it made all filmmakers, not just those filmmakers, look at Harvey and his bravado and say 'Wow, that's a guy with balls, and that's a guy who's not afraid to take a risk and will take your movie out there and really gets behind independent films.' That's how they kept their competitive edge."

Schamus says there are two ways of looking at it. "One is being overly cynical and stepping away from a potential home run. And the other one is just being so competitive that you forget what you're competing over, from a buyer's point of view. 'Did I really want X for ten million dollars?' The buyer's remorse moment. So you're constantly trying to test your own feelings, and emotions, and sort out your own relationships from the actual experience you had at the film, the gut instinct. As you know, festival audiences are not retail audiences; they're different. All festivals have different kinds of festival audiences. Sundance has its kind, etcetera, so while watching a film with an audience is a wonderful thing, clearly certain festivals have audiences with a track record of overresponding to specific kinds of movies that prove disastrously uncommercial [laughs]. Every festival has its own kind of thing."

Donnie Darko is an example of an overhyped film that many cited as a classic case of Suicide by Buzz. "It was the most overhyped film at Sundance the year it was there," said Picturehouse president Bob Berney. "Which is the classic problem: If you overdo it, people's expectations [are grossly inflated]. That was one where the distributors, and everyone, were like 'You're kidding? This is the best film?'"

"*Donnie Darko* Syndrome," said Sloss. "That was one of the clearest examples I've seen. But when the dust settled, most people thought it was a good movie."

"That script had been around and people really loved it," said producer Christine Vachon, "so there was a lot of anticipation for that script, and you could argue that the hype around *Donnie Darko*, at least at that particular Sundance, backfired because it did not meet expectations. The film's gone on to have an incredible life [including a huge cult following, an afterlife on DVD, and even a theatrical re-release in its 'director's cut'] but if you remember, specifically at that Sundance, most people were very underwhelmed, which just goes to show they were blinded by their expectations; they weren't really seeing the movie for the great thing that it was."

Berney added, "That one was really damaged [by expectations]. For us, it was a great thing, because three months later we bought it on the cheap side, and ultimately it was one of those films where the audience was absolutely there for the film."

If a film is good, will it find its way eventually?

"I used to feel that," said Vachon. "And I think that you have to feel that to a certain degree, because otherwise it's just too depressing of a world. But I also do think that the marketplace has gotten so crowded that, sadly, there's a possibility now that a great movie may not find its audience, at least theatrically. Of course, now there are so many other ways to find an audience, so I feel like even if it doesn't find one theatrically, it will find one somewhere. . . . *Velvet Goldmine* is a good example. It didn't have any theatrical life to speak of, but it has had an extremely strong, very vital DVD and video life."

Sometimes a film is victimized by the sheer fact that it's in a festival—it's a double-edged sword. In a festival environment, and people may not want to admit this, films are seen differently. They are judged by different, sometimes harsher, standards; they are seen with impatient, bleary eyes. No film is meant to be seen either as an 8:30 A.M. screening (particularly if you've been up till 3:00 A.M.). And no film is meant to be seen as the fourth or fifth film of the day. That said, *Donnie Darko, The Pianist*—which was almost universally disliked when it made its premiere at Cannes in 2002 (although it went on to take the Palme d'Or)—and many others did get a fair second chance and were reviewed well when they opened in theaters.

How to Make the Cruelest Month (1998) and *Clockwatchers* (1997) are examples of films that suffered from a massive hype glut. These titles had some of the coolest up-and-coming actors or stars around, and a variety of well-liked and well-connected producers. The films, even before going to Utah, could not live up to the buzz. Festival programmers also highlighted these films, which only added to the noise and expectation levels.

"I discount a lot of feedback from programmers," said Paul Federbush, but not everyone does. To that point, Laura remembers riding in a car with Geoff Gilmore at Sundance, and "we were rhapsodizing about *American Splendor*, which had not yet screened at the festival. We shared our enthusiasm for the film, talked about our love of Paul Giamatti and Harvey Pekar. And then I asked him, and asked him to tell his staff, to stop talking about *American Splendor*. He knew exactly what I was talking about."

Sometimes, many times, you cannot help buzz getting out about your film. But there is no good reason to add to it, and there are ways to help temper it. (*The Motorcycle Diaries* is a case in point; see page 135.)

"Our most vivid example of artificially reducing hype," said Sloss, "was on *Napoleon Dynamite*, where we basically made a decision internally not to talk about it with buyers before the film festival. When they asked about our slate, we talked about every other film we had, and when they asked about this one, we said 'It's small.' Because essential to that film's success was going to be the sense that people discovered it, and it was their film, and they were champions."

Often, Sloss continued, "in situations like these, the culprits are the programmers, for no other reason than the fact that they love movies, get very enthusiastic, and go on about them.

"The starkest example of where I felt we had to hype as much as possible was with *Capturing the Friedmans*," he said. "Because it was Friday night, it was a documentary, and it was about a child molester. I called distributors and John Horn of *The Los Angeles Times* or whatever and said, 'This is going to be a historic screening.' And that served the film well."

Sometimes, said *The New York Times*'s Sharon Waxman, "You can be really misled by what you think the hype and buzz is."

"There's this unbelievable sense of hype just about getting tickets," said Shari Springer Berman, codirector of *American Splendor*. "It can really throw off your sense of importance—you feel like you have a ticket to the Beatles reunion. Like your movie is that. But it's just that no one wants to miss the movie that *could* be, it's not that your movie *is* that. It's just about information.

"We were pretty quiet," she added. "We definitely weren't the movie that everyone was writing about before the festival. And we were the last movie in competition to premiere, which was really horrible. We would be sitting there and keep hearing, 'I just saw this brilliant movie. . . .' We just thought, 'Well, we might as well just go home now.' It's human nature to want to be the one that's written about, but I think it's better before the festival to be the surprise movie that gives people a sense of discovery."

"Our philosophy," said Springer Berman's codirector Robert Pulcini, "was always, 'Let's go in as quiet as possible, and if it hits great, and if it doesn't, nobody will notice, and we can move on. . . .'"

But you don't want to move on; you want to move up. You want to generate the right reaction to your film, and you want to tune the public vibration to something pitch-perfect for your career plan. So you don't hide under a rock; you just use information to best serve your film.

Perhaps your movie has been bought somewhere in the in-between season of festivals. Or at a festival that may be lower on the radar. Announcing the acquisition of a film during the first few days of a major festival can help get the film on the press's radar. And this is important, because there are so many films that many journalists won't see unless they already have a release date.

Marcus Hu described a recent pickup. "We made up a story about how we had acquired *Tony Takitani* out of Sundance, when in fact we picked it up in Vancouver. We delayed the news for months so that we could announce it at Sundance, to give the film a better profile. It happens a lot. Picking up a movie, saving it for a festival, and then making a big announcement right at the beginning, so you maximize your coverage. That's been a really good way of getting really good exposure for your film. You have everyone there; they're sitting ducks, they have to read this trade announcement. It's a great thing to do. Then people might come and see it, since they know it will have a release date. It only helps the film. It actually appeared on the first day of the festival—'Strand Picks Up *Tony Takatani* at Sundance.' It's not lies. It's just about timing."

Now is a really good time to mention that in creating buzz and trying to get publicity, it is really important to know that you don't necessarily need or want lots of big stories to run on your film. In fact, that huge story in the big paper may be what you don't want. Most independent film distributors know that most papers won't write about one film in a big way more than once. That story (or buzz in general) is best used for the film's good, when it's opening, and is coming to theaters for ticket-buying audiences. No distributor is going to buy your film because *Entertainment Tonight* did something on it or because *USA Today* wrote about it.

Buyers just want to know that critics like the film and that the chances are good, when the film opens, that writers will want to write about it and that audiences will really respond to it.

Remember. Buzz is the excitement that surrounds a film, and is best when it is honest-to-goodness buzz and happens organically, because a film deserves it. Hype, like crime, often doesn't pay: Anyone who's been around for a while in independent film and has been able to make a go of it has probably done so by being pretty honest.

Manners and Mis-manners
How Not to Alienate Potential Supporters

A s we've said before, albeit in fewer words: Unless you've already attained a certain amount of notoriety—unless you've mounted a *Blair Witch Project* prerelease, Web-site-driven publicity campaign (when such things were novel), or, like director Andrew Jarecki and *Capturing the Friedmans*, have a family as newsworthy as those Friedmans to help publicize your film—you need the press and the audiences more than they need you. Consider the following guidelines. Repeat them, memorize them, love them and live by them.

You Are Your Biggest Ally

Conveying enthusiasm for your own film is vital, as is the way you are able to articulate for buyers, press, and audiences the virtues of the film. If you can't do that, how can you expect anyone else to? Besides the film itself, you are perhaps the biggest tool in the film's success and you have the most to lose or gain by how it is received.

Friedmans director Andrew Jarecki said, "There is some preparation you can undertake to make the process of getting your film distributed easier and more focused. Assuming you have a good film, and in this context that means one that is compelling to a reasonably wide range of viewers, it requires, above all, a sense of what you are trying to get out of the process.

"I talked to a young filmmaker recently who had made quite a good documentary about politics. Not something salacious or innovative enough to make Sheila Nevins or David Linde snatch it up on first viewing," he said. But it was "interesting, subtle, and intellectual, though somewhat limited in its appeal. It would have to 'find the right audience.' Or, more accurately, if this filmmaker wanted her film to be seen by a large number of people, she would have to locate the right distributor, and then charm and cajole him into helping her bring the film to the right audience.

"I asked her what her goal was for this film, and she told me that she wanted to 'use it to make her next film'—that she wanted to build her reputation so she could get the funding to make her next film, which was going to be amazing. I immediately knew she was in trouble. The goal she had set for her film undermined its chances of success from the start. She had fallen into the terrible trap of getting tired of her own film. And even though I was not a buyer, and already liked her film enough to take the time to talk to her, she didn't realize that her role was to let me know through her actions and words that she felt her film was the greatest film in the world; that it was up to her to maintain the high level of enthusiasm it would take to push through the many closed doors she'd inevitably find along the road toward getting her film distributed. I'm not suggesting that filmmakers should be actively 'selling' their films, but rather that filmmakers must, in all of their interactions, express a love for their films that is so potent it's highly contagious. And if the filmmaking process or its duration has sucked the life out of it, they've got to go back and find the optimistic idealist they were when they started out, and channel that person into the present.

"This enthusiasm is important for at least three reasons. First, it gives others their first sense of the film and of you as the filmmaker—if you aren't excited about it, why will they bother? Conversely, if they like you and what you say about your film, they are more likely to give it a chance."

Secondly and very importantly, particularly for a film as challenging in subject matter as *Capturing the Friedmans*, Jarecki explained, "When you are describing your film to distributors and others, you are giving them their first sense of the language and approach they might use to market the film if they decide to take it on. You've had a few years of telling friends and relatives what you are working on, and honing your description based on their reactions to make it sound compelling so you're their first marketing consultant.

"Third, it tells the distributor something about you. When a distributor buys your film, they are making an investment in you as much as anything else. Since independent distributors don't have studio-sized ad budgets, their films typically find awareness in the marketplace through publicity rather than advertising; and publicity has to be created through one-on-one interaction with journalists. Whatever the terms of the deal, the distributor is becoming your partner, and needs to know that you'll be able to participate actively in spreading your enthusiasm about the film."

And, as Ringo would say, "Act naturally." As Beck would say, "I'm a loser, baby, so why don't you kill me?" Depending on what your real personality is, remember when speaking to buyers or press that you are actually trying to curry favor and win their affection. While you should be yourself and not solicitous, it should be a mutual honor for you to be sitting with the media. In many cases, they are, in effect, auditioning you. There are many other films they could support; make them want to support yours.

There are examples where this helps more than it should. James Toback has gotten a lot of mileage out of being a colorful character. That he goes about his business, and does whatever he feels without filters, is his shtick and it has won him support, even when his films don't necessarily deserve it. He's earned life credits. Kevin Smith, by being a sincere, honest, no-nonsense kind of guy, has done the same. And everyone can use goodwill sometimes.

Take Your Meds: Humor Pills and Humble Pills

"One of the things we always say," said PR veteran Mark Pogachefsky, "is every morning, when you get up, take a humor pill and a humble pill."

Good advice. It is very easy to become inflated about your film, and it shows in how you interact with people and the press. Confidence is fine. But it's important to take your medication.

Once upon a time, there was a filmmaker, one who had a film in Cannes. The film was, well . . . if a French medical student had opened a free colonoscopy kiosk across from the Palais du Cinema, he might have gotten more business. "Universally disliked" wouldn't be an overstatement. So much so that most critics didn't sit through the entire movie.

What did he do? Re-edit his film? Rethink his next project? Reconsider his choice of career? No, no, no. Nothing so conservative. Or sensible. Or untheatrical. He did what any self-respecting, self-destructive egomaniac would do: He waited and waited for the Critics Panel at the American Pavilion and got himself a seat and when it came time for the audience-participation part of the program, he participated—pointing fingers and challenging the critics, broadcasting to all present just who among the panelists did not like his film and letting people know, in a very public way (and for all of those that hadn't known anything about the film), that nobody liked it, and everyone had walked out.

This, of course, made the critics uncomfortable. The publicist was horrified—which is, perhaps, neither here nor there. Far more importantly, his performance certainly didn't make anyone like the film more than they already hadn't. And it publicized the negative reaction to people who hadn't even seen it.

One filmmaker, after leaving Sundance—where his little film had won a very big prize—flew to Los Angeles for meetings. Upon arrival, he went to Enterprise Rent-A-Car, and, when the reservation for his car could not be found, began throwing a fit, yelling about his Sundance Jury Prize. As if they cared.

Another filmmaker, on his way to Toronto, forgot his passport and began berating the airport staff. He screamed, "Don't you know who I am? Call Bob Berney! Call him!" He could have used a humor pill.

One filmmaker, at Cannes, suggested making an extreme form of sacrifice for his art. "Maybe if I get into a car accident, that will get people to write about it?" he asked his publicist. "Not really," the publicist said. "Unless you get hit by Sylvester Stallone." Nurse! Humor pill!

"One of the big mistakes," said *Variety* critic Todd McCarthy, "and it's happened a couple of times, is filmmakers who have careers, they'll call you up and they'll yell and scream at you because of some review. One filmmaker who was so upset, and wrongly upset, because it was a mixed review, screamed at me and told me everyone else loved it and it was going to do twenty or fifty million dollars, and I said it wasn't going to do any business. He said 'You're my enemy now. You're my enemy.'

"It's shortsighted to personalize a review instead of realizing that there's going to be another day, and another film," said McCarthy. "So don't muddy the waters like that. I just don't understand why someone would do that.

"We have a film," said RJ Millard, "where the script is so inflammatory and so incendiary and so fun on so many levels. But we do a big creative meeting, and the director comes across as arrogant—not somebody you want to talk in public or have talking to the media. He also comes across as defensive: When people ask him questions, he sort of barks at them. What we're doing, is retooling, and putting interviewers on the phone with the writer instead."

"Be humble and take your criticism and praises like an adult," said publicist Jeff Hill. "If you're at a festival, talk to everyone that you can. If you cannot handle criticism, don't read."

What's one of the biggest turnoffs for a distributor?

"Unfortunately, arrogance," said Eamonn Bowles of Magnolia Pictures. "You need a great deal of self-confidence and determination to get any film made, but nothing turns a distributor off more than having to deal with someone who has unrealistic notions about his movie. I've walked away from films I've liked because the prospect of dealing with the filmmaker fell into the 'life's-too-short' category."

Carl Spence, Seattle Film Festival's director of programming, added, "Just like with many distributors, when the filmmaker in their initial dealings with us, seems demanding and like they have impossible expectations, a distributor may decide not to pick up the film, for that reason. They do not want to pick up a film that's going to take more time than they have to give. Don't wear out your welcome before you get here. You should expect a certain level of professionalism from the festival, any festival, but at the same time, realize that you're not the only film. Be cognizant to not overwhelm the staff—expectations need to be realistic. It is a small business and people all talk."

Even before a film screens at a festival, in the way a filmmaker thinks about his or her own film, having the right attitude matters.

"There's an internal feeling that the world has to see this movie," James Schamus of Focus Features said. "And one of the first things I was always able to do in that situation was say, 'No, that's not the first thing you need to do. The first thing you need to do is find a way to present this film fairly, but in such a way that you're presenting it in the most favorable light to the people who you actually want to, eventually, distribute the film.'

"So there are a couple of mistakes people make. One mistake, at one end of the spectrum, is, 'Oh, I'm flattered you want to see it, let me give you a tape.' Three months before Sundance—'I don't know if we're in yet, but here, take it.'"

The other mistake, he said, is to go in the exact opposite direction. "'My product is so groovy,'" Schamus joked, "and so hot, so unique, and so exciting, that I'm not showing it to anyone—thinking that they will only show it after so much hype and after so much pressure and with everyone knowing that they have to decide if they want to buy it within thirty seconds of having seen it, and knowing that all their competitors will be sitting on every aisle with their cell phones on, waiting. 'The film is going to be so fucking great, and I'm going to sell it to the highest bidder, so you better be prepared to bring your checkbook.'"

To say that such an attitude would have a chilling effect on incipient deal-making is to put it mildly. As Schamus—and others—have said, if a movie is good enough, a distributor will kiss the biggest ass in the world. But if your movie is on the fence, obviously, egomania can push it the wrong way.

"Look," said Schamus, "in our business you often have to deal with people who are having their moments. And our job is to go, first and foremost, to find those films which we think we can distribute better than anybody else. So we're not going to say, 'Oh you're such a jerk, your publicist is so mean, they didn't make me feel good so I'm not coming.' You don't do that."

The World Does Not Revolve Around You

It may feel like everyone's talking about you and your film, but in fact that's only the people around you. And you. There are other films in the festival, and the experience is happening to them, too. Remember: People who like your film come up and tell you. People who don't like your film, don't. So even if you believe everyone likes your film, it's generally never true.

You shouldn't revolve around you either. Go see other films, talk about other things, ask people about other films. Be interested in what's going on around you. Try to keep in mind that you were probably a pretty interesting person before your life was consumed by your film. Try to find that person.

"Filmmakers should realize that they've already had their success, just by having their film invited to one of the principal film festivals," said William Morris agent Cassian Elwes. "It is an enormous achievement in itself. So to go there thinking, 'I'm going to make ten million dollars with my film,' that's a big mistake. Few films sell for that kind of money in this particular kind of environment, practically none, except for *Hustle & Flow*, which was close to that last year. The success is just being there."

If you keep your expectations in check, he added, and realize that what you're bringing is a small film that is artistic in nature, finding distribution is "the icing on the cake."

"You should bask in that part of it, and enjoy the festival, because you're never going to have that again—your first festival and your first movie. You have to enjoy that part of your success, which is that you've managed to make a film that has been invited and you've brought it, and it is going to be put up on a screen and seen by your peers, and seen by people who can make a difference. That's an enormous success just in itself."

Rally the Troops

Be nice. To your publicist and your distributor. They are your mouthpieces, and it will only benefit you if they think highly of you. You want to curry favor with them, so don't let them grow to hate you. It will translate into their performance on the film. Ask a lot of questions. Be involved in a collaborative way—be tough, communicate your needs, desires, and fears, but inspire the people around you to feel invested in your success.

Remember: There are a lot of personal friendships among press and publicists. When a filmmaker acts out, and treats the critic's publicist friend like shit, the critic knows the publicist can't do much about it. But he can.

Laura remembers, with affection and fondness, being at the Toronto International Film Festival, and waiting with eager anticipation the arrival of the entourage involved with *Another Day in Paradise*, which was on its way from the Venice Film Festival, where Larry Clark [*Kids*] had physically assaulted one of the producers during the film's press conference.

This is an extreme case of bad behavior, of course, and Larry Clark, being Larry Clark, well, perhaps that's just part of his charm? But the talent involved with the film felt threatened, and it created a great deal of strategic planning in keeping the gang separate. Security, for instance, had to be brought in. The fact that Clark urinated, publicly and poolside (not in, but poolside), didn't help matters. Also, when the New York Film Festival called him to say that *Ken Park* did not get in, and Clark started screaming, "You guys are a bunch of fucking assholes!". . . Ah, the memories. A film would have to be incredibly special for an independent distributor to put themselves through that kind of crap. We love the idea of the artiste, but dating them is just too much drama.

Journalists Are People, Too

"There's this one really annoying guy," said *Newsweek*'s David Ansen. "An aspiring filmmaker who's gotten himself so much publicity, and who keeps calling me and begging me for a quote. Which I didn't give him. But he's really obnoxious."

"It started on the plane," said critic Amy Taubin, recalling one all-too-physical encounter. "There I was, semicomatose, on the plane to Cannes, and someone is touching my shoulder. This total stranger, telling me, 'I have a movie in the market.' I tell him, 'I don't go to movies in the market, I have enough to do at Cannes, but if you want to, you could send me a screener after Cannes.'

"Every single fucking day, I would feel this arm on my shoulder or around me. 'My movie! You have one more day to see it!' Or 'We got an extra screening.' Or whatever. Don't touch me.

"I don't mind people being persistent," said Taubin. "But I mind people expecting that you will do something just because they're persistent. It's hard, I know, because the filmmakers have everything in it, their whole lives, and they don't like to hear 'I have one hundred movies on my floor, and I'll try to get to it.' And I understand that. But a lot of people feel, 'You're obliged to look at my movie.' I'm not obliged."

Roger Ebert added, "I've written stories from festivals about filmmakers who didn't rest until I had seen their films—for example, at Sundance 2005, *The Talent Given Us*, by Andrew Wagner. However, I won't go to a film simply because of a director's chutzpah. Some other kind of element must be present."

A lot of the problems stem from misinterpretation or mistranslation: It's as if the filmmaker has taken a Berlitz course in Swahili, gone to Africa, and asked an otherwise very nice person, "How much to buy your sister?" Things can get ugly. Similarly, the reaction of press to filmmakers who don't understand the rudiments of journalism, distance, and ethics. Mistakes may elicit an overly passionate, and negative, response, but that's because the two parties are speaking different languages.

"Filmmakers will write to critics," Taubin continued, "and say, 'My movie is not playing anywhere, I read your writing all the time, I think you'd like it. Please send me back your thoughts on my movie. . . .' Or, 'Could you write something that I could include in my press kit?' Those are very big no-nos. If I'm in love with your movie, I will write you back, and I will tell you that if it's ever going to screen anywhere, and I have any kind of reason to write about it, you must let me know. But that's a rare movie."

Fifty percent of filmmakers, she said, will not accept a no. "They will say, 'Why?' or 'But couldn't you do something?' or 'Jane and Bob think it's a great movie,' at which point I usually hang up the phone.

"Another thing, as long as I'm on this rant, it won't make me like your movie any more. I like movies independently of the people. There are filmmakers who I think are wonderful human beings and I'm so glad they're successful, and there are filmmakers who are shits, and I love their movies—and I want to get behind their movies, too. . . . You get a lot of points in my book, and I'll always look at your movies in this case, if I say 'I don't think this movie works for me, and I'm not sure it's going to work for anyone else, thank you very much' and they say, 'If you have some time, is there anything you could tell me?' Or, they just say, 'Thank you very much,' and they talk about something else. And they don't seem like they want to kill me because I don't like their movie. It's very hard to not want to kill someone because they don't like your movie, because it matters. But I don't want to have to deal with someone's fury because I don't like their movie. And I probably won't catch their movie first thing next time."

Another thing, Taubin said, ranging into more delicate territory: "It's because I'm a woman—Jim Hoberman, for example, never got this—The guy who tells you either to your face, or tells everyone else you know, 'She's not writing about my movie because she wanted to fuck me and I didn't fuck her.' Or, 'She didn't like my movie 'cause she's an old hag.' After you tell someone you can't write about their movie, or you don't want to write about their movie, that should end it. The filmmaker should think, 'This is painful,' but you really can't convince me to do otherwise. And you probably will make another movie, so you really don't want to antagonize me so I just get a headache thinking about seeing your second movie."

Manners 101

Behave, even when nobody's looking. The walls have ears. Remember: All of those people around you, whom you think you don't know—they may know you, and how you behave can make a lasting impression on them.

Laura saw a famous filmmaker berate his writing partner in a fairly public setting (backstage at the Independent Spirit Awards) and in an aggressive, mean way. That impression will never leave her, and she will never think he is a nice person, even though she's heard he is. Your behavior when you think no one's watching is most telling.

Say "Please," "I'm sorry," and "Thank you."

You would be shocked, but these are probably the least-uttered words in this business. Thus when they *are* used, they have twice the impact.

Yes, the lessons your mother taught you about being polite apply here, too. A thank-you goes a long way in this business and can reinvigorate energy for your film. It is hard work all around, and sometimes a few words of gratitude will go a long way.

"When you go up to introduce your film," said mPRm's Mark Pogachefsky, "thank the festival and the programmers. If you're in a festival like Sundance, Cannes, or Toronto, you're in a very privileged situation. And, as a filmmaker, you should kick back, have a good time, enjoy meeting other filmmakers and take advantage of what the festival has to offer. Let your sales and publicity team do their job—be informed of what's happening, but let them do their job. Don't drink too much. And get enough sleep."

Keep Your Perspective

"As John Cheever wrote somewhere in his journals, 'It helps to be relaxed,'" said longtime New York publicist Jeremy Walker. "The world premiere of one's film at a festival is a truly daunting experience. Leading up to the Festival there is usually a huge amount of work to be done and the screenings themselves can be nerve-wracking, but they can also be insanely rewarding.

"Try to take things in stride. Delegate where possible. Try to keep in mind that if something goes wrong, do not react immediately. Take a deep breath. Seek counsel from the talented people with whom you have surrounded yourself. Move forward.

"Conversely, no matter who you are or how great your film is, keep in mind that there are probably others around you whose films are more commercial, or have bigger stars, or have more fans on the jury, or have more heat for whatever reason. All of these things will be easier to take, and will be potentially less damaging to the way you and your film are perceived, if you are a sane and humble person.

"By the same token, if you have a film that is in a festival and things are going reasonably well, you are now a member of this community. Try to think in those terms. See other people's films. Get to know your colleagues. Take advantage of this very cool time in your life. Be open. Generous. Empathetic. Do not be an asshole."

"Keep some perspective," said Kirby Dick, director of *Sick: The Life and Death of Bob Flanagan, Supermasochist* and *Twist of Faith*, both of which were at Sundance. He agreed that "talking to other filmmakers, forming relationships with other filmmakers—especially on your first couple of films—is probably as important as forming relationships with distributors. Because they are people you can call on, or ally with in some way. I think it's really important and sometimes you forget about that."

Finally: Real people may like your film, but that doesn't mean critics will. Breathe a big sigh of relief if you have good reviews, and let go of the bad ones.

Don't Be a Turtle

Being chosen for a festival is, as many filmmakers seem to forget, a huge step up. "But when you go up," said *New York Times* reporter Sharon Waxman, "be open to all of the experiences that are going to go on around you. Be around. Be in the lobbies. Be in the hotels. Be in the bar. Because there are all kinds of moments you can have. You can have fun at Sundance; there are parties all night long. You can be in the hot tub. But if you want to use it as a chance to get your movie career going, be in the public places where other people are. There are opportunities all day long, twenty-four hours a day, everywhere you go, in the public spaces."

People Want to Help People Who Need Help

Each time you have a conversation with a journalist or do a Q&A, try to remember how you felt before and after your very first screening. Be excited that people are seeing it. Be grateful if they like it. Be thankful for the opportunity.

At the 2002 Sundance Film Festival, HBO's Maud Nadler set up a meeting for all of the filmmakers and cast of *Real Women Have Curves*, just before the film would make its world premiere. Laura was on the film and they did a run-through of the week's events, a brief outline of how the festival works, and went over everyone's schedules. Then Laura and Maud also described for them what would happen at the film's first screening: When the film was done screening, the audience would, they hoped, erupt into applause and cheers.

They were asked to remember exactly how they felt in this moment, before the film's first screening. And to try to come back to that place before each and every one of the screenings. It is important to remind people of this, because even if the reactions to a film are positive, it's a turn-off to see people on stage who expect it.

"Nothing is more off-putting to media and festival audiences," said publicist Chris Libby of B|W|R, "than a filmmaker with newfound success who appears ungrateful."

It may not feel like it, but remember, hundreds of films open every year, and only a few are critically acclaimed, and only a few of those break even, let alone do well at the box office, but many if not most films are enthusiastically received at festivals.

This is the beginning, not the end, of a long road of trying to win people over.

Treat Yourself with Respect, Too

"Drink lots of water, don't stay up too late, don't try to get into every party," said Jeff Levy-Hinte. "There are plenty of opportunities in one's life to pick up crass goods emblazoned with logos. I wouldn't waste my precious time at Sundance trying to chase that. It's simply, patently absurd.

"Try to be ready to put the best face for the film forward," he said. "Do the press opportunities that are there, avail yourself of the structured events that Sundance offers. This goes for any festival, but Sundance can be the most distracting. The most insane."

Try really hard not to get caught up in the hype, he said. "Stay realistic and use it as an opportunity for the next step instead of overly reveling it. A lot of people get there once, and then dip into obscurity. They get too full of themselves. Similarly, in that environment, if you're one of the few whose film people really liked, you get pursued by agents, etc. My feeling is to really take the time to sort through them; if you do well at Sundance, you will have plenty of opportunities."

DIY-PR

If You Can't Get Something Done Right . . .

Lindbergh did it. So did Amelia Earhardt. Yo Yo Ma does it every time he plays the Bach Cello Suites. Hall did it to Oates. And Tenzing Norgay did it, too (if you discount Edmund Hillary). What they did was go solo—a gesture to the breadth of the human spirit, and, occasionally, in FilmLand, to the depth of the pocketbook.

THIS CHAPTER—DIY, which, FYI, means "do-it-yourself"— is meant to be a guide for those filmmakers who either don't have the resources to hire a publicist for their film, or don't feel it's necessary. In determining whether or not it's necessary, you might want to consult Chapter 1, "Evaluating Your Film." But during that hopefully short time in your film's life before it has distribution, you will certainly need materials, but you may be able to get by without a publicist.

How do you know if you need to hire a publicist? Here are a couple of general guidelines—not absolutes, more like signposts to help guide you down the rutted highway of self-promotion.

If your film is "available" (for sale) and you are going to a festival where there is at least some press and buyer presence, you have to be honest with yourself:

▲ Do you believe that there's a very real possibility that your film
may get a theatrical release? (A difficult question to ask—
or answer—but if you think that the chances are slim, answer
"no" for the time being.)

▲ Does your film have well-known actors in it *or* does the director,
writer, or producer have any sort of profile, or track record?
(Have any of them worked on anything else that has been well
received by critics, and received even a modest release?)

▲ Are you in a high-profile section of a festival, where you will need help working with the press, or are you in a sidebar (subsection), where it will help to have someone with experience and relationships pushing on your behalf?

If you answer yes to any of these, then you may want to think seriously about hiring a professional.

Working with a Festival Press Office

On the other hand, if you are going to a festival where there is very little press or buyer presence (that is, one where even *Variety* doesn't send a critic), you can work with the festival's press office. The following are essential steps to take:

Contact the festival's press office a few weeks before the festival, and introduce yourself. Tell them what film you have, and let them know that if there's anything they need, to feel free to contact you. Make sure they have all of your contact information—both at home, and where you'll be (and reachable) once you've arrived on the scene.

Send your materials ahead. Having at this point dealt with the materials called for in Chapter 7, "Materials" (and if you haven't, get crackin'), send them, along with whatever other materials might be requested, to the film festival office, as soon as you can. There are many times that the media covering a festival will be doing prefestival stories, and need materials to do so—and if your materials happen to be the ones on hand, you may be the one chosen to be written about. It's happened, believe us, more than once. In cases like this, sometimes the early bird gets the worm, even if the worm is made of ink and no one's even seen your film.

Check the festival's program or catalog copy. Before the festival program goes to print, ask the festival if you can see the description of your film that they are going to use in the catalog, or on the festival Web site, in order to proofread it, for both accuracy and tone. If you disagree with its content, or even its attitude—if you think that, in fact, it might actually turn people off (this has happened, too)—ask nicely if it's too late to make changes.

Ask about prefestival screenings. Ask the press office if they will be scheduling prefestival screenings. If you will have a print ready (or have the film in another appropriate format), and if you *honestly* believe your film will have a good response from the press (and will play OK in a fairly empty room), offer your film up for a prefestival press screening.

If you're unsure, weigh seriously the pros and cons of this decision. What are you trying to achieve? Generally, if your film is available and will make its world premiere at a festival like Sundance, Cannes, or the Los Angeles Film Festival, conventional wisdom would say *don't* prescreen your film, particularly if you are in a competition situation. In fact, in most cases, prescreen only if: (1) you're at least 98 percent sure the reviews will be good (who wants to see negative reviews or capsules before your film even screens?), (2) if your film is in a remote sidebar of the festival program, (3) you have no cast of note, and no track record, (4) your film is a foreign language film, or a documentary whose subject matter, on paper at least, will have uncertain appeal, and/or (5) if you have nothing to lose (you've played elsewhere and have attracted very little press or buyer interest). In most cases, a film will be received better in a public screening, so if yours is a world-premiering film up for sale, you may not want to risk a prefestival screening.

Make the right media contacts. Ask the festival if they have a list of accredited press, and if so, could it be e-mailed it to you. If there is a press screening of your film at the festival, or before the festival, ask the press office whether there's a sign-in sheet. This enables you to get a sense of who has seen the film, and you can follow up with them if you choose to do so. It will always be helpful to you to know who has seen your film, and whether they liked it.

If you do plan to contact the media:

○ Draft a winning note—either to mail or e-mail—introducing yourself. Include a short blurb on the film, screening dates and times, and your local contact info, including cell number. A Web link to where they can download photography is always a plus. In the subject line, put the name of the festival and your film's title, so they can refer back to it easily. Include who among your cast or crew will be coming into town for the festival, and what dates they will be there. Make your note as short as possible, while still having all the information one could possibly need (an enigma, but not a tough one). For e-mail, a clear, informative subject line is vital. You want recipients to be able to go back and find your message, even if they don't remember the name of the film. Here's an example:

> Re: Seattle Film Fest—*Movie Name*: Director Smith
> and cast member Jones in Seattle from June 2–5.

○ Do not send large attachments unless someone asks for them. Imagine crashing some journalist's computer when he or she is at some film festival, seeing movies, writing about them, and trying to send copy to the paper.

○ Though you may be very excited that your film is in the festival, do not spam the press repeatedly, but do update them with important changes—clearly and simply. That way, they can either open your e-mail, or delete it with little bother. And when they're trying to go back to find it, the hunt will be easy. Sample subject lines:

> Re: SXSW Update: Patricia Clarkson coming to Austin!
>
> Re: SXSW: *Your Great Movie* Screening Time has CHANGED!

○ As you progress, and your film screens, and if, by chance, you get closer to a theatrical relationship with a distributor, start shifting your focus. If you're asked to do an interview, do it—but let the writer know that the film will most likely open in theaters—say, in spring 2007. This will let journalists know that they can hold the story until your film opens.

Getting ready for theatrical release. As your film is getting ready to go to theaters—whether it be with a distributor in place, or in the self-promoting situation known as *four-walling*—dealing with media becomes a more complicated, time-consuming, impersonal bit of business. At a festival, after all, everyone's in the same place and the atmosphere might even be congenial. Out in the real world, getting press exposure or, God bless you, airtime requires a different skill set, nervous system, and attack strategy.

Ergo, there are things you should know.

Deadlines for monthly magazines are usually way ahead of the publication date—for reviews, at least three or four months out, earlier for feature space, and even earlier for cover stories—so plan accordingly. Know that unless your film is going to open in at least the major markets, you will have a hard time getting national publications to pay attention.

Consider each one carefully: Does the audience for your film suit the readership of the magazine? If you are pitching a story, pick the appropriate seditor and send a letter, screening information, and a tape or DVD. Your account should give real reasons why this story should interest them, and not just because the film stars X or because "It's a good movie." It's almost always a good idea to write your pitch with the publication's specific audience in mind rather than just provide general information on the film.

"Know what constitutes a story from their perspective," said Los Angeles publicist Fredell Pogodin. "Don't call and say, 'I have this new movie,' or 'new project,' and then have no clue as to what's newsworthy or interesting or different about it, or him, or her."

And be sure that any information you give them is accurate. "If you don't," Pogodin said, "you make them look bad, and they'll never trust you."

If you are looking to have your film reviewed by the magazine's film critic, mail or e-mail them with screening dates and times; send a tape or DVD if appropriate, including the release date, where they can find art, and your contact information.

Newspapers are a bit different. When you're working toward getting newspaper reviews, you will want to notify film editors two to three weeks before your film is opening, letting them know when and where it'll play, and alerting them of press screenings. For feature stories, you will want to pitch writers or the editor at least three to four weeks in advance. (Sometimes feature stories are planned and assigned months in advance.) For papers such as *The New York Times* or *The Los Angeles Times*, give yourself even more time. And, again, remember your pitch should be *an idea*, original and compelling, and not just a synopsis. A good idea for a *story*. Not just a story on your movie.

Either include screening dates and times, or a tape or DVD, and where they can find photography. (We can't say often enough how important pictures are.)

For national weekly publications, pitch story ideas to one of their editors (check the masthead). Send information, and tape or DVD, four to six weeks in advance. Know the format of the magazine, and pitch ideas for particular columns and sections.

Most major cities have alternative weeklies. Pick one up and check out the masthead. Pitch your film story to the film editor, and send opening information and your contact info. For reviews, make contact two to three weeks in advance. For feature story ideas, give yourself three to five weeks.

If you don't have stars, or a compelling news angle, we hate to tell you: Television is worse than a long shot. Unless you're a local-kid-makes-a-movie story (outside of L.A. or New York), or there's a good local hook you can dig up, your chances for TV coverage are slim.

For an independent film, there's very little chance that you will get TV coverage on entertainment shows unless you have stars, and for foreign films with subtitles, it's even more difficult.

That said, Zana Briski, who made *Born into Brothels*, did get on some big shows, but only after Briski's 2004 documentary—about the children of Calcutta prostitutes—had won an Oscar.

Although the *Brothels* case is an example of the value of using a professional, there are disgraceful little tricks of the trade that doughty little filmmakers can appropriate for themselves. Just as a for instance: *Let It Snow* was a very small but charming independent film. Bob Myerson was the publicist on it when it was screening at the American Film Institute Festival in Los Angeles. So he and the filmmakers brought in "snow" and had it fall on Hollywood Boulevard. That got the film onto the ABC affiliate and some other local television. A sense of the outrageous never kept anyone off television.

Some stations or network programs have reviewers. This is one way you *can* get covered. If they have such a personage, send him or her information with your opening date, a copy of the film on tape or DVD, and broadcast clips from your film. The clips of your film are essential, as the station must illustrate the story, and, in virtually all cases, a piece on your film will never get on air unless you have broadcast materials to support it.

What radio shows are appropriate? What kind of entertainment stories do they do? For most art films or independent films, there are not that many shows that make sense. Many public radio stations have culture and politics shows that can be pitched. What are the questions that your film raises? Is there a dramatic question that can be debated? Some radio stations also have film review programs.

Send info and tape or DVD to the program director three to four weeks out, and follow up. Having separate audio clips from the film can be handy, although, in a pinch, they can usually use the screener and pull audio clips.

Up Against the Four-Wall

So let's say your film is going to open in a theater, be it through a distributor, or by being four-walled. You will most likely want to make sure either that your distributor has retained a professional publicist or that the theater's publicist is working on your film's behalf.

"Almost all films, whether they have a distributor or not," said Manohla Dargis of *The New York Times*, "have a publicist working on them, whether it's one hired by the distributor or one that works at the theater, even if it's the Two Boots Theater"—the Two Boots being a valiant little movie house in Manhattan's East Village. Dargis added, "I would not recommend anyone do it themselves," she said of such self-promotion. "People send me tapes and I'll never get to them. When I was at the *LA Weekly*, we actually stopped reviewing movies that were four-walled. They were usually so bad.

"There are some things that are going to look good to David [Ansen] and me," she said, using the *Newsweek* critic as an example. "Like, if it's playing at the Film Forum, I'm generally going to assume it's a notch above; we know that it's probably of good quality." Of Karen Cooper, Film Forum's director, Dargis said, "She's like a curator. I feel that way about some small distributors, too—Kino [the New York City–based distributor], for instance, has really interesting taste."

But even if the self-distributing moviemaker is in a theater whose own reputation enhances the film, every theater's publicist operates differently, and some may be set up only to get reviews. And since you're not paying them, they don't work for you; be sensitive: Collaborate with them without crowding them. Keep them enthused about your film—brainstorm with them, creating story ideas and angles. But always remember: This is their area of expertise. Learn how to be involved, and, at the same time, motivate.

And don't think money will make all the difference, either. Greg Laemmle, president of Laemmle Theatres and cofounder of Laemmle/Zeller Films (with Steven Zeller), a new alternative in distribution for filmmakers, has seen filmmakers who are self-distributing spend their money unwisely.

"You see filmmakers who come in," he said, "and they've collected a bunch of money somehow, and they think this levels the playing field, because now they can have big ads. The reality is, they need to do the groundwork to establish that the film is worth seeing.

"Yes, they have big ads in the paper," Laemmle said, "but it doesn't translate into box office. The most successful four-walls have often been ones where people don't have a lot of money to spend, so they're forced to do a lot of the grassroots publicity work that pays off for the 'smaller films.' It's not to say that having a little extra money on those films wouldn't have helped, but the filmmakers did the appropriate groundwork, and really aided the success of the film."

What makes the difference, as he and others well know, is the personal touch.

"One that sort of went out in a quasi-distribution arrangement, but where the filmmaker was actively involved, was *Broadway: The Golden Age* by Rick McKay," Laemmle said of McKay's 2003 tribute to Broadway greats. "Rick had played a lot of film festivals—not necessarily A-list film festivals, but very appropriate festivals for the film. And he collected e-mail addresses of people who would come up to him after the festival screenings and say, 'We loved your film. What's going to happen with it?'

"He'd get their e-mail addresses," Laemmle said. "And he was also collecting addresses on his Web site, which was up and running very early. It wasn't a super fancy site, but it served a purpose. And he was able to use direct e-mail as an incredibly effective tool to let people know where the film was playing, when it was coming, and how to garner support. Because it was all personality driven—he met the fans, asked them to 'Tell your friends.' He recognized that every person who said they liked the film was a potential representative of ten more customers. He engaged them in that way, and brought them into the fold, and that's a very effective use of new media, or whatever it's called, by using the Internet in that way."

Broadway: The Golden Age was aimed at a particular demographic, and McKay played to it.

"There was some advertising," Laemmle said. "It's not like there was no money. But the advertising disappeared after a week or two, and the grosses would still kind of be pushed by another e-mail blast—'We've moved from Theater X to Theater Y in Los Angeles. Also all you L.A. fans be aware of that, and by the way I'm going to be at the theater doing a Q&A with whoever.' And you would see the numbers all of a sudden pop. So it was not just the Q&A, but using a combination, as a direct outreach to an audience base. And that's something that someone who's self-distributing a film can do. If people like the film.

"Actually," Laemmle added, "Sandy Dubowski did it before Rick, with *Trembling Before G-d*," a 2001 documentary about the quandary faced by gay orthodox Jews. "That's a case," Laemmle said, "where there are very specific niche audiences, and though they had a distributor, and they had a publicist, all that grass roots stuff is really time-consuming, but works more if it comes from the filmmaker personally. It makes people feel connected and invested."

Laemmle added, "Recognizing that your film is a niche film doesn't have to define it, or limit it, necessarily, to that niche. But you want to make sure, first and foremost, that you cover that ground. As much as they wanted to say—and did say—that *Trembling Before G-d* was for every audience, they recognized that you had to hit Jewish groups, you had to hit gay groups. It's the old political adage, Mind Your Base."

Nothing beats filmmakers pressing the flesh, or making themselves available to do Q&As after each showing. "*Paris Is Burning* did tremendous business," said Karen Cooper, "and really hadn't been seen except at a couple of festivals. Nobody made much of a fuss over it and [director] Jennie Livingston, to her credit, realized the film had tremendous potential.

"She did a fabulous job making appearances with it," Cooper said of *Paris*, the 1990 doc about the cross-dressing balls of uptown New York. "She was smarter than I. We had just opened here [on Manhattan's Houston Street] and now had three screens—Watt Street [the old locale] was two calendared screens—and Jenny really was part of my education in how to keep a film running. And it ran six or seven months. And in its last week made more than twenty thousand dollars."

Andrew Jarecki did the same, running to and from theaters in the opening week of *Capturing the Friedmans* (2003) in Los Angeles. Jarecki, an exceptionally smart fellow who knew that Los Angeles is a rough place to open an art film, did what he could, with a film largely about pedophilia and how it affected public perception during a late '80s case in Great Neck, New York.

For smaller films, Dargis said, "If you're not attached to some sort of name distributor, a lot of critics are suckers for the underdog, and they will absolutely grade on a curve. They won't actually say 'This movie's terrible.' And if you can start with a few good critics, and build from the bottom up, they start thinking, 'Well, these people liked it. . . .'

"And there are definitely ways to work it," she added. "There are definitely filmmakers that can really get their films out there. Greg Pak had a film called *Robot Stories* [2003] that he got to play in major houses, and he went to lots of different film festivals.

"It's amazing you can work people's sympathies to keep building momentum for your movie," she said. "And after building and building, he got on [NPR's] *Fresh Air*—and I still don't know how he got half an hour with Terry Gross. It's really how you decide to work these angles."

Even if you have a distributor, the company's marketing dollars will most likely be carefully budgeted. So personal appearances with your film can only help generate exposure for the film. It also helps to get audience members personally invested in seeing your movie succeed, and can really help it rise above the others. Face it: There are five to ten films that will open in a city like Minneapolis every weekend—a handful of studio films and a few independents. Visiting the city can help compel the press to write about your film, as opposed to some of the others. If you have a distributor, they will organize this for you in a strategic way, timed to your film's release there.

Laura said, "When we worked on Peter Greenaway's *The Pillow Book* [1996], we really wanted to put Peter on the road to the major cities, so we put together a tour through which he could present his movie to film societies, museums, and cinematheques. Dennis Bartok of the American Cinematheque in Los Angeles put together a retrospective that could travel to any city or establishment that was interested. We mapped out and organized a tour of some twenty-odd cities, through which we could elevate the profile of both the film and Peter, and Peter could do press in all of these markets. We literally worked with all of these film centers, museums, and schools and asked that they split among them the cost of Peter's travel, literally dividing up the cost of the ticket, and requesting a check. By doing so, money that would have been spent on airfare and hotels could then be used in advertising for the film."

The Pillow Book was released by CFP (Cinepix Film Properties), now Lions Gate Films, and though Greenaway was a filmmaker who was well known, it was mostly by cinephiles, other experimental filmmakers, and critics. Although he is prolific and his work is admired, it is esoteric and for a very defined audience. Miramax had released one of his previous films The Cook, The Thief, His Wife and Her Lover (1989), so sophisticated audiences knew his name.

For John Maybury's Love Is the Devil—a 1998 film about the life of the painter Francis Bacon, starring Sir Derek Jacobi—a similar tour was put together for the film, and again the costs were split. And though Greenaway and Maybury are arty filmmakers, it has become extremely important for the filmmakers and/or cast to go and tour for their film. Most films do not fit in this museum–film society category, but most cities have film festivals, cinematheques, schools, etc., that can contribute to travel and accommodations.

Be creative, and ambitious—there are groups that would love to screen your film, and would help pay to get you there. Plan it so that you're in that market a few weeks before your film will open, so that you can benefit from the word of mouth, and do press before your opening.

12

The Marketplace
Finding Your Audience

Although far better known for his intellectual thrillers and even his collaborations with filmmakers (notably Carol Reed and *The Third Man*), Graham Greene was also a sometime film critic—a sideline during which he once cited the "totsy" allure of Shirley Temple's "ample rump" and got sued for it (and lost!).

Had he not been a world-class novelist, Greene would probably have wielded his critic's pen in darkest obscurity. Although his reviews were strictly in the mainstream, his collected targets include a huge number of films that even the most serious cinephiles would have trouble remembering now, nor would they want to. (The same can be said of the collected criticism of James Agee.) Even content-hungry cable has yet to unearth a lot of these masterpieces. What this means for today's novice filmmaker is not good, not good at all.

THE MOVIES—those for which one actually left one's house—were the chief source of mass entertainment in Greene's TV-less, DVD-less, iPod-less world. But if there's a common plaint among critics today, it's that too many movies are opening now—too many, at least, for the good ones to get the attention they deserve.

This doesn't seem to be an accident: The pipeline of product from Hollywood needs to remain a conduit in action—the plumbing needs to stay regular, so to speak. Clogs will not be tolerated. Neither will sluggishness: If you don't kill 'em on your opening weekend, you're off the screen the next. (In New York, and perhaps elsewhere, films have been bumped from screens on their opening *night* to make room for the latest Hillary Michelle Lohan epic that has them spilling over from Theater 3.) A movie that needs time to build an audience—or doesn't have a multimillion-dollar P&A budget or a star to kick-start the release—is in a dire predicament indeed. To point out that the imperiled film is very often an independent one is to state the obvious, especially to us conspiracy theorists.

Whether a filmmaker gets a full-on theatrical release or not, he or she should know this: The theatrical marketplace has changed immensely over the past ten years, and there are so many movies opening that it's hard to make a ripple. Though they may have gotten a decent theatrical distributor on board, this is only the beginning.

"The reality of the marketplace is that a very, very small percentage of films actually become successful in terms of making money," said agent Cassian Elwes. And yet, he said, "success is relative. To me, a successful release of a movie is a movie that creates enough excitement about it that people eventually will see it either in theaters or in other ways. . . . Your expectations have to be tempered; you can't compete with *War of the Worlds* and *Batman Begins* and whatever. It's just not going to happen. So success for an independent film means a film that does more than three or four million dollars. People get caught up in [the fact that their film] didn't make a hundred million dollars, but that's not what success for an independent film is. Success for an independent film is just actually getting distribution in the first place, and then it's getting good reviews, and for people to be talking about it. The big box-office success is just the icing on the cake, really."

Filmmakers should brace themselves. "For many films, it's important to manage expectations as to how well a film will do, and to disconnect one's opinion of the film and its worth from its ultimate success or failure at the box office," said Jeff Levy-Hinte, producer, Antidote Films. "There are films that have done better than I thought, and films that I absolutely adored that didn't do as well. It's always so hard to know."

Sometimes, the context of what's happening in the world can affect a film's impact, in a good or bad way. Sony Classics copresident Michael Barker remembers a particularly drastic case.

"I saw *In the Bedroom* at Sundance 2001, and I found it an extremely well-made film, brilliantly acted, brilliantly directed," he said. "But I was very hesitant about what a picture like that would do in the marketplace, because it didn't feel like the right moment for a film that dark—it had a lot to do with revenge, which I thought might divide audiences. And what was interesting was at Sundance there was a critic—who will remain nameless—who basically reflected that which I have just said. And between the time it showed at Sundance, and the time the film opened, was 9/11.

"And after 9/11," Barker remembers, "I was reading a review by this critic and it was an incredibly positive review—this same person who told me very different things early on. And I spoke to this critic and he told me, 'You know, we're in a very different place after 9/11. This idea of revenge has different ramifications at this moment, and I'm thinking of this movie in a different context.'

"That's probably something that couldn't ever be replicated—let's hope—but the fun is in the speculation of where audiences are. In that particular story, I remember after that horrific event occurred I saw deeper, darker more dramatic movies as being more accessible than they were before. And there are certain movies we had after that event that we felt did really, really well—*Last Orders, 13 Conversations About One Thing*—and there seems to be, in the last few years, more of an openness on the part of the audience for deeper, darker subjects. I saw that in *War of the Worlds*. I don't think Steven Spielberg would have made that same movie with that same script five years ago."

The argument as to whether the movies change with the times, or actually change their times, is an endless one. The answer is probably a bit of both. But this is a cultural question, not a business one. The rules of business are a bit more stable. Good films don't necessarily do well; filmmakers may not, in the end, really do themselves a favor by hitting the theaters.

Manohla Dargis of *The New York Times* recalled that Przemyslaw Reut, the guy who did *Paradox Lake*, won a lot of awards and money at festivals. "I think it's a lovely movie," she said, "but I don't know who would pay to go see it." And Eric Eason, the guy who made *Manito*, said something interesting, perhaps even perverse: He said he would actually rather go to festivals than have a small distributor. "'What am I going to do, get a week at the Quad?'" he remembers thinking. "And who's going to show up? Less than a thousand people? If you go to festivals, you get to share your film, and the audiences really love you, maybe get money at the gate, maybe win something, travel all around the world, and get put up."

A good reality check is supplied by Cinetic Media cofounder John Sloss. "Unless you have a slamming film that's going to blow a theatrical distributor away, you are basically mortgaging whatever ancillary value you have to underwrite the P&A [prints and advertising], the theatrical P&A. So you should understand: The distributor will act like it is their risk, but basically what they're doing is, they're taking the assured ancillary value and they're applying it— since they get to recoup the P&A—against the P&A risk. So if you don't want to roll the dice on whether a film succeeds and recoups its P&A, then you may have to look at the idea of not going out theatrically."

That's a lot of pressure. Obviously, even if you have a theatrical deal, that may not be enough: The film has to reach some level of notoriety in order to generate revenue in its other avenues. But as so many have pointed out in this book, the lure of theatrical release is all but irresistible—and even essential, some say, to profit.

"The profile of a theatrical release heightens the value of a film, especially with specialized film," said Sony Pictures Classics copresident Michael Barker. "In other words, there isn't a revenue stream that can't be enhanced by a theatrical release. The good news is, there are more streams.

"In the old days, when you didn't have video, you did all your business theatrically," Barker pointed out. "What's changed is the flow of the money. Now it's from all these other places. And now the windows between them will be getting shorter because piracy is a real problem. It may not be such a problem with our documentary about Robert McNamara [*The Fog of War*], but it is with *House of Flying Daggers* and the next Almodóvar. With the next Almodóvar, we're going to open it closer to Spain. And the windows are getting narrower and narrower, from opening to video, and from video to pay."

It's hardly the case that every distribution story is a tragedy. In many cases, things actually go right. "I think the most gratifying thing," said Cassian Elwes, "is when a movie finds the right partner, where there's a real excitement on both sides to be in business with each other. The most important thing is to find somebody who's passionate about your movie, then if you can make a good deal with them, even better."

Justin Lin's experience with his film *Better Luck Tomorrow* was, he said, a good one. "I was very involved, and I know I was lucky in that, because MTV was a great partner," he said. "They were very willing to try, and I felt like we got a lot of support, and that's all I could have asked for. I don't know if we did everything right or anything, but the effort was there and people were very passionate, and I was really very involved in everything from the marketing all the way to the platform strategy, and I know that's not always the case."

Director Bill Condon remembers similar experiences with both *Gods and Monsters* and *Kinsey*, which were released by Lions Gate and Fox Searchlight, respectively.

"The actual experience of working with these really talented people at these companies," said Condon, "the marketing people; the publicity people;

Mark Urman and Tom Ortenberg at Lions Gate; Megan Colligan, Nancy Utley, and Peter Rice at Fox Searchlight, all of that in both situations was as close to ideal as I could ever imagine. Just completely open and responsive. Lions Gate was struggling with the trailer, and I brought in a friend. He did one, and they used it—and they wound up using him for years and years. That kind of openness I'd never experienced before.

"I remember such a feeling of pleasure," Condon said, referring to the time after his 1998 *Gods and Monsters* caught on with the public, "because it reminded me of being a kid again when I opened up the *The New York Times*, and there was a tiny little ad, it was like one inch, but it was for *Gods and Monsters* at the Quad, and it said 'seventh month.' It was great. It's so the opposite from the way studio movies are released, to find a home like the Quad in New York, which I had questions about. But Mark Urman and Tom Ortenberg [both then of Lions Gate] argued for it, and were right. It was just amazing."

But once a filmmaker is working with a distributor, he or she should stay engaged, and be an active participant.

"They'll want to and should be involved with everything from the trailer to the poster," said marketing exec RJ Millard, "and the publicity, but we also work with them for talent relations. If we run into any problems, the first person I'm going to call is the director or producer. Beyond that, we really need them to be there to be a resource to talk about the film—because they will have a longer history with the film than we ever will. They will know more about the back-story and about how the actors came aboard; they will know where everyone's from. All of that kind of stuff helps, and it's stuff we can't discover working on a film for six months."

Producer Matthew Greenfield agreed. "It's really important for filmmakers to work closely with the distributor and to completely trust what they do and their process, and work with them to make sure they understand your movie, and listen carefully to how they believe that the audience will respond. You can also help the distributor understand how the director, and the creative people involved with the film, see both your film and your experiences with audiences so they have a better picture of how you think an audience will respond to or will not respond to the film. And, similarly, to help the filmmakers and the people on the movie's side understand what the distributor's plan is and help them feel comfortable."

As a producer, Greenfield continued, "It's important to coordinate your team—your director and all the others involved have to speak with one voice to your distributor so that the distributor isn't hearing from a million different people. Because that's the way you'll get heard the best, and create the best relationship."

Like many distributors, Barker has experienced the dark side of this. "What I have found is that when the filmmaker has other people always be the messenger to or from his or her distributor, that's where things get miscommunicated. One of the biggest problems I've had lately—I kid you not—we had a film not long ago with fifteen producers. And the only way I can beat it is to say, 'I will talk to the filmmaker, but you all have to decide among yourselves who's going to be the spokesperson.' Otherwise, there are so many crossed wires it can be an organizational disaster.

"And that's something that's only occurred recently," Barker said "probably in the last five years. These films come with so many producers that you don't know who has the power and who doesn't. The only way to get by that as a filmmaker is to figure out your presence in the scene and create some kind of mechanism that organizes those producers into one voice, one spokesperson."

In other words, the kind of individuality, singularity, and personality that mark the better films should also mark the better business campaigns. But be real. "You may have a terrific film," said Magnolia's Eamonn Bowles, "but that doesn't automatically mean it's worthy of a full-on Academy campaign or a 2,500-print release. Distributors spend every day trying to figure out how to maximize a film's potential in the landscape of a super-competitive marketplace. And while there are varying degrees of effectiveness, the odds are pretty overwhelming that they are going to have a more levelheaded take on its prospects than the filmmakers would. That being said, get involved and be informed about the release and ask questions."

"The filmmakers may know the most about their film," Millard said. "They are, of course, the creators of the film, and they will have opinions on how they see their film, how it should be positioned, etc. But they have to realize that they see their film one way, and we're trying to sell it in another way."

Filmmaker Kirby Dick (*Sick, Twist of Faith*) recommended starting the "relationship" early. And not to be timid.

"I think it pays—in negotiations or discussions with a distributor, especially early on—to ask a lot of questions," he said. "If they are definitely interested, and the deal looks like it's going to happen, it really helps to be involved and, either through your producers rep or directly, to stay in contact with a number of people there, so that you can be involved in the decisions they are making on your film's behalf. Each film is different, and a filmmaker's perspective is valuable. Just because a filmmaker may not be experienced in distribution doesn't mean he doesn't have a really important role to play."

It can happen that a film is a good film, but people don't know what to do with it—they don't know how to market it—and, sometimes in the midst of all the struggle between strengths and weaknesses, the distributor, instead of concentrating on the strengths, gives up and throws in the towel. Which almost happened on one of producer Scott Macaulay's films.

"The distributor decided to shelve it and go straight to video," he said. "We convinced them to let us go back and do more work on the film and bring on a new editor. We did that work and were also able to show it to another distributor who agreed to pick it up from the company that originally financed it. But it was a film that was otherwise destined to vanish off the face of the map.

"It can be a very short distance between success and failure," he said. "I've certainly been involved with films that had really bleak and dark moments. But sometimes, when it seemed that no one was ever going to see a film that we had worked very hard on, something has turned around. And the film has gotten out in the world in a good way."

Would it be an understatement to say that even if you have a distributor, an ideal relationship, and a unified field theory about where, when, and how a film will be marketed, that things can go awry?

"A director said to me recently," recalled Macaulay, "'All I thought I had to do was make a good film. I didn't realize there was all this other stuff.'"

"Just be aware," said director Gregg Araki, "that finding a distributor, doing publicity, and overseeing distribution is another, sometimes onerous, part of the filmmaking process—like production, post, etc. It's a long haul, but very important to the life of your movie."

"If you're releasing an independent film, you will most likely not have a budget to buy a lot of media," said RJ Millard. "Your primary way to let audiences know about the film is through publicity. For most art films, it's all daily newspapers and alternative weeklies. We've had filmmakers and actors who have done the festivals, have done lots of interviews, and they hit this point where they feel like, they're the director, they're actors, they don't want to be doing interviews. They shouldn't have to be doing them. All the questions are the same. They feel like they've been having the same conversation for days.

"But this is two-thirds of the job," he said. "Promoting the movies is the only thing that can make them work, unless you don't care if nobody sees it.

Don't try to find a buyer, don't take it to a film festival, don't try to get it released, if you're not up for it. If you want it to get out into the world, and you want people to see your film, that is a six- to nine-month process."

In Hollywood terms, it's often more the rule than the exception that a star or director is doing press long after a movie has wrapped, and it's quite often obvious that the enthusiasm of the filmmaker has, shall we say, been tempered by time. The same is true in Indieville, except there's more at risk. And the feeling of enthusiasm on the part of an interviewer, or even a public audience, shouldn't be dampened by boredom on the part of the filmmaker, just because he's been flogging his product for months.

"The director, the actors—they need to be really prepared to work in order to make the film successful," said independent producer Jeff Levy-Hinte. "The distributor will have its publicity plan and needless to say, it generally doesn't include a press junket at the Four Seasons. It generally includes a lot of little hops, skips, and jumps all over the country in sometimes obscure places, and sometimes only for a handful of people. But it's like running for public office: Every single person you see, if you're able to affect them in some way, and positively predispose them to see the film, that's another vote, another ticket that's going to sell. That kind of on-the-ground, aggressive, tireless energy is critically important. I really try to impart that to the directors, that you really can't rest on your laurels, no matter how good people say the film is. At least with films of this level."

Sometimes working it too much can be discouraging to a distributor, but pure perseverance can pay off.

"Julie Dash had this film, *Daughters of the Dust*, and she couldn't get arrested," recalled critic Amy Taubin. "I can't remember if Sundance was the first place it played; maybe it was. People didn't respond, and everyone told her it was dead. Then she got into Chicago, and she really worked it. I think she got there two weeks before and called every community center, every radio station, and there was a market there that was underserved for exactly that film. It was middle-class, extremely well-educated African-Americans who read Toni Morrison but did not have a single film they wanted to see.

"The film sold out its first screening," Taubin said, "it sold out its second screening, and there were lines of people that were turned away."

And what did distributors say? "You've used up your audience."

"At one point, Kino got involved," Taubin said of the respected New York distributor and film catalog company. "I can't remember if they got involved before or after it got to the Film Forum. But Dash came to New York, I put her on the radio three weeks before; it took off incredibly. I think Karen [Cooper] could only show it for two weeks; they didn't have the tickets computerized then. People would come in to buy tickets at seven A.M., and they were busing in matinee ladies from New Jersey. Up to two years ago, it ended up being, I think, the largest moneymaker Kino had had up to then. This was a film that people said, 'No one's gonna touch it.'"

But she added, "There are also people who are working it who don't look like they're working it. I think Jonathan Caouette [director of *Tarnation*] really worked it. He had a fantastic story and he had a fantastic movie. That movie could have easily gotten stuck at gay and lesbian film festivals and could have never gotten out of there. But I think he knew that he wanted something else for that movie, and he went out and got it."

A filmmaker once said to an audience before her film unspooled, "Thank you for coming. I have always considered the act of filmmaking in two parts. One is making the film, and the other, which completes the process, is sharing it with an audience. Thank you for coming to see the film, and thank you for completing me."

OK, she didn't say this in English, and we're not even sure if she really even said it, because we heard it through a translator. But the idea is something to be remembered—unless a filmmaker is making a film purely for him- or herself. The film opened in theaters, nobody went to see her film, so perhaps she's out there somewhere, kind of half a person.

But if you want to be "completed" as a filmmaker, you have to identify your audience. And you have to come up with something more specific than "the arthouse audience" or "independent film lovers." Unless your film is *Sideways*, it's simply not enough; very few films achieve that level of critical recognition. Say that there are eight to ten other independent films opening the same day as yours, and imagine that most people will choose only one film to see on a given weekend, if that. Which film will they choose? Identify specific core audience(s) that will be motivated to see your film for reasons other than "I like independent films." Is it about the Holocaust? Is it about any ethnic groups? Does it appeal to nerds? Older women? Where do you reach those people who are interested in this subject matter?

"Core audiences will come out the first weekend if you're doing your job," said independent film consultant Peter Broderick, president of Paradigm Consulting. "And, hopefully, they'll come out the second weekend, and they'll keep the movie in theaters long enough to give it the chance to cross over through word of mouth. If nobody comes the night a movie opens and the distributor gives up on the movie by midnight, you're not going to have time for word of mouth.

"*Napoleon Dynamite* is a great example, because Fox Searchlight decided its core audience was nerds," he said. "So Searchlight tried to get every nerd in America to see the film multiple times and did remarkably well.

"Many other recent successes—*Bend It Like Beckham* [2002], *The Passion of the Christ* [2004], *My Big Fat Greek Wedding* [2002], and *Y Tu Mamá También* [2001]—also began by attracting core audiences. Even if it isn't obvious at first, there may be a core audience out there that can be reached with enough imagination and effort.

"If you've got a core audience, they're probably already organized online, probably hanging out at certain Web sites."

The truths are sometimes harsh—it is very difficult to connect with a certain group of filmgoers and, even if you do, will that audience be enough to keep a film in theaters long enough to reach a broader demographic?

"If you look at the numbers of the people who actually pay attention to the ads," said RJ Millard, "you'll find that our segment of the audience, they read the articles, and they've been trained to ignore advertising because they are skeptical; they know it's trying to sell them something. If they're reading an article, they take it as an endorsement—whereas an ad is paid for, and they know it. If you did a survey of the mainstream audience, and you asked them questions to gauge whether or not they're going to see a movie, it's all about advertising. If you look at a specialty audience, it's the reviews, word of mouth, and trailer play."

You can't get a specialized audience—which is generally more highly educated, and far more discriminating about what they like and where they choose to eat, and how they choose to spend their time—to go see a film they've heard is bad. The word of mouth that happens around these films happens so fast, and the indie film community is too small. Yet "if you create a really bad poster or really bad trailer, those things can be overcome if the reviews and the word-of-mouth are good," Millard said.

Think about it. "By the time the movie hits theaters, you've heard whether it's good or bad. And so have they," he said. "You can't fool the audience anymore. Not for arthouse films. You go to see *Super Size Me* [2004], because friends tell you it's hilarious, or *What the Bleep Do We Know* [2004], because someone told you it changed their life.

"Never underestimate your audience," Millard said, "and don't ever think you really know your audience."

Sometimes a film comes out of nowhere, and, because it's something people simply want to see, it works. *What the Bleep Do We Know*, which was about modern spirituality, is a good example. For this film, Millard said, "The audience was indefinable. We had no idea where these people came from, but they were everywhere. The film grossed over eleven million dollars."

And yet, all the reviews were two stars or worse. "No paper in the country would cover the film, until it was a huge success," he said. "But the audience spoke and said 'This is something we're interested in; we are interested in this subject, we like the way it's presented.'"

"Your film is your best marketing tool—your film and the people around it," said Millard, who helped bring success to films like *Super Size Me* and *Ladies in Lavender*. "Sometimes the only chance you have is good word of mouth. It is the cheapest form of marketing you can get.

"If you're afraid to give it away to eight hundred people in New York City, then forget it," he said. "If you're worried about eight hundred people or eight thousand dollars—well, you're not going to succeed on eight thousand dollars. For a modestly budgeted film in New York, you're talking at least sixty thousand dollars in advertising for one week. You've got to bring in a lot more than eight hundred people to make that money back, and in order to establish longevity and generate word of mouth, that takes time. You can't compete with television advertising or with stars that may draw people in."

Generating publicity for the smaller films has become more and more difficult—it's simply harder and harder to break through the clutter. The reality is that there can be ten to fourteen films opening on a given weekend, and editors do not necessarily feel they need to assign a review of *every* movie on that list, let alone a feature story.

Do good films slip through the cracks?

"It's a paradox," said John Sloss. "Too many films get released. Nobody could argue with the fact that the market can't support ten films a weekend, and there are deserving films that don't get picked up."

"Absolutely," agreed Michael Barker, copresident of Sony Classics, "especially in this environment, when so many companies are looking for the home run and that's all they're looking for—that picture that will make a fortune. So they don't pay attention to the smaller pictures. They write off smaller pictures much easier than they would otherwise, if they weren't in that frame of mind. I'd actually say we pick up fewer films, believe it or not, than we used to—it's about half our slate now, between a third and half our slate now.

"We're starting a lot earlier in the process," he said, meaning the script stage. "But you know, no one really ever had a perfect record on picking films or predicting the marketplace. It's about applying your own expertise and your taste to the quality of the film and then to the speculation about whether the public will see the film. And in that speculation, two things go on: It's speculation about the history of the public's taste in going to movies and about the moment in time when the decision's being made.

"So often," he said, "when a film's released, the moment in time might be really good for that film to succeed or it might be really bad. It could be about surprising world events, it might be a change in taste among people who go to art films, or even among teenagers—I think that's what makes what we do exciting. But I think if you're a filmmaker there are some very important things to be aware of: What's going on at the moment, what's doing well, hazarding a guess about why it's doing well, and the context of the marketplace at the time you're selling the film. It's very important not only what the public is going to see but also what films are selling to companies, what they're selling for. Is it a buyer's market at that moment? Or is it a seller's market?

"Even if you don't have solid answers to those questions," he said, "just the fact that those questions are being asked will help you make much more informed decisions on your own film."

It's a jungle out there—an independent–art film survival of the fittest. But hasn't it always been? And isn't the distribution network widening?

"One of the basic questions I always get asked," said Sundance director Geoff Gilmore, "or rather, one of the arguments that is often made to me, is 'Oh God, we need more distribution companies.' I say, 'Do you know how many distribution companies are out there?' They'll say twenty-five. I'll say, 'Eighty. Let me show you the eighty film companies that released a film last year.'"

Gilmore conceded that "forty of them had no resources whatsoever. And only the top twenty-five or so usually have some reputation or connections and network. So if your purpose is to figure out a way to get to those companies, you may, in some cases, be better off going directly to a Wellspring or to Marcus Hu and letting them look at your work personally, rather than deciding that you have to put your film on a festival platform."

But the point is there are options. "It seems to me that eventually, anything good does get picked up," said Manohla Dargis of *The New York Times*. "It does seem like, with all the micro distributors, people I've never heard of are just coming out of the woodwork. Does anyone need to see all of these movies? I personally feel there's just too much product at this point. I don't know. I think if a movie is good, and enough of us have seen it, someone will find that movie because there are too many of us looking for them. Whether the film will make money, now that's another thing. But I don't believe there are any real undiscovered treasures. The net is so thick with so many people. Everyone's hunting."

Paul Federbush of Warner Independent agreed. "For the most part, I do think good films find their way into the marketplace," he said. "Of course, there are going to be some things that slip through the cracks but by and large the good things rise to the top and find a release one way or another."

When a film that deserves to be seen is not, Federbush added, "it's usually a well-made, beautifully directed film that's completely inaccessible to an audience, that would probably make one hundred thousand dollars. There's a cost to working on those movies. Mostly they're really good, but really arthouse."

"I think that theatrical is such a crapshoot these days," said Scott Macaulay. Decisions are not so much related to the quality of the film but the perceived marketability of the film, or its perceived value in ancillary markets. A number of business decisions that go into whether something should be a theatrical release or not— I think a lot of those things don't actually have much to do with the artistic merit of the film. The presence or [absence] of certain kinds of companies—like Cowboy Releasing, the [now defunct] company that released *George Washington*," he said of David Gordon Green's acclaimed 2000 indie. "If that film were to come out today, who would be releasing it?

"People need to throw away the status symbols of the past, like theatrical distribution, and realize that there are new technologies and new markets, new ways that people want to have their films delivered to them, and the audience actually wants interesting content that gets to them in that way. I think that there's a real opportunity for people to make an impact through these new distribution channels, and people should learn to think creatively about these new outlets."

Amy Taubin agreed. "Peter Broderick has been going around the world and telling people, 'This is a new idea, this is how you could make it work. Why do you want to give up your first film to a distributor? You'll have no control over it, and it will most likely disappear. If you see any money, you'll be lucky.'

"People can make money," she said, "and I think it works well with documentaries—putting up a Web site, doing their own distribution out of their garage on DVD. There's this guy who made this documentary about motorcycle racing [*Faster*], who made eight hundred thousand dollars selling DVDs out of his garage. And *then* he got a DVD deal from a regular distributor who didn't think he had exhausted his audience."

Peter Broderick believes that before making any distribution deals, filmmakers should develop for each film a unique proactive strategy designed to maximize audience and revenue.

"In the old days," he said, "filmmakers were very reactive. They did the best they could to position the film, create a press kit, get journalists excited, get into festivals, find a [producers] rep, and then hopefully attract distribution offers. They'd basically accept one of these offers. By and large, these offers were pretty conventional in terms of the sequence of things. The distributor would start in a few theaters, see how it played, then have a video release and sell to TV. It was paint by the numbers."

Today, he said, each film has some unique potential in terms of distribution possibilities.

"If a distributor says, 'I'll give you a $150,000 advance for all North America rights for fifteen to twenty-five years,' that may appear to be a pretty good offer," he said. "But your leverage will be much greater if you know you can sell 20,000 DVDs directly from your Web site, making a $20 profit per DVD. If someone offers you $150,000 for all rights but you know that you can bring in $400,000 just from sales from your Web site, then the offer will have to be substantially increased or won't be that appealing.

"For the first time filmmakers have the opportunity to go around the traditional gatekeepers and reach audiences directly, across the United States and around the world. Rather than making overall [all-rights] deals, filmmakers should consider splitting up the rights.

"When you make an overall deal, the distributor determines which company will release it on video (usually either their video subsidiary or the video company they have an output deal with). Video is where most of the revenue is these days. If people can break even theatrically, that's considered a success. The revenue from TV sales is often limited.

"If filmmakers split up the rights, they can select their video distributor. They can consider possible video partners, trying to find ones that have successfully distributed films like theirs. Then they should talk to filmmakers who've worked with those distributors, trying to find one that has been really effective and responsive and paid them the money owed. They can't make this critical choice if they make an overall deal.

"If filmmakers start with solid distribution strategies aimed at significant core audiences, their chances of attracting private investors to finance their films should be much greater."

And that will increase the filmmaker's chances of raising money from nontraditional sources, because any investor who's been offered the opportunity to invest in various independent films also knows that getting zero back on his investment is a high probability—in the traditional way of doing things. If that investor knows that there is an avid core audience for this subject matter, and the filmmaker has convinced the investor that he or she can sell 20,000 copies off the Web site—making $400,000—and if the budget of the film is $800,000, then the investor's risk has just been halved.

And in a way, the business gets easier each time out. Or at least you are equipped with more experience.

"As you continue to do it, you do understand the system more," Scott Macaulay said. "Producing, to some degree, is about making mistakes, and then not making them again on your next movie, and then, at a certain point, you've been through enough situations that you know how to handle every kind of situation."

But even if you've made a great film, making your next movie doesn't necessarily get easier—which makes following your vision all the more valid a course.

"It sounds like a fable or something," said Richard Peña, who, besides directing the New York Film Festival, is professor of film at Columbia University, "but I think the most successful students I've had at Columbia are the people who really made the films they wanted to make. Nothing kills an artist more than trying to make what you think the market wants. Or what you think distributors will like. I think those films are easy to see through, and while they might be made with a certain amount of skill, they really have no life.

"Those filmmakers who've had a certain vision or idea and have been able to pursue it and get it out there have been successful. For example, the couple who made *American Splendor*, Robert [Pulcini] and Shari [Springer Berman]. For most people they'd be considered a great success. I mean, the film really did well, won prizes at international film festivals, it was well reviewed, but on the other hand, I know they're still struggling. Yes, the doors may be a little more open to them, but even a success like that doesn't mean now you can write your own ticket. Nowadays, unless you have a mega-hit, something legendary like a *Pulp Fiction* or something like that, and have someone behind you like Harvey Weinstein, it's going to be a continuing struggle. You can't just sit back and go into cruise mode."

Still, Springer Berman said, it's important when making your next film to "think of something different and new that's very specific to you and your personality and your experience. It's just not that exciting to see carbon copies of things that have happened already. Try to do something different and interesting. And don't make a calling card for Hollywood. Make something that's really unique to yourself that you couldn't make in Hollywood. Don't look at last year's Sundance and try to make a movie that's like the movie that won. Make what you want to make."

Case Studies
Things You Can Learn Just by Looking at 'Em

How do you spell success? Sometimes it's L-U-C-K. Sometimes it's S-W-E-A-T. Sometimes, in fact almost always, it's a C-O-M-B-O P-L-A-T-T-E-R. The following are general anecdotes. You may just be able to glean some good knowledge from the experience of others.

Finding Champions: *The Cruise*

Laura. You may or may not have heard of *The Cruise*, which is why I'll begin with it. The moral of this story is that some films are really harder than others and have a lot of disadvantages. A black-and-white documentary about an eccentric, albeit profound and poetic soul who happens to be a tour guide on a bus in New York City does not scream box-office jackpot. But all it takes is one person at a time to see it, be won over, and make the little engine just a little stronger.

The Cruise is about Timothy "Speed" Levitch, a philosophical motormouth whose stream-of-consciousness bus-tour spiels around Manhattan were the kind of thing you might script, but probably couldn't. As a character, he was sublime, eccentric, a super-active presence with his mind in fifth gear.

The film did not get into Sundance, which was a huge disappointment. It was then submitted to the Los Angeles Film Festival, and was accepted. Bennett Miller, the film's director, and Kevin McLeod and J. B. Miller, the film's producers, and I started urging buyers to come to the film's first screening.

The festival also gave the film a prefestival press screening, which we accepted with some apprehension: Would it be well received in a half-empty room? Would it get buyers to pay attention? The screening went off fairly well, getting the film good reviews in most of the daily publications, *The Hollywood Reporter*, and the alternative weeklies.

Then it was time for the film's first public screening, to which any potential buyers could come. Looking at the festival screening schedule, we found that *The Cruise* was screening at the same time as a world premiere of a narrative feature. All of the buyers except for John Hegeman, then with Artisan Entertainment , went to that film and missed a really enthusiastic screening of the film. Without missing a beat, we asked all of the buyers if they could make a screening the following week, a few days after the festival was done. We booked a fifty-seat room, let all the buyers know when and where the screening was, and packed the room with friends and anybody we could get to come. The film screened really well there—the buyers liked it, but nobody was convinced that there was an audience for it.

From there, the film went immediately to New York for DocFest. I invited a few journalists to come and see it—people that could make a difference, or "champion" the film. John Anderson from *Newsday* and Jeff Gordinier from *Entertainment Weekly* came out on a hot Saturday afternoon to see it, and they loved it. Slowly the momentum was building. Meanwhile, Hegeman, who already liked the film, heard those positive reactions and that helped win him over.

The film went on to win huge victories—one critic at a time, one screening at a time. Then came Toronto.

For a number of reasons—including the fact that it had played a few other North American festivals—the press screening for *The Cruise* was scheduled for the first day of the festival, at 9:00 A.M. As most journalists were just arriving, very few could have gotten credentialed in time to make a 9:00 A.M. screening. The hour would have been bad enough on a regular day, much less on the first day.

It was the day before the press screening and I was desperate. I had put flyers in all of the press boxes and hung out by the press office, trying to catch anyone walking through, but nobody had checked in yet. I called journalists in their hotel rooms, but had no luck reaching anyone—they simply had not arrived in Toronto yet. So, that night, I did what any desperate film publicist would do. I took a deep breath and called Roger Ebert in his hotel room, gave him twenty words about the film, told him it was screening at nine the next morning. He said he just arrived and that he did not have his credentials yet. I told him I would be at the theater and would make sure he got in without a problem. He was really nice and said he would try, but after I hung up with him, I had doubts. I slipped a polite note and press kit for the film under his hotel room door and went to bed.

The next morning, I got to the theater nice and early so I could introduce myself to the theater manager and explain that I was expecting a journalist, but he hadn't had time to get his credentials yet. I was really nervous, because sometimes festival staff, particularly early on in a festival, can be really strict. They let him in, thankfully, because that morning the only people in the 350-seat theater were Roger and one other journalist, Amy Longsdorf from the *Allentown Morning Call*. I remember this distinctly because it was a horrific thought. There were only two journalists in the whole room.

Roger enjoyed the film, wrote about it, and more theaters across the country booked the film because of it.

Stacking Your Deck: *Kissing Jessica Stein*

Laura. A producer I'd never met, Brad Zions, called me one day and asked if I'd look at a film he was involved with, *Kissing Jessica Stein*. He was referred by an old colleague in New York named Nathan Nazario.

He asked me to come and see it at an edit bay where they were still working on it. Eden Wurmfeld, someone I had known for years, was one of the producers on the film. I asked Eden and Brad if I could bring Jeff Dowd along.

Jeff and I both enjoyed the film and felt there was something there. It was smartly made—well written, and the performances were top-notch. It was still a difficult film in many ways—no stars, and potentially tricky subject matter: A romantic comedy involving a bisexual woman and a straight woman. But it was good. Jeff made notes on how it could be an even better film, and he and the filmmakers collaborated on making it just that.

The screening we went to in that edit bay was also a research screening, of sorts, but with friends of the court. Their comments, as well as Jeff's, were really useful and could help make a good film even better.

As soon as we got out of the edit bay, I asked the producer if they'd considered sending it to the Los Angeles Film Festival; the deadline was quickly approaching. Eden and Brad and I met to talk about the festival, other options, etc. They submitted the film, it got in, and Jeff and the filmmakers went back to work on the film. With only a few weeks, they had reshoots to do, some cutting. . . a lot of work.

Some other interesting tidbits: Though the festival offered the film a press screening, we declined. For a film like this, where audience reaction would really help win the press and buyers over, a press screening held before the public screening was not worth the risk. We would forgo the prefestival write-ups, the capsule reviews, etc., so that we could try to get any press that would come into a public screening.

So we hand-picked twenty or so journalists (gay and straight) and carefully—

and personally—invited them to see the film. We let them know it was a fun, smart film, and that they should come and just enjoy themselves.

Luckily, reactions were solid and the audience response was really enthusiastic.

Jeff Dowd explained: "*Kissing Jessica Stein* is a really good example of a film that almost worked, three weeks ahead of the world premiere. It's about a straight woman, Jessica Stein, and a bisexual one, and they enter this courtship and the courtship goes on and on and then all of a sudden bang, boom, they break up. One guy at a screening, just forty-five people at somebody's house, said, 'I didn't get the breakup.' And we went, 'Holy shit.'. . ."

What they did involved some very easy fixes, including giving the bisexual woman a scene where she just looks in the mirror. "She had a private moment, and [the audience] knew there was trouble in paradise," Dowd said. "The other thing was, the worst scene in the movie, the final scene where Jessica went meandering to the stoop of her ex-boyfriend's apartment—it was an absurd scene, because it just didn't work."

"One of the things that was recognized very early was right on the surface: Jessica goes and has this relationship and at the end of the movie sends out a message that she's probably not going to be gay. Which could send out a message that it's a choice, it's something you do in college, have a little fling, but it's not a legitimate lifestyle.

"But what they did, in one day of reshooting, was to give the other woman a new girlfriend—they wake up, she has a new mate, which legitimizes how she can have a happy new life after she and Jessica break up. That, and changing the boyfriend scene."

But the changes, as small as they were, were critical because "the film was in danger of alienating the entire gay community, some of the very people the filmmakers had hoped would champion the film."

Our festival strategy had always been to get a good body of support from journalists and editors. I told the actors, the writer, and the director that our objective was not to get all these interviews and photos, that it was not about the publicity, but to get a handful of working journalists, editors, and critics in to see and, hopefully, "champion" the film. This means a lot to buyers, particularly if they are seriously interested in a film. They want to know that there is support for a film when it opens, before they buy it.

In this particular case, *Variety* assigned a new young male critic, Scott

Foundas, to review it. We were disappointed—we were hoping it would be Lael Lowenstein, who by all accounts would have been perfect as an audience for this film. It was the day of the 10 P.M. world premiere screening, and a strange twist of fate would have the review reassigned to Lael. For this film, it was a miracle—all that strange twisting of fate paid off. She loved the film, and, thankfully, so did all the buyers that were at the Directors Guild of America that night, including Nancy Utley of Fox Searchlight.

Norman Baits: *Raise the Red Lantern*

John. This is an example of why persistence can actually be beneficial.

Norman Wang is an impish sweetheart of a man who has a long history in the world of New York film publicity. He originally worked with the late Francine Trevens, a PR legend, on a team that included Sophie Gluck and Cynthia Schwartz—the latter of whom would become Miramax's magician of awards nominations. (Cynthia's all-time coup? Getting director Krzysztof Kieslowski an Academy Award nomination for *Red*.) Norman then had a long business partnership with Sophie. He currently lives in Hong Kong and works for director Wong Kar-wai. He is the guy I would always go to with questions about Asian cinema.

At the Sundance Film Festival 1992, Norman had the unenviable task of promoting a non-American film at America's premiere celebration of American cinema. Never easy: as we've said elsewhere, the press focus there is firmly on U.S. features and docs, and getting anyone to look at, much less write about, an Asian movie was about as likely as avoiding Mormons in Utah.

Norman kept telling me I had to see this movie. "You've got to see this movie," he said. The director was relatively unknown in the United States, but that wasn't likely to remain the case for long, Norman told me. And the fact is, I trusted Norman: Had it been a lot of other publicists, I wouldn't have taken the offer so seriously. As it was, tantalized by the prospect of being ahead of the curve on a Chinese director (Chinese cinema was just about to come into what would be its '90s vogue), I said OK.

"What time?"

"It's at the Prospector Square; I can give you a lift."

"What time?"

"Ten o'clock."

"P.M.?!"

"Uh huh."

Now, in most world capitals, 10 o'clock is not late. In Barcelona, it's about the time they start thinking about dinner. In Park City? It might as well have been 3 A.M. When your first screenings are at 8:30 in the morning, and you're cold, hungry, wet, and tired for much of the day (the oxygen deprivation, Park City being at about 8,000 feet above sea level, has an insidious effect), 10 P.M. is like a parallel universe. You can get jet lag just driving to the theater. It was above and beyond the call of duty. But what the hell.

So we went, and the screening, somewhat predictably, started about an hour late. So now we're at 11 P.M., and the movie starts. The most beautiful woman in the world is on screen for most of it. The movie fulfills that oft-abused word, masterpiece. I'm a happy man.

The film? *Raise the Red Lantern* by Chinese auteur Zhang Yimou, who would go on to make *Story of Qiu Ju, To Live, Shanghai Triad*, and, in more recent years, *Hero* and *House of Flying Drag Queens*. I mean, *Dragons*. The star was Gong Li.

I was very happy I'd not gone to bed.

Thus began an ongoing relationship, of sorts, between me and Chinese film. I wrote about Zhang whenever the opportunity presented itself. Norman never again had to push me to go to a Zhang Yimou screening. Some of his films haven't quite measured up to *Red Lantern*, but who is so consistent? The point was that Norman insisted that I go and I went, and it paid off for everyone.

Especially me.

Steering Into the Clear: *Blue Car*

Laura. *Blue Car* is a good example of a beautifully told but difficult film. It was written and directed by first-timer Karen Moncrieff. It had fairly good indie names in it—David Strathairn, Frances Fisher, and a fantastic new actress named Agnes Bruckner. It was difficult because the subject matter was dark and challenging and also because it had no big stars. It was also difficult because it was in the American Spectrum section of Sundance, which just doesn't get the traffic that the competition does.

In this case, it was a good thing—it kept the expectations low and helped the film become one of those gems to discover. It would just take some persistence in getting press off the beaten (competition) track.

We discussed having a prefestival screening for press, but knew that would be risky. The print would only be ready literally hours before it would need to be shipped to Utah. We had a three-hour window that the film print could actually be in Los Angeles.

We decided to screen for Kenneth Turan before the festival and gave him the heads-up that we'd have a print on this particular day and that we'd love for him to see it, if he had the time. Unfortunately, it was smack dab in the middle of the Christmas–New Year holiday period, but he did make himself available. He, like a few other critics, can be a real supporter and is often really generous with his limited time.

Turan remembered, "It was in the middle of the Christmas holiday vacation. First of all as a film critic, if you take your job seriously—almost every major critic I know takes their job seriously—if you have the time and you're there, you see the film. You sacrifice part of your life to see all these films, because that's the only way to do the job correctly."

It was his seeing the film and writing about Agnes's astonishing performance that gave the film a bit of a lift. And then David Ansen from *Newsweek* came to see it. And one journalist or critic at a time—literally—eventually came.

Miramax bought the film and though it took a while for the film to be released, when it was, the reviews were terrific.

Ed Trip: *The Brothers McMullen*

John. Sometimes you don't have to see a movie to write about it—not if the back-story is good enough. Take the case of Ed Burns and *The Brothers McMullen*. Long before Sundance '95, the festival *McMullen* would win, Burns was getting ink. I'm sorry to say I contributed.

But it was one of those Cinderella stories—sort of—that make newspaper editors salivate. Burns had been working as a techie on *Entertainment Tonight* and put together *McMullen* on a relative shoestring. Then, he had gotten into Sundance. That he was from Long Island made it all the more appealing to *Newsday*. In a preview story about that year's festival, I devoted a lot of space to Burns. He seemed like a nice guy.

And the film got a lot of people's attention, as did Burns's ingenuity. In a laudatory article I found online, you get this type of thing: "Ed did not get permits to film on the New York subway system—he merely carried a hidden camera onto the trains. Likewise, he was fortunate not to be stopped by police when he was filming on New York streets with his conspicuous crew (cameraman, sound man, lighting technician, and actors), since filming in New York requires permits (money) from City Hall."

What Burns wasn't going out of his way to talk about was the fact that his father was a police officer and had been in charge of media relations for the

New York City Police Department. No wonder the cops didn't stop him.

No wonder Jimmy Breslin wrote a rave review of the movie, without ever having seen it.

But back to Sundance: Having already written about Burns, and there being 150 other films to occupy my attention, I had set up an interview appointment with the young director for a few days before the end of the festival. Arriving at the designated time and place, I was met by Burns and by Jeff Hill, his publicist.

"John," Jeff said, "we're really squeezed for time today. Is there any way you can do the interview back in New York?"

I calculated: Deadlines being what they are, there was no way of getting Burns into the paper before the awards ceremony. If he won, an interview back home would probably be better—in fact getting him preawards would almost be counterproductive, especially if he won something. Although no one expected him to win.

Sure, I told Jeff. Yes, I'd wasted time getting to the interview that wasn't happening. I'd missed a movie I might otherwise have seen. But jamming the interview into what then seemed their overloaded schedule wasn't a very appealing prospect, either.

So awards night comes. Burns wins the top prize. We get back to New York. And my editor wants an Ed Burns story. No problem, I say: They've promised me the time.

Call Jeff Hill. Ask about interview. Am told, "Tom Rothman said no more interviews until the movie opens."

Rothman, at the time, was running Fox Searchlight, which had picked up the movie. His thinking made sense—why blow all your publicity before the movie was even close to opening? Still, I wasn't thinking particularly fondly of him at that moment. I was thinking what he might look like pinned to the grille of my car.

And I also wasn't thinking too kindly of Jeff Hill or Ed Burns. I had given them the break—I had an interview set up in advance with an unknown filmmaker and had been asked to postpone it. Once the advantage went to the *Brothers McMullen* people, they had, essentially, screwed me.

The critical thing is, this experience ruined my relationship with Jeff Hill for years.

As a sidebar to this, the features jury at the '95 Sundance was about as loose-lipped as any I've ever encountered. None of them could say enough, later on, about how their decision had been reached—how they'd been so severely split over Tom DiCillo's *Living in Oblivion*, Matt Harrison's *Rhythm Thief*, and James Mangold's *Heavy*, that they'd decided to give *Rhythm Thief* and *Heavy* special jury prizes and the Waldo Salt Screenwriting Award to DiCillo and let a compromise choice, *McMullen*, walk away with the top prize.

Lunacy. To say nothing of what they did for the career of Edward Burns. And to the moviegoing public.

Market Placing: *Waking Ned Devine*

Michael Lawson from mPRm had been hired by First Look to work on *Waking Ned Devine* in Cannes. The film was not in the official festival, but in the market, and getting journalists to pay attention to films in the market, when the festival is more than they can already bear, is not an easy feat.

Market screenings, first of all, can be a waste of time for journalists, particularly critics. Many of the films are not that good; if they were, they'd have been accepted into the festival. Also, without a U.S. release date, why spend the time? And finally, many of the market screenings are private and they don't allow press in, so after running to the Palais and waiting in line, just to be turned away—well, most press don't even bother.

In any case, Michael did ask Kenneth Turan of *The Los Angeles Times* and Lisa Schwarzbaum from *Entertainment Weekly* to come to a screening and made sure they got in. Fox Searchlight—which had had a lot of luck with *The Full Monty*—ultimately bought the film.

Turan explained, "*Waking Ned Devine* was an interesting case. It was in the market at Cannes, which I don't really go to. It's often hard for me to get into market screenings, because I don't get a market badge; we don't always have the budget for it. The interesting thing about being in that room is that there were buyers in there with me. You could feel how commercial this film could be while sitting in this room, and you could almost see dollar signs in the buyers' eyes, leaving the room, but in a good way because it's a wonderful film. It's so rare to come across a film that is available and also commercial."

Knowing When You've Got the Stuff: *L.A. Confidential*

In 1997, Mark Pogachefsky was retained by Warner Bros. to handle *L.A. Confidential*. The film had no stars (at the time, Russell Crowe, Guy Pearce, and Kim Basinger were not big names).

Once the film was accepted into Cannes—which was a surprise for everyone—Mark and former mPRm publicist Eric Kops decided that, rather than hold onto the film and screen it for key critics in France, they would begin screening aggressively in New York and Los Angeles before the festival, allowing the press to free up their schedules a bit and allowing them to forgo the madhouse that is the Cannes press screening. When you have the goods, why hide them? Plus, this tactic definitely engendered good feelings about the movie.

"The movie was opening in the fall, and it was the beginning of May," said Pogachefsky, "and we had just started screening the movie for magazines. And it became apparent really quickly that we had a film that was working in a big way. Then the film got into Cannes, which none of us had planned on. So we decided to open it up right away to press that were going to Cannes and got people in—people who would normally not have gotten in to see it until a few weeks before it would open—dailies, weeklies, etcetera. We had nothing to lose by giving the home team an advantage in going to Cannes. And really: What would we have gained asking them to go and see the film at 8:30 A.M.?"

Buzz Kill: *Dogma*

Laura. Mark (Pogachefsky) and I had been hired by Harvey Weinstein to lend our PR help in selling Kevin Smith's *Dogma*, when Miramax was unable to release it due to its parent company (Disney). It had never been seen, and it was slated to world-premiere at Cannes, under a cloud of controversy with the Catholic Church.

We were told that we wouldn't be able to see the film until Cannes, at the press screening. We insisted that we needed to see the film first if we were expected to work on it, and literally got on a red-eye flight to New York where we saw both *Dogma* and Atom Egoyan's *Felicia's Journey*, and returned the same day to L.A., just in time to catch our flight to France.

Having seen the film, we decided the best way to handle the film was to try and help deflate the controversy before people saw it. Why? Because we believed that the controversy would create a level of expectation that would, in the end, not help the film. How do you deflate controversy? When the subject of the film came up, someone would invariably ask, "So is it really controversial?" And answering very casually, we would say, "Controversial? No, not really. Have you seen it? (knowing they hadn't). . . . It will make you think, and it's full of ideas, but no, I wouldn't say it's controversial." Almost dismissively, just to let a little air out.

They were sincere, real conversations, but the words were carefully chosen to dampen a charged environment.

Dogma sold to Lions Gate.

Everything but the Girl: *Girl 6*

Laura. Arguably, *Girl 6* was not one of Spike Lee's most memorable films, but it was my first Spike Lee film, and I was honored.

Knowing the reaction to the film would be something to overcome, I did the math and figured that that year marked ten years since his groundbreaking *She's Gotta Have It*. I put together a time line and a list of all of his films that included actors and actresses whose careers he launched and gave it the heading "10 Years of Spike" and passed it out at all the screenings. The idea was to draw attention to Spike's career and contributions and to write about him as a figure. Also, as the film's star Teresa Randle was not well known, we tried to find interesting places to do interviews to entice people, as well as to up the chances that the stories would run. We did interviews in wig salons. (It was not easy to convince the Korean wig store owners . . . "Um, no it's not a porn movie. Uh, well yes, it is about phone sex operators. . . ." but that's another story.)

Coalition of the Shilling: *Amélie*

Laura. Mark (Pogachefsky) and I were hired to work on *Amélie*, and as it had already opened to great success in France, it would be ineligible for Cannes. Miramax decided to screen there anyway, as the film was early in its French theatrical run, and the awareness of the title was high. And since Jean-Pierre Jeunet and Audrey Tautou lived in France, it was logistically simple to get them and the press together. The film was not in Cannes, remember, but screening rooms were booked at the Olympia Theater anyway, and we invited journalists to come and see it. We also offered time with the director, in a press roundtable setup. As time in Cannes is always at a premium, when you schedule something, you are always going smack-dab against something else of interest. This was the case—the people with Hal Hartley's film *No Such Thing* would be conducting their interviews at the same time.

We coordinated our efforts with Jeff Hill, who was working on the Hal Hartley film. We joined the two and created a scenario where you could interview them all at the same location, and be done in an hour.

What this enabled us to do was establish a foundation for the film, and also save Jean-Pierre from some wear and tear further down the line.

Tran Figuration: *Cyclo*

Laura. While most have probably never heard of *Cyclo*, I bring this title up because I really loved it and because the late Adam Rogers, the film's distributor at Cinepix

Film Properties, now Lions Gate, had very little in the way of resources to spend. This combination makes you think hard and be resourceful though it's always more work. What we were able to do, however, is worth mentioning.

When Tran Ahn Hung, the film's director, was appointed to be on one of the Cannes juries, this created an opportunity for him to sit down with some of the key press from the United States who normally go to Cannes, and that would be helpful when the film opened.

Sure, it would take some wrangling: getting journalists to see the film before leaving for France months before they would normally need to, working with the festival's protocol office to make sure it was okay with them (as jurors are not supposed to give interviews), and finding a translator and having them see the film so they could translate. Not to mention finding journalists who would, in the height of the Cannes frenzy, be willing to think about a film that would open a few months down the line, and give their time to it.

What was done was devised as a safeguard—if Tran Ahn Hung could not come to the States to promote his film further down the line, it wouldn't be the end of the world. Also, it saved him travel to a few cities, saving the distributor money that would instead be spent on getting the film out.

By the way, speaking of translators, it is very hard to find a good one and asking journalists when they've had a great translator is a good way to find one. Few translators really speak the language of cinema and, should you need one, it pays to find a translator who knows how to translate technical information about filmmaking in general.

Films That Require a Little Ingenuity

Laura. Sometimes, when you don't have a lot of resources, you have to be clever. Sometimes the media just isn't interested in covering your film. For the following films, which had young, up-and-coming casts, but not a lot of hooks to hang anything on, this is what was perpetrated by the always-clever Bob Myerson (currently copresident, dada, and executive vice president—publicity, Tartan).

For Gregg Araki's *Splendor*, a dark but sexy romp, he had the cast do their interviews in bed—just to help make it unusual and different. For *Smiling Fish*, he secured the house where the film was shot and did all of the interviews there. (Luckily, the house was conveniently located in Hollywood.) For *Skins*, Chis Eyre's tale of two Native American brothers, he found a company that had mobile theaters and brought the film to reservations. And he got news out of it. For *Unmade Beds*, he pitched a story that was irresistible: As he was declined on feature stories on any one involved with the film, he pitched *The Los Angeles Times*'s Kathleen Craughwell a night on the town with three single men, including himself. They all went to the *Happiness* premiere in search of—and got—two hits in one, one for *Unmade Beds* and one for *Happiness*.

For a film called *Cemetery Man*, Jeff Raymond put dirt in all of the invitations. When people opened their invites, it sure made an impression, and it did get written about. We sent out pork buns for *Double Happiness*, served Yoo-Hoo! at screenings of *Hold Me, Thrill Me, Kiss Me*, mailed bugs and spiders for *nowhere*, chocolate for *Chocolat*, Jelly Bellies for *American Splendor*, flan for *Real Women Have Curves*. These things are not to sway people, but cheap and fun ways to get attention. I remember Liz Manne, who was at Fine Line, had me working on *Bodies, Rest and Motion*. She had this great idea to have the premiere for the film at IKEA, which was thematically perfect for that film. That kind of thinking helps get additional coverage for a film, though I wouldn't say it brings people to theaters. It's just about getting people to pay attention.

These types of stunts are not groundbreaking, but can help get you coverage where you otherwise might get none. Sometimes they don't work. I sent bananas to journalists with invitations to see *Johnny Stecchino*. By the time the packages got to people's homes and mailrooms, the bananas were rotten, the packages were oozing and fruit flies were swarming. It actually infuriated some people (one being Bob Strauss of *The LA Daily News*, who was not amused.)

A Plain Brown Envelope: *The Cockettes*

Laura. Marcus Hu released *The Cockettes* theatrically and though it was well liked by some critics, it performed modestly at the box office. It was also the year of *Bowling for Columbine*, a tsunami of a documentary. Still, Marcus wanted to do his best at year's end to remind critics about his film.

Marcus did not create fancy packaging or special DVDs—he copied DVDs in his office and just wrote on them with a Sharpie—*The Cockettes*. He had sent screeners a few years earlier for a film by André Téchiné that many had missed called *Wild Reeds*, and it really helped the film—not in terms of box office, but just in terms of acknowledgment. In any case, he just mailed *The Cockettes* in plain envelopes to members of the Los Angeles Film Critics Association, the New York Film Critics Circle, and the National Society of Film Critics. No cost but postage really—in all, less than seventy-five dollars. It really helped—in fact, the film appeared on many top ten lists as well as winning best documentary in many of the critics' races.

Not in New York, though: What became clear during the Film Critics Circle deliberations that year was (1) there was a solid bloc that would vote for anything BUT *Bowling for Columbine* and (2) a lot of critics hadn't seen anything but *Bowling for Columbine* and *Jackass: The Movie* (which came dangerously close to winning). Ultimately, *Standing in the Shadows of Motown* took the prize, basically because the opposition to *Columbine* was so fierce. But *Jackass* was a real contender. Imagine. The winner of the New York Film Critics Circle's Best Documentary award might have been *Jackass!*

On the other coast, sending these DVDs probably got *The Cockettes* the Best Documentary Award from the Los Angeles Film Critics Association.

Going Out for Lynch: *Mulholland Dr.*

Laura. You never know what's going to happen when you're working with critics. There are no guarantees of the outcome. But that said, you can always do what you can to better your chances.

I was hired to work on a film called *Mulholland Dr.* which at that time did not have a distributor, and though the idea of working with David Lynch was what I'd consider a career highlight, in this case, we would not be able to see the film until we landed in Cannes, where there are literally just hours for you to process what you've just seen, decide how you're going to talk about the film, and figure out how best to present the project in a way that will give it every chance.

So we see the film as soon as we arrive and are mesmerized. *Mulholland Dr.* is a film that—who knows?—could have gone either way, particularly at a really early morning press screening (a competition film press-screens at 8:30 every morning during the festival). So we decided to sneak a few critics into a private market screening of the film, allowing them to skip the early showing. That way, we could at least feel as if the film would have the chance it deserved, to be seen with fair eyes at a civilized time.

This is not to say that the same critics wouldn't have loved the film either way. It's about making sure you screen under the best possible conditions within your control. The time of day, the chance to see it early—that was a risk worth taking, and it really laid the groundwork for the film. Focus Features bought it shortly thereafter.

Picking Your Battles: *Last Summer in the Hamptons*

John. It was an instance where you could see the publicist's point, but that didn't mean it wasn't a pain in the ass.

Henry Jaglom is a filmmaker who scores high for consistency, because his movies are so uniformly bad. Kevin Thomas is a long-time critic for *The Los Angeles Times* and a very knowledgeable source on movies. He can also be very generous to filmmakers.

To take this setup one step further, there was a point in time when *Newsday* and *The Los Angeles Times*, which are and have long been owned by the same company (*Tribune* now, the now-defunct *Times-Mirror* then), had two film critics each: Kenneth Turan and Kevin in L.A., Jack Mathews and myself in New York. Being the subordinate critic (or perhaps, the lesser of two evils), I was fated for the hellish pits of Henry Jaglom.

The film was *Last Summer in the Hamptons*, in which no one gives any indication he or she can act, Jaglom certainly can't direct, and the entire project reeks of self-indulgence and posturing.

But despite all this, I was having trouble getting into a screening. It either simply wasn't working out timewise, or I was being led up the garden path by the film's publicist, Jennifer Morgerman, who went on later to work for Lions Gate. With one screening left—one of those "courtesy" screenings that was being held at a film class by Richard Brown or one of those pre-release screening moguls—she was erecting the great wall of Jaglom.

Why? Well, I finally figured it out. If I couldn't get to the film, *Newsday* would be forced to run Kevin Thomas's review—which was guaranteed to be a four-star justification of incompetence. Whether Jennifer already knew what Kevin was going to write, or whether he had already written it, or whether she was just speculating, I never knew. But she also knew, through instinct and experience, that I was going to eviscerate the film.

When I did figure it out, I was, of course, furious. And even more determined to get to that last screening, which was held on what had to be the coldest night of the New York winter of 1995. Blistering winds, breath-sucking cold. And still I was given a hard time at the door (Jennifer's boss, Mark Urman, now of ThinkFilm, did the right thing, apologized and calmed me down. Which was great. Although a cup of cocoa would have made it nicer.)

The thing was, Jennifer was actually doing her duty for the film, trying to prevent what she was sure would be a nasty review out of a New York paper. The question is, Did she really want to go to all that trouble just to alienate a critic she was going to have to work with on a lot more movies? And did she want to do it on behalf of Henry Jaglom?

Bujalski and Co.: *Funny Ha Ha*

John. Andrew Bujalski's *Funny Ha Ha* is a charmingly innocent, guileless, unpretentious romance about college-age friends that opened theatrically in summer 2005. But it had been around for a while.

In fact, the selection committee of the New York Film Festival, of which I was a member, had seen the movie a few years earlier, and were completely won over by how genuine and gentle the whole film was. Wow, we thought, wouldn't it be something to put this obviously low-budget, low-flying feature in one of the world's most prestigious film festivals?

And what would that something have been? It may have been a major success, but would it have been the semiprecious gem in the Tiffany's of cinema? It surely would have changed Bujalski's life. But would that have been for the better?

"There are a lot of arbitrary calls," said Richard Peña, the program director of the Film Society of Lincoln Center, and a permanent member of the committee. "I really enjoyed *Funny Ha Ha* but it's a very small movie—and its charm is its utter simplicity. I mean, the people are barely actors—you can't even call them nonactors, they're barely actors—and it's a big screen at Alice Tully Hall, and a lot of people, and there are films that just wither under that kind of attention. I think that would have been one of them."

Richard is, and was, probably right. Ultimately, the committee decided not to risk a young director's heart with a shot at the New York Film Festival, and that's something he probably won't ever thank us for.

"I have a pretty laissez-faire attitude about all of it," said Andrew Bujalski. "I just haven't allowed myself to get all stressed out about all the festival politics—the 'if you go to this festival, you cannot go to this festival' thing can all be very frustrating.

"I tend to look at these festivals less as industry stepping-stones and more as venues for showing the films to an audience," said the director of *Funny Ha Ha* and *Mutual Appreciation*. "It's kind of actually saddening to me when you think 'Because I showed the film to this audience, I cannot show it to that audience.' We ended up premiering the new one at SXSW, which they offered, and we got the film done just in time for that. I like that festival a lot. I love Austin. I used to live there. It is a noteworthy festival, but ultimately I think we went there more because the timing worked, and for personal reasons, than for any timing or strategy—not a whole lot of thought went into the 'Well, this is going to be the place to maximize our industry noteworthiness.'"

Bujalski is something of an anomaly in the often cutthroat world of indie film. And the idiosyncrasy is apparent in his movies.

"He's an amazing filmmaker," said veteran critic Amy Taubin. "He's the only young American filmmaker that I've been really out of my mind excited about. And *Funny Ha Ha* has the weirdest history. Two years ago I saw it, it never opened then, but Andrew just went around the college circuit and did that for two years. And then finally, someone came along with money, to blow it up to 35mm and make the soundtrack better, because it was just terrible. This guy who just adores Andrew's work put up the money to have a New York and Los Angeles release. It played four weeks at the Cinema Village. Actually, it did extremely well. And then to have Wellspring come along and put it out on DVD."

Bujalski said *Funny* was shot on 16mm and made "on favors and almost everybody working on the film worked for free. Almost all of the equipment was lent to us. Pretty much made in a vacuum. There was no eye toward anything and we weren't thinking about strategy when making it."

As if in defiance of the very premise upon which this book is based, Bujalski said he had no master plan.

"There was a six-month period before I could get anyone to show it anywhere," he said. "I think we finished the film in March of 2002, and it didn't have its first public screening until September of that year. So it was a very scattershot approach. We sent out tapes to whoever we could think of that might be interested and applied to a lot of film festivals. In the festival world, so many of the ones we did get into had so much to do with the film by then having acquired a reputation, or having people recommend it to one of the programmers. It happens so rarely. Only a couple of times did we get into a festival just based on a blind submission. And so what I was doing at first was just applying, and I got quite a lot of rejections, so there was no real grand strategy, except to get the film to whoever we could think of. Slowly it started to acquire a few key supporters who were the kind of people who did know film festival programmers, and who did have that kind of influence or ability to help us in getting dates."

Almost predictably, after getting no invitations anywhere, they got three in one week.

"It played at the Coolidge Corner Theater in Boston, which was doing a series of local filmmakers, and then it played at the Woodstock Film Festival, and then it played at the Sidewalk Film Festival in Birmingham, Alabama," Bujalski said. "And that was all in September of 2002, and it bounced around to a few more festivals over the course of the next several months.

The last one he applied to was the Los Angeles Film Festival.

"At one point, I had called a moratorium on the submission to festivals, but I applied to LAFF and was surprised to get in," he said. "We got a really nice review in *Variety* as a result of going to that festival, and it really took the exposure of the film to another level. That was the festival where the whole world of Los Angeles film industry people became aware of the film."

Bujalski said the Los Angeles Film Festival was "a very nice festival"; it treated him very well and he had three successful screenings. Which, from the filmmaker, sounds like a rave.

"I was a little surprised," he said. "I didn't know what to expect from L.A. audiences, but they were very friendly, and we got a nice review in the *LA Weekly*, which also helped a lot in getting people out to the theater. Because we had been to a number of festivals before that, we had already been acquiring some sort of reputation—a few film critics, and a lot of hardcore cineaste people, were aware of the film. But it was the *Variety* review that made us a commodity to the industry.

"I had a lot of e-mails from agents and production companies and people like that requesting screeners, and so I sent out a ton of screeners," he said. "And, of course, in the immediate term, it didn't lead to much because, nice review or not, the film is still a tough sell, and I think most of the people did indeed watch the first five or ten minutes and say, 'What is this? There's no way for anyone to make a profit.' But I did find a producers rep, who ended up being a huge help in the life of the film, and so I was eternally grateful for that."

He said it took a while for his rep, Houston King, to come on board, and, because he had started production on the next film, "I was so overwhelmed I didn't have a lot of time or energy to really think about the business life of *Funny Ha Ha*. At this point I didn't think there was that much further to go with it, because it had been around for a while and a lot of distributors had seen it. I figured they'd all seen it."

Bujalski and Co. did a little industry screening in New York in January before the Los Angeles Film Festival, and Bujalski said he was getting the kind of response he figures you get with a film like his: "People telling you how much they love it, but no one lifting a finger to get into business with you.

"Looking back," he recalled, "I might have spent less time and energy on the blind submissions to festivals, just because so little of that went anywhere. That said, the Sidewalk Film Festival did accept the film on its merits, and I was really happy to go there, and I'm really glad and grateful for that. But it did end up being the case that almost everywhere we went was because someone somewhere mentioned it to someone who worked at the festival. It was a little demoralizing to think that that's the way of the world. I think it's because they get so many submissions. Especially with a film like mine, where there's this kind of conventional wisdom that when you're submitting to a film festival, your film has to have something thrilling in the first five minutes or they might not watch it past the first five minutes. My film, as it happens, builds pretty slowly. But I resented the notion that I'd have to change the structure of the film, or that I'd have to reconceive the film, just so that I could please a film festival programmer."

Bujalski is not a role model for anyone reading this book, even if his indifference is inspiring. Take his attitude toward producers reps, for instance.

"Perhaps instead of pursuing festivals," he said, "I could have been pursuing those sort of people. But the way that everything worked for my film, everything was a slow build and eventually a rep did come along and those sorts of people did sniff around. But it was only after that *Variety* review that suddenly those people started to be interested in the film. I don't even know how I would have attracted them before that, because it is a tough sell of a film. No movie stars and a very difficult film to describe and make it sound any good."

King came on in November of 2003—"the rep started plugging away"—and in February of 2004, Bujalski won an Independent Spirit Award—which, like the *Variety* review, was a shot in the arm. "So I went out to Los Angeles for the awards certainly not expecting to win and that was a very nice surprise," Bujalski said. "The film has had such a peculiar life span. There were so many points where I've thought, 'OK, we've had our run, it's over now.' I probably thought that three months after our first festival, and every time I think it's over for this film some other strange turn of events happens, and it gets a new breath of life."

A *Variety* review, a Spirit Award, and then a sale to Sundance Channel. With each, *Funny Ha Ha* got re-resuscitated.

"Television is a whole other world in terms of exposure," he said. "I have no idea how many people have seen the film, but every time it shows on the Sundance Channel I get another handful of e-mails—and that's pretty strange to have people out in the ether communicating with you based on that."

On the film's theatrical release: "It's another long and complicated story, but after being on the Sundance Channel, I thought the film's life span had come to a close. But there's this guy who I had been vaguely in touch with who was a music industry guy, and after the Spirit Awards, he came around asking what we were planning to do with the DVD release. And we didn't have anything lined up. We were obviously trying; our producers rep Houston was trying. But this music guy said, 'I have friends who are starting up a DVD label,' so we got in touch with them, and that didn't work out. And after that, this very strange turn of events, this music guy who loved the film decided that he loved it so much that he wanted to get the movie seen even though he'd never done anything like this before. So he decided he wanted to put his own money behind self-distributing the film theatrically, so that's been our big project for the last year."

The music guy invested. Bujalski said they probably needed about $150,000 to do it "comfortably," and had about half of that. "But that's what we're working with. We've made two 35mm prints of the film; earlier I'd been traveling with 16mm prints. We were in New York, Los Angeles, Boston, Minneapolis. The film's in Dallas right now and we're just booking those two prints through the summer. Wherever they'll have it."

On what he'll do differently with his new film. "I think I'm in a different position now. The process with *Funny Ha Ha* was getting to learn a little bit about how the film industry works, and how the festival world works, and all their quirks. My new film is finished, it's called *Mutual Appreciation*, and it's already started a festival run. That said, my strategy is not that different, but I know more people and I can get their attention quicker. But the film itself is still a very difficult sell. I have Houston on board now, and we're already flirting with distributors, but because it's still not a terribly commercial film, it's still as much of an uphill battle. Having made a film now that people have heard of, we've eliminated that part of the uphill battle. I suppose."

Sundance?

"I did apply and sent a rough cut of the new one," he said. "We didn't get in, which was good, because our film wouldn't have been finished in time for it anyway. There are festivals like the Sidewalk Film Festival in Alabama, which largely exists to serve an actual regional population of people who come and check out new films. And there are festivals that consist of . . . a couple hundred industry people who travel from festival to festival. For those, it makes sense that they can't screen all of the same films because it's literally the same people, and they've already seen it."

Beating the Odds: *Gods and Monsters*

"Most of the things that can go wrong at a festival did go wrong for us," said Bill Condon, director of the Oscar-nominated *Kinsey*, and—back in 1998— *Gods and Monsters*.

The story of director James Whale—director of the horror classics

Frankenstein, Bride of Frankenstein, and *The Invisible Man*—*Gods and Monsters* starred Ian McKellan and, as his love interest, Brendan Fraser. (Whale was one of the more "out" directors of '30s Hollywood.) The movie was eventually declared among the best of its year; McKellan got an Oscar nomination. The movie did incredibly well.

"We were just finishing our film when the deadline was looming for Sundance," Condon remembered. "And perhaps because it had been such a struggle to get the movie made—it had taken a number of years—and because we didn't have distribution, everyone, the financier, Paul Colichman at Regent, and all of us involved in making the movie, we thought Sundance was the perfect place to expose it."

So they submitted it to the festival. "And the first disappointment was that we didn't get into competition," Condon said. "We got into something called American Spectrum, which is sort of the junior-league division, and everyone kind of pretends there's no big difference, but there is. So that was a disappointment. But still, the most important thing is the fact that we were going to be there"

Condon had been granted the rights by Universal Pictures to use clips from *Frankenstein* and *The Bride of Frankenstein* and, in return, the studio got a first look at the movie. "So we'd been very careful," Condon said. "First of all, the movie was one of those classic festival cases, typical in a way—the festival print was not done until two days before we showed it in Sundance, but we had to show it to [Universal] before."

The company involved was the Universal offspring, USA Films, which had formerly been Gramercy Features and is now Focus Films. Not that it matters much now, especially after what happened.

"We get there," Condon said, "and the buyers, whoever they were from USA, had passed on the movie; they had talked about it on the airplane, about passing, and why they didn't think it would work, and all that stuff. And that was the first thing we heard. You arrive, you hear the buzz, that the word going around is not that good because it's been passed on by the only people who had seen it."

Strike two, he said, was that they were in American Spectrum. "Strike Three was that our first showing was Wednesday at midnight—it was clear we were not loved by the programmers," he said. "But there we were, bravely premiering, and everything about it—the lack of heat, the late hour—it just didn't feel great. We had two subsequent screenings that went extremely well. But that first one felt a little dead. There were the typical things—every cliché—executives leaving halfway through, people on the phone."

But there were supporters, too. "While there was all this disappointing stuff happening on the business end, there were people who came out of that first screening having liked the film quite a bit," Condon said. "One of them was Harry Knowles [aintitcool.com], who had been in touch with my boyfriend, Jack, on line, and Jack had gotten him into the first screening and he became a great advocate for the movie. There are a handful of people who put the film on the map, and I always think of him as one of the most important ones. The next week, Ken Turan, Lisa Schwartzbaum, and Owen Gleiberman, all of them in their festival wrap-up articles, spoke highly of the movie, and specifically about the idea that it should have been in competition. And that was a nice thing that came out of that experience."

In retrospect, knowing what he does now, Condon says he wouldn't have put such importance on his first screening. "I have much more knowledge now, but knowing we were in Spectrum, and where and when our first screening was . . ." he said, "I would probably not have put all the pressure on myself. With Sundance, you get the news, and you hear you should be grateful for even Spectrum, and John Cooper, I think he even had to fight to get us in Spectrum; unfortunately, the whole committee wasn't into the movie. So you're both disappointed and anxious about it, and because you believe in your movie, you sort of put aside those fears that you have. But maybe you should take a step back and ask, 'Is this the right way?'"

Part of Condon's problem may have been the added stress he suffered during production. "The company that was going to finance the film, Regent, wasn't up and running quite as quickly as they thought they were going to be," he said. "And we had a stop date on Ian McKellan [meaning they only had the actor for a certain amount of time] and about three weeks before production, we had a million-dollar gap. So they brought in Showtime."

Suddenly he had another set of pressures, "which was really intense: After a certain period of time, if we had not sold it to a distributor, it would go to Showtime. And that was my biggest fear—that even though it had not been made as a Showtime movie, because they put some money in, they could take it over if we didn't get a distributor."

It was a weird year at Sundance. The previous one had seen some big deal-making and sanity seemed to have prevailed—for a while. But at the same time, Condon said, "*Next Stop Wonderland* sold that year for six million, *Smoke Signals*, there were quite a number of films that sold. We all know there's this ebb and flow to the Sundance deal-making heat."

Gods had an IFP screening when they got back to L.A., "and that was a really good screening." They slowly started showing it to all the distributors who hadn't seen it and got passes from all of them except for Lions Gate, which was then a new company, formed out of the old Cinepix. "They were willing to advance a lot less than the financiers wanted, so during that time, things like the IFP screening going so well helped to keep the heat alive and helped build a sense that the film was worth pursuing."

At the same time, his representation was bailing out from under him. "I had two agents at CAA," he said, referring to Creative Artists Agency. "Both were instrumental in getting the movie made, but one, Ken Hardy, had left just before we were getting into Sundance. It was time to see who else might be willing to take me on, and to test the waters there, so we had a big screening for the department at CAA, plus my one remaining agent—who called the next day with the bad news that of all of the people who had seen it, no one had stepped forward and said that, based on that film, they couldn't do anything with me or for me. So I was fired from CAA based on *Gods and Monsters* having done nothing notable up to that point. I had them as agents fifteen years, after having written *Strange Invaders*, so I had been there fifteen years and got dropped once they saw *Gods and Monsters*."

Condon said his current agent, Adam Shulman, had been at that IFP screening, "and he came after me and said he loved the movie, and he'd love to represent me. And I've been very happy with Adam.

"It took forever," Condon concluded, "but we finally made the deal with Lions Gate. During that time we went to the Seattle Film Festival, which was good. I think we did suffer, in that our film definitely didn't fit into the hipster aspect of Sundance."

But it fit in elsewhere at other festivals, such as Seattle, and was finally given the launch it deserved at the New York Film Festival, "which was spectacular."

What the Hell Happened to *What Happened Was. . .*?

One of the suspicions surrounding Sundance, especially in earlier years, was that the competition winners were generally the films that needed the attention— films without distribution, for instance, or whose marketing was destined to be problematic. This could be good: In 1991, for instance, Todd Haynes's *Poison* took the grand jury feature prize, and while there might have been more popular movies in that year's festival, the jury's wisdom helped boost the career of one of America's best filmmakers.

Things got nuttier. "The first film I ever produced," said Scott Macauley, "was called *What Happened Was. . .*". The 1994 film was also the first film produced by Macauley together with his producing partner, Robin O'Hara, whose Forensic Films would later make *Raising Victor Vargas, Joe the King,* and *Gummo*.

"We were just excited that it was in focus, and there was sound," he said. "The film was based on a play, and we loved the play. When we saw it, we thought, 'If we can make a film as good as the play, we'll have a great movie.' And we felt like we did, that we'd made a film that was as good as, if not better than, the play."

The author of the play, and the star and director of the film, was Tom Noonan, who would later make *The Wife* and had been a featured actor in such horror films as *Manhunter* and *Robocop 2*. Not exactly a conventionally charismatic guy, but a challenging writer and an idiosyncratic and provocative presence.

"We had submitted it to a number of festivals before Sundance," Macauley said. "And we had gotten rejected everywhere; starting with Cannes, New York, Mill Valley, we got rejected everywhere. So this was back in 1994, and we submitted to Sundance, and we got into the competition. We were really excited.

"After the film's first screening, which went extremely well, Goldwyn was interested. After the second screening, Ira Deutchman, who was then with Fine Line, said, 'Look I'm only going to be able to see half of the film, because we have our movie screening in an hour, so don't feel offended when I walk out. I'll come back and catch the second half later.' He had someone else sitting in the screening to watch the whole movie.

"And after the film, the other person came out and said, 'Wow, I really liked that movie.' And the next day, Fine Line made an offer on the film. They said, 'We'll give you X as an advance, but our offer is going to expire at the end of the festival.' They also negotiated a bump if we won an award. We were thrilled."

Macauley and O'Hara were the producers; James Schamus and Ted Hope were the executive producers. "The screenings were getting better and better," Macauley said. "It got to the awards night and the film won the grand prize and the screenwriting prize, so we were wondering what that meant. Does that double the bonus? It was unclear. Of course, in this situation, and because the film wasn't one of the super high-profile films, not every distributor had seen it."

As we said, this was an earlier Sundance era; these days, everyone's at the first screening. "So everyone who hadn't seen the film descended on us," Macauley said, "saying, 'We have to see the film now.' At the same time, we had this Fine Line offer that was ticking away. One of the huge, major companies said, 'We need to see the film, you need to send the print to L.A.' So we collectively decided to take this gamble and screen the film for everybody."

To make a long story short, he said, the company that needed the print in L.A. was Miramax. "Harvey walked into the screening room, sat down, the film started, and he said, 'You know what, we're not going to wind up buying this film.'"

They only had one print. "That print had to come back," Macauley said. "Fine Line's offer had expired. They said, 'Of course we're still interested, but our offer has expired.' But Ira also said, 'You know, I never saw the second half of the movie. So we're still interested, but I need to see the second half of the movie.'"

So back the print went to New York, where they held a screening for another distributor. "And they were very aggressive with us and made it sound like they were going to buy the film," Macauley said. "They had three partners, and the third partner hadn't seen the film. So the third partner saw it, and didn't like it. So that distributor was gone. Miramax was gone. We only have Fine Line."

Deutchman then saw the rest of the film, but by himself—not in the company of an enthusiastic festival audience. "He walked out and said, 'The film gets really sad at the end. The first half is so funny, and then it really takes this darker turn. I thought I could sell this as a comedy, but it's not a comedy. It's more like a tragedy. I have no idea how to market this film.'

"So we went from being this little film that we thought no one would care about," said Macauley, "to having all this distributor interest, to us winning the grand prize, then to us having zero. No offers, nothing. It wound up with Goldwyn—Sam had seen it and liked it, and they picked it up. But for a moment there, it was very scary."

In Nomine Padre: El Crimen de Padre Amaro

Sometimes you want people to love a movie. Sometimes you want them to hate it.

RJ Millard was vice president of marketing and publicity for IDP Films when the company had *El Crimen de Padre Amaro*, a movie about corruption and Catholicism starring Gael Garcia Bernal as a priest who has an affair with a 16-year-old girl.

"Nobody wanted this film because they thought it was a melodrama," said Millard. "It is a bit melodramatic, but it worked for the audience. It got medium to positive reviews, like two and a half stars, mostly. But we knew the audience, and we knew to take this sliver and hit the Mexican-American community."

They played the film in all the major markets, "but where the film really worked was in the Southwest. So we reconfigured our distribution pattern to match that."

Where they really went right was to position the film as the year's most controversial. "Mainstream America may not have read about the film," he said, "but certainly people who had Catholicism in their background or were Latino knew about it. We got the Catholic League, Focus on the Family, and these types of organizations, just invited them in and showed them the film—and then we watched them hate it and condemn it. That got us a lot of mileage."

And that, of course, opened the doors to bigger coverage: "pieces on CNN, etcetera. Unless there was controversy, we would have never gotten that kind of exposure for a foreign language feature. Just doesn't happen."

Millard said, "We figured out who our enemies were, and who our friends were, and went after both of them hardcore."

There Are No Road Maps:
Robert Pulcini and Shari Springer Berman

Writer-directors Robert Pulcini and Shari Springer Berman are best known for the feature-doc hybrid *American Splendor*, but their earlier documentary, *Off the Menu: The Last Days of Chasen's*, had gotten them considerable attention. And it all started with a guy in a tuxedo.

"We got our first agent based on screenplays," said Springer Berman. "We had written spec screenplays while we were still in school, and we wrote one that got rejected by every agent in Los Angeles. One agent who had rejected us, her assistant, Eric Kim, had read our script and really liked it. And when he got promoted to be an agent, and he was looking for clients, Eric called us."

Kim called the New York couple from L.A. "He told us, 'I have a lot of confidence in you guys. Do you have an agent yet?' So we signed with Eric, who was a new agent, which was good because we were new writers.

"A lot of times," Springer Berman said, "people think the fancier the agent is, the better off you'll be, but it's almost better to have someone who's going to come up with you, who's really going to focus on you, than someone who's got huge clients, and you're almost like an afterthought. We kind of worked together and kind of came up together.

"The first time we went to Los Angeles for work," she said, "it was because Eric said, 'You have to come to Los Angeles. You have this script, and I want to go out with it as a spec, and I want you to do meetings. Even if we don't sell it, you'll meet people in the industry.'"

They had no money. They were still in film school. They didn't have a place to stay. "Bob found a bed-and-breakfast online in West Hollywood that was way less expensive than the hotels," Springer Berman said. "So we wound up staying in this bed-and-breakfast, this pink beautiful house in the Hollywood Hills, and by day we were doing meetings about this screenplay we had written, and we'd come home to the bed-and-breakfast."

The guy who ran the bed-and-breakfast was a captain at Chasen's.

"And he'd come home with his tuxedo on, and he'd come home and fight with his friend Neil about kissing up to Mrs. [Aaron] Spelling, and all about how Chasen's was closing, and how one of the waiters was on oxygen, and how he comes and still tries to work with his oxygen tank.

"We were having a miserable time," she said. "Nobody wanted to buy this script and our meetings were going really badly. But we were getting fascinated with this restaurant world, which seemed to represent this dying era of Hollywood, this old-school era. And this restaurant. We were kind of depressed, and Bob turns to me and says, 'We gotta put this guy Raymond in a documentary.' I called my friend who had some money and wanted to make a short, and I said, 'Forget about the short, I think we have something here.' And that's how we made Chasen's. And we never sold the script."

"The Last Days of Chasen's was pretty interesting," Pulcini said, "because we financed it with money from a friend. We had a lot of short ends [of film stock], we had access to our film-school equipment, so we kind of pieced together the shoot. But then we really had no money to finish. But we had enough money to develop the film, and we were able to cut a trailer. So we cut a fifteen-minute trailer that gave highlights of what the movie would be."

And then they didn't get into Sundance. Twice.

"We applied with a pretty bad cut one year," Pulcini said, "and when it was done the next year, we applied again, and we were rejected."

"Once we knew we weren't accepted into Sundance," said Springer Berman, "then it became, 'What's the next best thing?' But because the movie was about a restaurant in Hollywood, we were invited to be the closing night film of the Los Angeles Independent Film Festival [now the Los Angeles Film Festival]. We were the closing night film at the DGA [Directors Guild of America], with two theaters and a big giant party, with food, catered by the people who own Chasen's—chili, and all that. They had a big high-profile event.

There were like 600 people there, and it was perfect because it fit into the theme of old Hollywood. Being in Hollywood, with a film festival that's related to Hollywood, it went over great. It was a great screening. Our mistake was, we did not have a producers rep."

Subsequently, there was a lot of interest in the movie, they said, and while they had a verbal agreement with a producer's rep, he was really not on board. So our producer Alicia Sams wound up having to field all the interest.

"We didn't have John Sloss," said Springer Berman. "We didn't have anybody who could really negotiate. With these films you have a window to close the deal, and we didn't have anyone to do it."

"In the event that there will be excitement about your film," Pulcini said, "you'd better have your ducks in a row to capitalize on that excitement. Because it fizzles fast."

They spent months with no distribution and a lot of meetings that went nowhere. They eventually signed with the small distributor, Northern Arts, but "I think we could have had different distribution had we been prepared," said Springer Berman.

"You have to have someone who knows what they're doing," she said about deal-making. "Unless they've made a lot of deals, like Ted Hope, if you have a producer who's a little bit green, that doesn't mean they're not a good producer, or that they don't have the best intentions. But there's an art to closing a deal. That is one of the biggest mistakes we made, going in there without anyone who knew how to do it. The event worked, all of our logic worked, we were really well positioned, but then we couldn't bring it home."

Europe was different. "Our European premiere was at Locarno, which worked really well for us," she said. "It's a really wonderful festival; we won an award there. We did have a sales agent, Jane Balfour, who isn't doing this anymore, who came on before the festival, and we made a lot of foreign sales out of Locarno."

The fate of Chasen's might have been different had they made it a few years later. "The mood of the industry has changed," Springer Berman said. "Documentaries have a different cachet now. People believe now that they can make money, but when we had Chasen's there was really no precedent for docs making money, except for people like Michael Moore, and that was seen as an aberration. Even the biggest festivals aren't necessarily good for documentaries, because they can really get lost. Going to a smaller festival like Locarno, there was a real open mind to documentaries and a lot of foreign buyers who were interested in buying the movie. We made a lot of sales—not tons, but we did well there. And then we went to IDFA, the big documentary festival in Amsterdam, probably the biggest international one."

"We went to the Hamptons and won best doc there, too," said Pulcini. "All those things helped us to make foreign sales. And at some point we sold it to Cinemax."

Cinemax is a subsidiary of HBO, where Pulcini and Springer Berman found a home of sorts. Although it had its disadvantages at the time.

"When we made *Off the Menu* in 1997, we never had any hope that the movie was going to make money getting released theatrically," said Springer Berman. "But at that time, when you released a documentary theatrically, it generated a certain kind of press, a certain kind of attention that really helped us. It got great write-ups and made ten-best lists and really put us on the map as filmmakers. When we made *The Young and the Dead* [about the Hollywood Forever cemetery], the option of a theatrical release was never on the table. It was at the point when HBO refused to release their films theatrically."

"Everyone told us, 'Millions more people are going to see this film,'" said Pulcini. "And we're really proud of that film, and we fought for that film to have a festival life. It played at the Venice Film Festival, a few places, but people always reference the *Chasen's* movie, they never reference *The Young and the Dead*, even though it got that kind of exposure on television. It's a different kind of exposure. When *American Splendor* opened, everyone mentioned, 'From the people who brought you *Off the Menu: The Last Days of Chasen's*.'"

The Young and the Dead had its world premiere at the Venice Film Festival, "and it was fun and it was amazing being there," recalled Springer Berman, "but that's a case where it was really hard to get attention for a documentary. I would venture to say that even today, it's the same. Barbara Kopple was there the year we were there with a movie. It's just really hard to get attention, because it's just a very feature film–oriented, glamorous festival. I wouldn't trade in that experience, because it was so much fun and because it was already really clear that they weren't going to allow us to have theatrical distribution."

It also played at Telluride—where they met HBO Film's President Colin Callendar, who loved their film and set the stage for them to return to HBO for *American Splendor*, their film about cantankerous but loveable comic book writer Harvey Pekar.

But the "can we?/can't we?" issue of theatrical release still hung over the HBO relationship.

"It just makes a different kind of cultural impact," Pulcini said of theatrical. "The exception is, of course, HBO. Their brand is so classy, it's kind of the one place if you do a documentary there you can get a lot of attention. But there's still nothing like having it play in a theater.

"Once it plays on television, it's over," he said. "When it's in theaters, even if people don't go to see it, there's talk about it in the media that is of a different caliber. I think it's changed a lot now, and I think people have been educated and documentaries now can mean box office and they can be profitable. When we were doing it, it was maybe one or two a year that might make profit. It was almost like a dirty word. All the promotional material would never say 'documentary' or 'nonfiction,' and there was a bias that documentaries were like medicine. Obviously, and fantastically, that has changed."

Going into Sundance—where they were not only finally accepted, but won with *American Splendor*—they knew theatrical was at least on the table.

"HBO Films had done it before with *Real Women Have Curves*," said Springer Berman, "so it was tantalizingly dangled in front of us."

"We were told when we were making the film 'Forget about it. It's not going to happen,'" said Pulcini. "So we didn't make the film with the intention of getting a theatrical release, although Ted Hope, the producer, always said to us, 'Anything can happen. Keep an open mind.' HBO, meanwhile, kept saying, 'It's not going to happen, that's not what we're about right now.' And then, once the film was getting finished, they were getting the theatrical bug."

At Sundance, "Bob and I were a nervous wreck," said Springer Berman. "I definitely wasn't as nervous before the Academy nominations, or the actual Academy Awards. . . . I was more nervous at Sundance, before the film was going to screen for its first public audience. We were working till the last minute, and because our movie was really tricky, there was a big question of whether the audience would buy it or not. It could have really flopped. It wasn't just a straightforward movie, so it was pretty scary."

Prescreening, she said, "We had a pow-wow in the condo, with [consultant] Liz Manne; Maud [Nadler of HBO] was a nervous wreck, Harvey was catatonic in the corner, Joyce [Brabner, Pekar's wife] was yelling at him to wake up. Liz talked about what the process is, and you [Laura] told us that, 'These things can get really dramatic; you're going to feel like everything's going to change but try to keep your head. This is a very emotional environment. Keep your cool, don't get too overwhelmed either way,' which was a really good thing to hear."

"It was crazy though," said Pulcini. "There's something about the

Sundance audience where you feel like, not only is the whole industry there, but I remember Hope Davis walking up to me, right before the screening starts, and she says, 'Al Gore is in the second row.' How weird is that? You don't find that at other festivals."

Peter Broderick Talks *Faster*

Faster is a documentary about Grand Prix motorcycle racing narrated by Ewan McGregor. "When it was in limited theatrical release," said film consultant Peter Broderick, "there was already a lot of demand for the film. People kept asking, 'When can we buy the DVD?'" Broderick told the filmmakers they could start selling it exclusively from their Web site. Labeled the Preview Edition, the DVD included the film and one short extra from Cannes. The filmmakers' Web site (www.fastermovie.com) sold five thousand copies in the first two weeks and then another eight thousand in the next few months.

"We made a video deal with New Video to distribute it to retail outlets. The retail edition consisted of the film plus two and a half hours of new material, including a whole new documentary and interactive POV footage of riders during the final miles of races (viewers could cut between them as they approached the finish line). This two-disc set was labeled the 'Ultimate Collector's Edition.' We e-mailed everyone who had purchased the preview edition to let them know that we really appreciated their buying the first edition, that an exciting new version was coming out, and that we'd give them a free T-shirt if they bought it.

"Although selling for $20 from our Web site, a T-shirt only cost us a fraction of that to make. Many customers returned to our Web site to buy the new edition and were pleased that we rewarded their loyalty with a free T-shirt. In addition to direct sales from our Web site, the Ultimate Collector's Edition was sold in video stores, on Amazon, and through other retail outlets. Within six months, fifty thousand DVDs had been sold in retail and another seven thousand from our Web site.

"Filmmakers can use hybrid strategies, combining traditional and innovative routes. They can release their films theatrically via service deals. They can make a retail video deal and at the same time sell DVDs directly from their own Web sites. Their largest revenue stream may come from direct sales. Once you see numbers like twenty to thirty thousand units, that is real money. Hybrid strategies give filmmakers more control over their fate.

"Alfred Hitchcock had a worldwide following but he didn't know the names and addresses of any of his loyal fans. They were all anonymous members of a mass media audience. Today, filmmakers have the opportunity to build a core personal audience by developing relationships with customers who purchase DVDs from their Web sites. The goal is to transform consumers of a product into patrons of an artist.

"If a filmmaker accumulates a list of twenty thousand people who have bought DVDs from his or her Web site, the filmmaker can appeal to them for financial support for a new project. For example, an e-mail message can be sent out, saying 'It's going to be really hard to finance my next movie. It's provocative, controversial, and not obviously commercial. I won't be able to raise the money from the usual sources. I need you to help me make the movie by pre-buying the DVD.'"

What Broderick is talking about is a variation on that old saw about cutting out the middleman—but, in this case, the middleman could well be the corporate film industry as we know it.

Index

ABC, 160
ABC World News Tonight, 120
Access Hollywood, 112
Acquisitions community
  buzz from, 133
  screenings for, 70–71
Affliction, 51
AFI Fest, 60, 67, 70, 160
Agee, James, 165
Agents, foreign sales, 30–38
aintitcool.com, 202
Alice Tully Hall, 196
Allentown Morning Call, 183
Allen, Woody, 15
Ally, self as, 144–146
Almodòvar, Pedro, 168
Altman, Robert, 85
Amazon, 39, 79, 211
Amélie, 191
American Cinematheque, 163
American Film Institute Festival.
  See AFI Fest
American Film Market, 61, 63, 70
American Graffiti, 45
American Pavilion, 146
American Spectrum, 64, 186, 201,
  202
American Splendor, 12, 47, 62, 75, 89,
  141, 142, 179–180, 193, 206,
  209, 210–211
Anderson, John, 18, 182
Anderson, Paul Thomas, 3, 4
Anderson, Wes, 3, 4, 45
Andreen, Scilla, 78, 79
Angelika, 18
Annapolis, 83
Annie Hall, 5
Another Day in Paradise, 150
Ansen, David, 65, 102, 103, 126,
  150, 160–161, 187
Antidote Films, 43, 166
Araki, Gregg, 20–21, 32, 43, 45,
  171, 192
Arclight, 30
Arlen, Alice, 91
Arteta, Miguel, 4, 9, 14, 87, 91,
  92, 99
Artisan, 78, 138, 182
Associated Press, 26

Bacon, Francis, 164
Bacon, Kevin, 97
Balfour, Jane, 208
Ballard, Carroll, 126
Barbieri, Tony, 44–45
Barker, Michael, 20, 38, 61, 89,
  104, 168, 170, 175–176
Bartok, Dennis, 163–164
Basinger, Kim, 189
Batman Begins, 166

Bearden, Keith, 39
Beatles, 45, 48
Beck, 146
Bend It Like Beckham, 174
Benson, Sheila, 126
Berlin Film Festival, 58, 61, 63, 64
Berlin Film Festival Market, 58
Bernal, Gael Garcia, 136, 205
Berney, Bob, 3, 5, 36, 37–38, 61,
  70–71, 72, 75, 78, 96–97,
  123–124, 129–130, 140, 147
Better Luck Tomorrow, 27, 28, 60, 83,
  87, 101, 112, 128, 130–131, 168
The Big Lebowski, 10
Billy's Dad Is a Fudgepacker, 38
Billy's Hollywood Screen Kiss, 45, 83
Biographical information, 115
Biskind, Peter, 35
The Blair Witch Project, 16, 118, 144
Bleak Moments, 110
Blind submissions, 72–76
Blood Simple, 14
Blue, 102
Blue Car, 186–187
Bodies, Rest and Motion, 193
Bodine, Sue, 26–27, 30, 32–33, 46,
  49–50, 60, 72
Bonds, Barry, 73
Born into Brothels, 81, 88, 159–160
Bowles, Eamonn, 29, 46, 63, 104,
  119, 130, 147–148, 170
Bowling for Columbine, 49, 193, 194
Boys Don't Cry, 36
Braun, Josh, 29
Breslin, Jimmy, 188
Brevity, with media, 100
Brick, 37
Bride of Frankenstein, 201
Bridges, Jeff, 10
Briski, Zana, 159–160
Broadway: The Golden Age, 161–162
Broderick, Peter, 24, 76, 104–105,
  173–174, 177, 178–179, 211–212
Brooks, Mel, 15
Brother's Keeper, 77
The Brothers McMullen, 12–13, 187–189
Brown, Richard, 195
Bruckner, Agnes, 186, 187
Bujalski, Andrew, 111, 196–200
Burns, Edward, 12–13, 187–189
Buzz, 133–143
B|W|R, 22, 23, 106, 111, 154

CAA, 22, 29, 42, 203
Callendar, Colin, 209
Canby, Vincent, 111
Cannes Film Festival, 1, 20, 57, 58,
  59, 60, 61, 62, 63, 64, 67, 69, 73,
  84, 85, 89, 95, 103, 104, 120,
  136, 141, 146–147, 150, 152,

157, 189–190, 191, 192, 194,
  204, 211
Caouette, Jonathan, 10, 173
Capturing the Friedmans, 17, 81, 142,
  144, 145, 163
Case studies, 181–212
The Castle, Happy, Texas, 139–140
Cast list, 115
Catalog copy, checking of, 156
Catholic Church, 190
Catholic League, 206
Celluloid Dreams, 30, 31, 36
Cemetery Man, 193
CFP, 127, 131, 164, 191–192, 203
Chain Camera, 88
Chasen's, 47, 71, 206–209
Cheever, John, 152
Cherot, Christopher Scott, 95
Cheshire, Godfrey, 104
Chicago Film Festival, 62, 109–110,
  172
The Chicago Sun-Times, 110, 126
Chocolat, 193
Chuck & Buck, 14, 87, 99
Chumscrubber, 5
Cinemart, 91
Cinema Village, 197
Cinemax, 88, 209
Cinepix Film Properties. *See* CFP
Cinetic Media, 20, 22, 29, 72, 167
Clark, Larry, 44, 150
Clarkson, Patricia, 158
Clean, Shaven, 138
Clein, Harry, 11–12, 113
Clerks, 104–105
Clinton, Bill, 74, 106
Clockwatchers, 141
CNN, 120, 206
The Cockettes, 193–194
Coen brothers, 10
Colichman, Paul, 201
Colligan, Megan, 169
Columbia University, 38, 179
Condon, Bill, 23, 50–51, 109,
  168–169, 200–203
The Confessions of Amans, 110
Contacting festival press office, 156
Contacts, media, 157–158
*The Cook, the Thief, His Wife and Her
  Lover*, 164
Coolidge Corner Theater, 197
Cooper, John, 68, 83, 128–129, 202
Cooper, Karen, 3, 73–74, 161,
  162–163, 173
Cottrell, Mickey, 23, 44, 139
Cover page, 115
Cowan, Noah, 59
Cowboy Releasing, 177
Craughwell, Kathleen, 193
Creative Artists Agency. *See* CAA

Crew list, 115
Crowe, Russell, 189
The Cruise, 138, 181–183
Crumb, 61
CustomFlix, 79
Cyclo, 191–192

Dana, Jonathan, 29
Dargis, Manohla, 18, 36, 65, 104, 107, 108, 109, 116, 118, 124, 135, 138, 160–161, 163, 167, 177
Dash, Julie, 172–173
Daughters of the Dust, 172–173
Davis, Hope, 211
Davis, Julie, 137
The Daytrippers, 127, 128
Dead by Dawn, 55
Deadline, 26
The Debut, 77
The Delta, 103
Dentler, Matt, 61–62, 67
Derrida, 88
Deutchman, Ira, 204, 205
Devor, Rob, 37
DGA, 52, 53, 185, 207
Diamond Men, 110
DiCillo, Tom, 189
Dick, Kirby, 88, 131, 153, 170–171
Directors' Fortnight, 136
Directors Guild of America.
  See DGA
Director's statement or Q&A, 115
Disney, 190
DIY-PR, 155–164
DocFest, 182
Dogma, 190
Donnie Darko, 88, 140, 141
Double Happiness, 193
Douglas, Deandra, 71
Dowd, Jeff, 7–8, 10, 12, 13–14, 15, 16, 18, 29, 59, 82, 106, 107, 183, 184
Down and Dirty Movies, 35
Down to the Bone, 73
The Dream Life of Angels, 104
Dubowski, Sandy, 162
Duma, 126

E!, 112, 138
Earhart, Amelia, 155
Eason, Eric, 167
Ebert, Roger, 21–22, 63, 97, 100, 107, 109–110, 126, 151, 182–183
Eccles Theater, 27
Ed's Next Move, 137
Egoyan, Atom, 190
Egyptian, 88
El Crimen de Padre Amaro, 205–206
Electronic materials, 119–121
Elevator pitch, 98
Ella Enchanted, 45, 83
El Mariachi, 63

Elwes, Cassian, 22–23, 28, 29, 61, 88, 130, 134, 149, 166, 168
Emano, Winston, 97
The End, 88
Entertainment lawyers, 30
Entertainment Tonight, 81, 112, 143, 187
Entertainment Weekly, 107, 182, 189
Epstein, Levinsohn, Bodine, Hurwitz and Weinstein, LLP, 26–27
Eugene O'Neill Theater Center, 7
Evaluating film, 5–18
Everly, Bart, 74
Eve's Bayou, 63
Exaggeration, 98–99
Extra, 112
Eyre, Chris, 56, 192

Fahrenheit 9/11, 112
Falco Ink, 23
Far from Heaven, 36, 65
The Fast and the Furious 3, 83
Faster, 178, 211–212
Federbush, Paul, 26, 135, 139–140, 141, 177
FedEx, 120
Feinstein, Howard, 104
Felicia's Journey, 190
Fellini, Federico, 95
Fessenden, Larry, 43–44
Festival circuit, 55–70
Festival press office, 156–160
Field, Todd, 88
Film Comment, 117
Filmex, 88
Film Forum, 3, 6, 73–74, 161, 173
Film Independent (FIND), 76
Filmmakers Lab (Sundance), 91, 92
Film Sales Company, 29, 50
Film Society of Lincoln Center, 38, 196
Fine Line, 75, 193, 204, 205
First Look, 189
First Love, Last Rites, 8–9
Fisher, Frances, 186
Fiss, Tracey, 138
Flirting with Disaster, 95
Focus Features, 19, 33, 59, 129, 139, 148, 194, 201
Focus on the Family, 206
The Fog of War, 168
Foreign sales agents, 30–38
Forensic Films, 6, 76, 204
Fortissimo Films, 30, 31, 74
Forty Shades of Blue, 103
Foundas, Scott, 184–185
Four-walling, 158, 160–164
Fox, 83
Fox Searchlight, 9, 87, 168–169, 174, 185, 188, 189
Frank, Barney, 74
Frankenstein, 201

Fraser, Brendadn, 201
Fredell Pogodin & Associates, 23
Fremaux, Thierry, 67
Fresh Air, 163
Frilot, Shari, 83
The Full Monty, 138, 189
Funny Ha Ha, 196–200

Gaines, Christian, 67
Garden State, 26, 81, 88
Garvin, Tom, 30
Genghis Khan, 19
George Washington, 177
Gere, Richard, 13–14
Gerrans, Jon, 103, 137–138
Get Over It, 45, 83
Giamatti, Paul, 141
Gilmore, Geoff, 58, 59, 60, 64–65, 65, 67–69, 82–83, 84–85, 89–90, 128–129, 141, 176
Girlfight, 95, 128
Girl 6, 191
Giveaways, 121
Gleiberman, Owen, 202
Gluck, Sophie, 23, 185
Goat on Fire and Smiling Fish, 107
Goddard, Jean-Luc, 114
Goddard, Robert, 114
Gods and Monsters, 23, 50–51, 109, 125, 168–169, 200–203
Goldman, William, 16
Goldwyn, 137, 204, 205
Goldwyn, Sam, 205
Gong Li, 186
The Good Girl, 14, 87, 99
Good Machine, 59
Good Morning America, 25, 100, 108, 111, 120, 127
Gordinier, Jeff, 182
Gore, Al, 211
Gramercy Features, 201
Gray, Jonathan, 30
Green, David Gordon, 177
Green, Micah, 22, 29, 31
Greenaway, Peter, 163–164
Greene, Graham, 165
Greenfield, Matthew, 9, 16–17, 18, 47–48, 59, 87, 169–170
Gross, Terry, 163
Groth, Trevor, 83
Guevara, Ernesto "Che," 136
Gummo, 204

Habit, 43
Hall, Daryl, 155
Hamptons Film Festival, 209
Happiness, 13, 63, 193
"Happy Birthday," 48
Hardy, Ken, 203
Harris, Ed, 92
Harrison, Matt, 189
Hartley, Hal, 85, 191

Hav Plenty, 95
Hawk, Bob, 24, 104–105
Haynes, Todd, 4, 203–204
HBO, 39, 75, 92, 154, 209–210
HBO Films, 75, 209, 210
Head-On, 138
Healthy Baby Girl, 95
Heavy, 189
Hegeman, John, 182
Heidenreich, Erin, 29
Helfand, Judith, 95
Help, 153–154
Hero, 186
Herwitz, Andrew, 28, 29, 30, 50, 118
High Art, 43
Hill, Jeff, 23, 25, 147, 188, 191
Hillary, Edmund, 155
Hitchcock, Alfred, 211–212
Hoberman, Jim, 151–152
Holden, Steven, 37
Hold Me, Thrill Me, Kiss Me, 193
Hollywood Forever, 209
The Hollywood Reporter, 127, 181
Holofcener, Nicole, 4, 70
Holyfield, Evander, 69
Hoop Dreams, 126
Hoosiers, 14
Hope, Ted, 8, 12–13, 20, 34, 204, 208, 210
Horn, John, 142
Hostess, 48
House of Flying Dragons, 168, 186
How to Make the Cruelest Month, 141
Hu, Marcus, 9, 25–26, 31, 35, 36, 63–64, 74, 83, 96, 103–104, 105, 116–117, 118, 119, 138, 143, 176, 193–194
Humor pills and humble pills, 146–149
Hustle & Flow, 135, 149

ICM, 30, 42
IDFA, 209
IDP Films, 23, 100, 116, 130, 205
IDP/Goldwyn, 137
IFC, 39, 70
IFC Films, 5, 92
IFILM, 39
IFP, 12–13, 76, 203
IFP Market, 69, 71, 91, 104
IHOP, 23
IKEA, 193
I Love You, Don't Touch Me, 137
IMDB, 116
"I'm Looking Through You," 45
I'm the One That I Want, 77
Independent Feature Project. See IFP
Independents Nights, 12–13
IndieFlix, 76, 78–79
Information, press, 98, 115
Innocence, 110
International Creative Management, 30, 42

International Festival of Horror, 55
Interview with an Assassin, 66
In the Bedroom, 81, 83, 88, 138–139, 166–167
The Invisible Man, 201
Irreversible, 31
I Stand Alone, 31
Iwashina, Kevin, 29

Jackass: The Movie, 194
Jackson, Michael, 48
Jacobi, Derek, 164
Jaglom, Henry, 195
James, Caryn, 9–10
Jarecki, Andrew, 17, 144–145, 163
Jarmusch, Jim, 85
Jeremy Walker & Associates, 23, 77
Jeunet, Jean-Pierre, 191
Joe the King, 76, 204
Johnny Stecchino, 193
Journalists, as people, 150–152
Ju Dou, 103
Juergensen, Heather, 14–15
July, Miranda, 90–92
Junebug, 81

Kael, Pauline, 105
Kamins, Ken, 28
Kathy Morgan International, 30
Kelly, Richard, 88
Ken Park, 44, 150
Kidd, Dylan, 70
Kids, 44, 150
Kieslowski, Krzysztof, 185
Kim, Eric, 206–207
King, Houston, 198, 199
Kino, 161, 172–173
Kinsey, 168–169, 200
Kinski, Natassja, 44
Kissing Jessica Stein, 14–15, 183–185
Klubeck, Rick, 30
K-Mart, 49
Knowledge, of journalists, 100–102
Knowles, Harry, 202
Kopple, Barbara, 209
Kops, Eric, 190
Korenberg, Rosanne, 29
Kramer, Jeffrey, 10
Kwik Stop, 110

L.A. Confidential, 189–190
The LA Daily News, 193
Ladies in Lavender, 175
Laemmle, Greg, 73, 77, 161–162
Laemmle Theatres, 73, 161
Laemmle/Zeller Films, 73, 76, 161
LAFF. See Los Angeles Film Festival
Last Orders, 167
Last Summer in the Hamptons, 194–195
Launching, 55–79
Laurel Canyon, 43
LA Weekly, 65, 96, 102, 160, 198
Law, Lindsay, 9–10

Lawson, Michael, 136, 189
Lawyers, entertainment, 30
LebowskiFest, 10
Lee, Ang, 4
Lee, Spike, 191
Legal matters, 41–54
Leigh, Mike, 110
Leno, Jay, 138
Let It Snow, 160
Let's Get Frank, 74
Levitch, Timothy "Speed," 138, 181
Levy-Hinte, Jeff, 21, 24, 28, 30–31, 154, 166, 172
Libby, Chris, 22, 106, 111, 123, 135, 154
Libresco, Caroline, 83
Licensed to Kill, 77
Lichter, Lisa, 30
Lifetime, 75
Lin, Justin, 27, 28, 60, 83, 87, 130–131, 168
Lincoln Center, 12–13, 38, 65, 196
Lindbergh, Charles, 155
Linde, David, 34, 144
Linklater, Richard, 3, 4, 56, 67, 131
Lions Gate, 31, 35, 45, 51, 78, 127, 164, 168–169, 190, 192, 195, 203
The Living End, 45
Living in Oblivion, 189
Livingston, Jennie, 46–47, 162–163
Locarno Film Festival, 208–209
Lohan, Hillary Michelle, 165
Longsdorf, Amy, 183
Long Way Home, 136
Los Angeles Film Critics Association, 193
Los Angeles Film Festival, 1, 15, 59, 60, 62, 63, 65, 70, 116, 131, 134, 157, 181–182, 183–185, 197–198, 207
The Los Angeles Times, 25, 36, 85, 96, 97, 98, 101, 109, 123, 124–125, 137, 142, 159, 189, 193, 195
Lost in Translation, 63
Love Is the Devil, 164
Lovely & Amazing, 70
Lowenstein, Lael, 185
Low-pressure tactics, 99
Luddy, Tom, 62–63, 67
Lynch, David, 194

Ma, Yo Yo, 155
Macaulay, Scott, 6, 8–9, 17, 27, 48–49, 76, 89, 171, 177, 179, 204–205
Mad Hot Ballroom, 97–98
Maggiori, Mike, 73–74
Magic Lantern, 137
The Magic of Marciano, 44–45
Magnolia Pictures, 29, 46, 63, 104, 119, 130, 147, 170
Mahieux, Michelle, 107
Mangold, James, 189

Manhunter, 204
Manito, 167
Manne, Liz, 193, 210
Manners, 144–154
Maria Full of Grace, 75, 81
Marketplace, 165–180
Martell, Cynthia, 116
Martin, Dean, 47
Materials, 102, 114–121
  advance sending of, 156
Mathews, Jack, 195
Maya Lin: A Strong Clear Vision, 77
Maybury, John, 164
McCarthy, Todd, 147
McDonald's, 49
McGeehee, Scott, 63
McGregor, Ewan, 211
McGwire, Mark, 69
McKay, Jim, 137
McKay, Rick, 161–162
McKellan, Ian, 201, 202
McLeod, Kevin, 181
McNamara, Robert, 168
Mean Creek, 31, 81
Me and You and Everyone We Know, 81,
  90–92,110
Media, 93–113
  contacting of, in DIY-PR, 157–158
Meds, humor and humble, 146–149
Memento, 78
Mickey Cottrell, 23
MIFED, 63
The Migration of Clouds, 103
Millard, RJ, 23–24, 39, 100, 116,
  118, 119, 130, 147, 169, 170,
  171–172, 174–175, 205–206
Miller, Bennett, 138, 181
Miller, J. B., 181
Miller, Rebecca, 4, 85
Mill Valley Film Festival, 204
Miramax, 35, 47, 70, 102, 106,
  127, 139–140, 164, 185, 187,
  190, 191, 205
Moncrieff, Karen, 186
Monster, 5, 77, 97
Moodysson, Lucas, 70, 105
Moore, Michael, 49, 63, 208
Morgan, Kathy, 30
Morgerman, Jennifer, 195
Morrison, Toni, 172
The Motel, 87
The Motorcycle Diaries, 81, 92, 136, 141
Mottola, Greg, 127
mPRm Public Relations, 23, 72,
  112, 152, 189, 190
MRC, 23
MTV, 168
Mulholland Dr., 194
Murphy PR, 23
Museum of Modern Art, 39
Mutual Appreciation, 196, 200
My Big Fat Greek Wedding, 5, 71, 77, 174

Myerson, Bob, 160, 192–193
My Life As a Dog, 111
Mysterious Skin, 43, 45, 81

Nadler, Maud, 75, 154, 210
Nair, Mira, 74
Napoleon Dynamite, 62, 81, 83, 88,
  141–142, 174
National Research Group, 15, 71
National Society of Film Critics, 193
Nava, Gregory, 110
Nazario, Nathan, 183
Neil (Chasen's), 207
Nenette et Boni, 138
Netflix, 10, 76
Nevins, Sheila, 144
New Directors/New Films, 39, 60,
  61, 63
Newmarket Films, 5, 75, 97
Newsday, 1, 182, 187, 195
Newsweek, 65, 102, 103, 126, 150,
  161, 187
New Video, 211
The New Yorker, 105
New York Film Critics Circle,
  193, 194
New York Film Festival, 37, 38, 59,
  61, 62, 64–66, 67, 84, 150, 179,
  196, 203, 204
The New York Times, 9–10, 24, 25–26,
  36, 37, 65, 68, 87, 96, 105, 106,
  107, 108, 109, 111, 116, 118, 121,
  124, 135, 136–137, 142, 153, 159,
  160, 167, 169, 177
Next Stop Wonderland, 202
Nielsen Entertainment, 71
No Borders, 91
Noe, Gaspar, 31
Noonan, Tom, 204
Norgay, Tenzing, 155
Northern Arts, 208
No Such Thing, 191
Nowhere, 45, 193
NPR, 163
NRG, 15, 71
NYU, 74, 109

Oates, John, 155
Obsessing, about press, 103
October Films, 16
An Officer and a Gentleman, 13–14
Off the Menu: The Last Days of Chasen's,
  47, 71, 206–209
O'Hara, Robin, 204
O'Haver, Tommy, 45, 83
Oldboy, 83
Olympia Theater, 191
One, 44
One False Move, 126
Online Testing Exchange (OTX),
  15, 71
Open Water, 26

Orion, 14
Ortenberg, Tom, 169
Our Song, 128, 137
OutFest, 55, 60
Overlooked Film Festival, 110
Overpreparation, for press, 103

Pak, Greg, 163
Palais, 189
Pallotta, Tommy, 90
Palm, 46
Palm Springs (shorts festival), 55
Paltrow, Gwyneth, 106
Panahi, Hengameh, 31
Paradigm Consulting, 173
Paradox Lake, 167
Paramount Classics, 98
Paris Is Burning, 46–47, 162–163
The Passion of the Christ, 5, 77, 174
Payne, Alexander, 4
Pearce, Guy, 189
Pekar, Harvey, 141, 209, 210
Pekar, Joyce, 210
Peña, Richard, 38–39, 65–66, 67,
  179–180, 196
People, 95, 96
Perspective, 152–153
Photography, 117–119
The Pianist, 141
Picturehouse, 5, 36, 61, 71, 75, 96
Pierson, John, 34, 105
The Pillow Book, 163–164
Pitch, elevator, 98
Place, Mary Kay, 91
Pogachefsky, Mark, 17–18, 72–73,
  100, 102, 112–113, 136, 146,
  152, 189–190, 191
Pogodin, Fredell, 23, 101, 109, 158
Poison, 203–204
Police Academy, 11
Police Beat, 82
Politeness, 152
Pordenone, 55
Posin, Arie, 5
Postcards, 121
Posters, 121
PR, DIY-, 155–164
Prefestival screenings, 72–73, 156–157
Presley, Elvis, 46
Press office, festival, 156–160
Private Practices, 88
The Producers, 5
Producers representatives, 26–30
Production notes, preliminary,
  115–117
Program copy, checking of, 156
Programmers, buzz from, 133
Prospector Square, 185
P.S., 70
Public Access, 83
Publicists, 21–26
  buzz from, 133

Pulcini, Robert, 47, 71, 89, 142, 179–180, 206–211
Pulp Fiction, 180

Quad, 167, 169

The Raftman's Razor, 39
Raise the Red Lantern, 185–186
Raising Victor Vargas, 128, 136–137, 204
Rallying troops, 149–150
Randle, Teresa, 191
Raphael, Steven, 19, 29, 36, 72
Rappaport, Irwin, 7, 30, 41–46, 47, 48, 50, 51–54
Ray, Bingham, 16
Raymond (Chasen's), 207
Raymond, Jeff, 193
Reading between lines, on press, 99–100
Realness, 99
Real Women Have Curves, 75, 128, 154, 193, 210
Recruited screenings, 71–72
Red, 185
Redford, Robert, 7–8, 80, 81, 82, 83, 136
Redick, Sean, 30
Reed, Carol, 165
Regent, 50–51, 201, 202
Reiner, Carl, 15
Release. See Theatrical release
Reporters, buzz from, 133–134
Representatives, producers, 26–30
Required Viewing, 19, 29, 72
Respect, self-, 154
Reut, Przemyslaw, 167
Rhee, Karen, 25, 100, 108, 111–112, 120, 127
Rhythm Thief, 189
Rice, Peter, 169
Riding Giants, 26
Rissient, Pierre, 62, 63
Rize, 45–46, 81
Robertson, Michelle, 138
Robocop 2, 204
Robot Stories, 163
Rodriguez, Michelle, 95
Rodriguez, Robert, 63
Roeper, Jim, 97, 126
Rofekamp, Jan, 30
Roger and Me, 62–63
Roger Dodger, 66, 70
Rogers, Adam, 191–192
Ronson, Rena, 29
Rosefelt, Reid, 137
Rosenblum, Ralph, 5
Rosen, Rachel, 67, 116, 118, 119, 134–135
Rothman, Tom, 188
Rotterdam Film Festival, 63
Roud, Richard, 84

The Royal Tennenbaums, 45
Rozen, Leah, 96
Russell, David O., 95

Sachs, Ira, 103
SAG, 52–53
Salles, Walter, 136
Sams, Alicia, 71
San Francisco Film Festival, 61, 62, 89
Sardi's, 37
Satter, Michelle, 91
Scandiuzzi, Gian-Carlo, 78
A Scanner Darkly, 90
Scarlet, Peter, 55–56, 57, 64, 66, 67
Schamus, James, 19–20, 33–35, 38, 59, 61, 129, 139, 140, 148–149, 204
Schultz, Howard, 68
Schwartz, Cynthia, 185
Schwarzbaum, Lisa, 107, 189, 202
Scorcese, Martin, 83, 109–110
Scott, A. O., 36, 136–137
Scott, Patrick, 103
Scratch, 46, 106
Screen Actors Guild, 52–53
Screeners, 122–131
Screenwriting Lab (Sundance), 90–91
Seattle Film Festival, 23, 56, 59, 60, 61, 66–67, 69, 70, 89, 148, 203
Sedgwick, Kyra, 97
Self
    as ally, 144–146
    as center of world, 149
Self-distribution, 76–78
Self-respect, 154
Shackles, 116
Shanghai Triad, 186
She's Gotta Have It, 191
Shooting Gallery, 44–45
Short films, 38–40
Show Me Love, 105
Showtime, 39, 51, 75, 202
Shulman, Adam, 203
Sick, 88, 131, 153, 170
Sidewalk Film Festival, 197, 198–199, 200
Sidewalk Stories, 110
Sideways, 173
Siegel, David, 63
Silkwood, 91
Sinatra, Frank, 46, 47
Singer, Bryan, 83
Siskel, Gene, 126
Skins, 192
Slacker, 61, 67, 131
Slam, 128
Slamdance, 97, 98
Slingblade, 70
Sloss, John, 20, 24, 27, 28, 29, 31, 34, 36, 37, 42, 43, 68, 72,

75, 77, 124, 130, 134, 135, 140, 141–142, 167–168, 175, 208
Sloss Law, 20
Smiling Fish, 192
Smith, Kevin, 4, 104–105, 146, 190
Smoke Signals, 56, 202
Sneak Previews, 126
Soderbergh, Steven, 3
Sollett, Peter, 136
Solondz, Todd, 4
Songs from the Second Floor, 110
Sony, 7
Sony Pictures Classics, 20, 35, 38, 61, 76, 89, 104, 166, 168, 175
Sophie Gluck & Associates, 23
South by Southwest Film Conference and Festival. See SXSW
Spanking the Monkey, 95
Spears, Britney, 81
Spelling, Mrs. Aaron, 207
Spence, Carl, 23, 56, 66–67, 69, 70, 148
Spielberg, Steven, 83, 167
Spitfire Grill, 120, 139
Splendor, 192
Springer Berman, Shari, 47, 54, 62, 71, 142, 179–180, 206–211
Spurlock, Morgan, 49, 88
Stallone, Sylvester, 147
Standing in the Shadows of Motown, 194
Starbucks, 68
Star Maps, 9, 14, 87, 99
Starr, Ringo, 146
The Station Agent, 43, 81
Steal Me, 39
Story of Qiu Ju, 186
Strand Releasing, 9, 25, 31, 35, 63, 74, 83, 96, 103, 105, 116, 118, 137–138, 143
Strange Invaders, 203
Strathairn, David, 186
Strauss, Bob, 193
Summit, 30
Sundance Channel, 39, 199
Sundance Film Festival, 1, 5, 7–8, 9, 12–13, 14, 23, 27, 28, 31, 32, 33, 34, 35, 39, 43, 44, 45–46, 55, 56, 57, 58, 59, 60, 61, 62, 63, 64, 65, 66, 67, 68–69, 70, 72, 73, 76, 78, 80–92, 96, 97, 98, 99, 103, 104, 109, 110, 120, 123, 125–126, 127, 128–129, 135, 136, 137, 138, 139, 140, 141, 143, 147, 148, 151, 152, 153, 154, 157, 166–167, 172, 176, 185–186, 187, 188–189, 200, 201–205, 207, 210–211
Sundance Institute, 80, 83
Sunshine, 18
Superman Returns, 83
Super Size Me, 49, 62, 77, 81, 88, 112, 174, 175

Surpin, Shelley, 30
Surrender Dorothy, 110
Suture, 63
Swingers, 63, 70
SXSW, 23, 26, 39, 60, 61–62, 70,
   88, 89, 130, 158, 196
Synopsis, 115

Tadpole, 139–140
The Talent Given Us, 151
Tarantino, Quentin, 3, 4
Tarnation, 10, 110, 139, 173
Tartan, 192
Taubin, Amy, 25, 46–47, 103–105,
   110–111, 117, 124, 150, 151–152,
   172–173, 177–178, 197
Tautou, Audrey, 191
TCDM, 23, 97
Team, 19–40
TÇchinÇ, AndrÇ, 193
Telluride Film Festival, 55, 60, 61,
   62–63, 64, 70, 89, 209
Temple, Shirley, 165
The Terrorist, 110
Theatrical release
   DIY-PR before, 158–160
   legal matters relating to, 158–160
Theron, Charlize, 97
ThinkFilm, 88, 195
The Third Man, 165
Thirteen, 43, 110
13 Conversations About One Thing, 167
This Is That, 20
Thomas, Kevin, 195
Three Kings, 95
Time constraints, media, 100
Time Out, 96
Times-Mirror, 195
Toback, James, 146
Together, 70
To Live, 186
Tonight Show with Jay Leno, 138
Tony Takitani, 143
Toronto International Film Festival,
   1, 8–9, 57, 59, 60, 61, 62,
   63, 67, 69, 70, 89, 97, 100, 107,
   112, 147, 150, 152, 182–183
Traction Media, 29
Trailer, 121
Tran Ahn Hung, 192
Transamerica, 66
Trapping press, 102
Trembling Before G-d, 162
Trevens, Francine, 185
Tribeca Film Festival, 55, 57, 60,
   61, 63, 64, 66, 69, 70, 116, 118
Tribune, 195
Trimark, 45
Troops, rallying of, 149–150
Truth, to media, 99
Tully, 110

Turan, Kenneth, 25, 85, 97–98,
   101, 104, 109, 110, 124–126,
   137, 187, 189, 195, 202
Turtle syndrome, 153
2929, 30
Twist of Faith, 88, 153, 170
Two Boots Theater, 160
Two Women, 110

Un Certain Regard, 63
United States Film Festival
   (U.S. Film Fest), 80
United Talent Agency. See UTA
Universal Pictures, 201
Unmade Beds, 192–193
Up for Grabs, 73
Urman, Mark, 169, 195
US, 95
USA Films, 201
USA Today, 138, 143
U.S. Comedy Arts Festival, 55
The Usual Suspects, 83
UTA, 30, 35, 42
Utley, Nancy, 169, 185
Uzzan, Jessica, 137

Vachon, Christine, 36–37, 51, 58,
   63, 65, 75, 76, 140, 141
Variety, 43, 127, 147, 156, 184–185,
   198, 199
Velvet Goldmine, 141
Venice Film Festival, 59, 61, 64,
   150, 209
The Village Voice, 96
The Virgin Suicides, 101
Volkswagen, 50
Volunteer Lawyers for the Arts, 54

Wagner, Andrew, 151
Waking Ned Devine, 189
Walker, Bart, 28
Walker, Jeremy, 9–10, 22, 23, 69,
   77–78, 99, 106, 111, 127–128,
   152–153
Wallace, Rona, 29
Walter Reade Theater, 12–13, 65
Wang, Norman, 185, 186
Warburton, Patrick, 37
Warner Bros., 189
Warner Independent Pictures,
   26, 76, 177
War of the Worlds, 166, 167
Waxman, Sharon, 24–25, 87, 88,
   108, 116, 121, 127, 142, 153
Weinstein, Harvey, 98, 103,
   139–140, 190, 205
Weintraub, Bernie, 109
Wellspring, 176, 197
Wendigo, 43
Westfelt, Jennifer, 14–15
WGA, 52, 53
Whale, James, 200–201

Whale Rider, 5
What Happened Was . . ., 203–205
What the Bleep Do We Know, 174–175
When the Shooting Stops<, 5
White House, 69, 106
Who's That Knocking at My Door?,
   109–110
The Wife, 204
Wilder, Billy, 5–6
Wild Reeds, 103, 193
William Morris, 22, 29, 35, 42, 149
Williams, Robin, 138
Wilson, Hugh, 11
The Woman Chaser, 37, 65
Wong Kar-wai, 185
The Woodsman<, 97
Woodstock Film Festival, 197
World, self as center of, 149
Writers Guild of America, 52, 53
Wuornos, Aileen, 97
Wurmfeld, Eden, 183

X-Men, 83

The Young and the Dead, 47, 209
Y Tu Mamá También, 174

Zeller, Steven, 73, 161
Zhang Yimou, 103, 186
Zions, Brad, 183